Arabs at the Crossroads

Arabs at the Crossroads

Political Identity and Nationalism

Hilal Khashan

University Press of Florida

Gainesville · Tallahassee · Tampa · Boca Raton

Pensacola · Orlando · Miami · Jacksonville

Copyright 2000 by the Board of Regents of the State of Florida
Printed in the United States of America on acid-free paper
All rights reserved

05 04 03 02 01   6 5 4 3 2

Library of Congress Cataloging-in-Publication Data

Khashan, Hilal, 1951–
Arabs at the crossroads: political identity and nationalism / Hilal Khashan.
p.cm.
Includes bibliographical references and index.
ISBN 0-8130-1737-8 (alk. paper)
1. Arab countries—Politics and government—20th century. 2. Nationalism—Arab countries.
3. Islam and politics—Arab countries. I. Title.
DS39 K43 2000
320.9174927—dc21   99-047602

The University Press of Florida is the scholarly publishing agency for the State University
System of Florida, comprising Florida A&M University, Florida Atlantic University, Florida
International University, Florida State University, University of Central Florida, University of
Florida, University of North Florida, University of South Florida, and University of West
Florida.

University Press of Florida
15 Northwest 15th Street
Gainesville, FL 32611-2079
http://www.upf.com

To Maha and Mazen:

keep the faith

Contents

Preface and Acknowledgments

Writing a book on the outcome of Arab political endeavors in modern times is not a heartwarming experience. It involves the recognition of the unfavorable climate in which the Arabs interacted among themselves and with the outside world over the past two centuries, a multifarious process that ultimately gave rise to the stark reality that currently prevails in the Arab world. Central to Arab travails in dealing with the Western-defined requirements of the modern age have been the issue of political identity and the challenge of solving the riddle of development. The objective of this book is to demonstrate that failure to come to terms with the question of political identity and subsequently to redefine the relationships between the state and society have necessarily doomed Arab prospects for development. The contemporary assortment of Arab states—a witness to inherent divisions and Western preponderance—has not been able to identify practical common interests and pursue them conscientiously. As a logical consequence, the Arabs have not been able either to cope with invading ideological challenges such as Zionism or to realize their own economic development and install institutionalized political processes. The book achieves its stated objective through a linkage process that traces the development of Arab identifications and subjects them to relevant theoretical scrutiny.

The unconsummation of Arab nationalism caused the crisis of identity (long attenuated by nominal identification with the Islamic caliphate) to position Arab leaders against one another and alienate the masses from state-sponsored economic programs. Elite insensitivity to pan-Arab issues and Arab publics' poor affective evaluation of state domestic policies coalesced to preclude inter-Arab cooperation. They also induced foreign infringement on Arab lands, resources, and strategic interests. Arab hopes for economic betterment became an immediate casualty of Arab infighting, absence of long-term planning for development, and survival of primordial tendencies in society. Political degeneration manifested itself by military adventurism and defeat, retreat in favor of the non-Arab states in the Middle East, and mounting domestic opposition that raises the slogans of political Islam. Operationally, the analysis proceeds as follows:

Chapter 1 recognizes the evolution of Arab search for identity from its inception some two hundred years ago until its current state of morbidity.

Chapter 2 looks into the origins of the nation-state as it appeared in Europe, as well as its utility in Asian and African societies. The chapter also considers the strength of religion as a competing source of identification, especially in countries where the idea of nationalism remains nebulous.

Chapter 3 discusses the factors that contributed to the rise and decline of Arab nationalism. It makes reference to the tenuous theoretical foundations of Arab nationalism and alludes to lack of commitment to pan-Arabism among Arab ruling elites.

Chapter 4 dwells on Arab failure to contain the rise of the Jewish state to regional preeminence, linking it to weak resolve to confront Israel and preoccupation with inter-Arab factiousness instead.

Chapter 5 addresses the plight of Arab development beginning with the defeat of liberalism and the ushering in of radicalism in the late 1940s. It notes that neither the army officers' approach to modernization nor that of the conservative elites proved successful in achieving the desired results. More ruinous has been the general failure of political development in the Arab world, including the arrest of transition toward democratization and rule of law.

Chapter 6 focuses on Iraq's eight-year war with Iran and the Gulf War precipitated by Iraq's invasion of Kuwait. The Gulf War and the area's security predicament highlight not just inter-Arab divisions but also the empty space in domestic politics and poor decisions by authoritarian rulers who squandered their countries' resources on grandiose projects and sui-cidal adventures. The first Gulf War and especially the second Gulf War reveal the decay of the Arab order of states and underscore the need to revamp it.

Chapter 7 deals with the appearance of political Islam and growth of the Islamists, largely a symptom of repression, economic crises, unresolved identity crisis, and defeat in war with Israel and the West. Political Islam presents a formidable problem to Arab ruling elites and a compelling warning for them to rationalize their policies and open up their systems.

Chapter 8 diagnoses the grave symptoms of contemporary decay in the Arab world by pointing to the impact of continuous defeats and ideological debacles on the central identity issue. It also refers to debilitating societal crises, intellectual stagnation, inability to define achievable objectives, and finding solace in the past.

Chapter 9 proposes basic steps that Arab elites and publics must endorse if they truly aspire to break the vicious cycle of political and economic backwardness, the legacy of defeat and disarray. The proposals include Arabs' need to understand the West, to believe in the myth of Arab nationalism, to define and pursue realistic objectives, to nurture respect for authority, and to realize the inevitability of political representation.

This book is significant in several respects. First, it dwells on the main problems that continue to afflict the Arabs in their bid to reassert themselves on the map of the modern world. Second, its analysis neither resorts to apology nor masquerades unpleasant realities. Third, the ultimate objective of the book is not to engage in self-flagellation, but to prescribe cooperation, rationality, ideological flexibility, and understanding as essential criteria for the Arabs to reenter history. This book is particularly useful to undergraduate students with little or no background in Arab affairs. It is essential for graduate students wishing to complement their exposure to the mainstream U.S. analysis of Arab politics with a dispassionate Arab perspective. Western nonspecialists interested in Arab affairs will find this book noteworthy in that it opens for them a gateway to better understand compelling issues pertaining to Arab identity, the Arab-Israeli conflict, and Islamic revival.

The genesis of this book owes much to the undergraduate course on modern Arab politics that I have taught for years at the American University of Beirut. Classroom discussion and students with insightful questions mightily contributed to the presentation of this work, and I thank each and every one of them. I am forever indebted for the steady encouragement and support of my children Maha and Mazen who had the capacity to stall the progress of this book but instead chose to help bring it to fruition.

1

The Search for Identity

Today, the Arabs are at a loss. They suffer from a severe identity crisis. Nineteenth-century reformers disturbed the Arab mind by sowing distrust in the Ottoman empire, without securing a tenable ideological alternative to that religious state and to Islam which it embodied. The disconcerted process of ideological reformulation and reindoctrination dragged into the twentieth century, breeding a disoriented and politically indecisive mind. Sa'dun Hamadi feels that the evolution of Arab character has, since the liberal age, produced a perplexed individual who cannot cope with complex reality. He attests to his opinion by referring to a succession of ideological changes that Arabs have witnessed during the last century: "An ideological wave prevails for some time then it dissipates, only to be replaced by a completely different wave. . . . Political ideologies often rise and fall depending on the international situation."[1] Reformers told Arabs that traditional Islam needed reform, and they believed them. Other reformers later gave them the impression that nationalism would cure their woes and lead them to modernity. The masses uncritically took the reformers at their word. Instead, the Arabs moved from one humiliating defeat to another, until the Islamists offered them messianic redemption. In few Arab places, the cycle of change seems to complete a full cycle, as traditional Islam reasserts its lost influence.[2]

For many centuries Islam had succeeded in submerging the ethnic identity of the faithful. Islamic universalism overshadowed group particularism as political authority slipped from one caliphate to another. Even the rise and fall of competing dynasties—with all the ethnic and clannish parochialism attached to them—did not seem to revoke the supremacy of religion over all sorts of visceral tendencies which abounded in the world of Islam. In the nineteenth century, however, the hold of religion on the temporal concerns of Muslims began to give way to rudimentary secularism. As it became obvious that the eventual collapse of the Ottoman empire was unavoidable, its Muslim subjects started to search for alternatives to political authority. Motivated by dynastic ambitions, Egypt's Muhammad 'Ali sought to annex Syria and Hijaz to his viceroyship. The declarations of his son Ibrahim Pasha, who commanded Egyptian regiments in Syria, clearly indicated desire to create an Arab national state. Claims about the pan-Arab orientation of this Macedonian military leader are beside the point.[3] The debate on the strength of Ibrahim Pasha's pan-Arab feelings appears inconclusive. What looks more definite is that within a few years of his ventures in Arab lands, the content of political discourse there marked a slow but steady shift from religion to nationalism. This tendency accelerated once it became obvious that the demise of the Ottoman empire would not lead to the rise of another state inspired by shariʿa.

Developments in the nineteenth century significantly altered the ideological components of the Arab-Islamic mind. Further change in the twentieth century accentuated the process of value and aspirational change. Nevertheless, the political transformation of Arab political thinking from one state of mind to another remains far from complete. The Arabs today seem confused. They loathe their political systems and distrust the ruling elites. They desire reform but disagree about the course of action. Thus political quandary and regime failure currently prevail in the Arab world. In the midst of ideological confusion and lack of legitimacy, Arab elites confine their agendas to regime maintenance and avoidance of controversy. They may repress or co-opt opposition groups, but they never integrate them by broadening the base of the political system. It is therefore the objective of this chapter to look into the factors that have interfered with Islamic political thought over the last two centuries. Specifically, to what extent and toward what directions has the Arab-Islamic political mind shifted from divine law to mundane contrivances? The aim is to decipher the implications of diverse yet partial ideological change on the Arab scene as the beginnings of a new political era in the Middle East seem to set in.

The Seeds of Change

The ability of traditional Islam to provide political continuity and a semblance of stability for the Islamic state lasted for at least a millennium. This seemed no longer possible by the end of the eighteenth century. Manfred Halpern regards Islam to have failed in responding to the requirements of modernity already sweeping into Europe by that time. He argues that while ". . . Islam could provide all participants with a universal language of terms and symbols . . . [it had] no renaissance or reformation."[4] The Ottoman empire simply failed to cope with increasing challenges, both from within and outside its borders. Nationalism rose among its Christian subjects in the peripheries, and many of them seceded from the empire one after another. Thus Serbia achieved its autonomy in 1830, and Greece won its independence in 1832. The Ottomans lost more territory, especially to tsarist Russia. Even lands nominally controlled by the Ottoman sultan—in North Africa and along the Nile Valley—started falling to other European colonial powers, such as Britain, France, Spain, and Italy. The Ottoman empire shrank alarmingly, and the specter of its collapse alerted both sultans and European powers. Britain and France worried about Russian expansionism and themselves failed to agree on partitioning Ottoman territory. They chose to allow the ailing empire to survive until further notice.

These dramatic changes forced Ottoman sultans to begin major reform plans. Their aim was to transform the empire into a Western-type monarchy. The initial reforms had a military nature. Sultan Selim III witnessed another Ottoman loss to Austria and Russia. As soon as he concluded peace agreements with these two adversaries in 1792, he initiated programs to reorganize the Ottoman army according to European standards.[5] His successor, Sultan Mahmud II, concentrated on centralizing the authority of the empire. Nevertheless, the most far-reaching reforms took place between 1839 and 1876, during the viziership of Rashid Pasha and Ali Pasha. These reforms, better known as the Tanzimat, aimed at reorganizing various aspects of Ottoman social and political life. They involved administrative, legal, and constitutional innovations that seemed to part from time-honored Islamic tradition. Two royal decrees of paramount importance encapsulated the entire reform process: the Hatt-i Sharif of Gulhane and the Hatt-i Humayan, enacted in 1839 and 1856 respectively. The second decree abrogated the *millet* system and extended substantial citizenship rights to Ottoman Christians that placed them on a par with Muslims.

Secular reforms in the Ottoman empire came too late to reverse its collapse. Influenced by European coreligionists, Ottoman Christians began to articulate their distinct ethnonationalisms. Syrian Christians, already emancipated by Ibrahim Pasha during his rule there from 1831 till 1840, introduced the idea of Arab nationalism and eventually succeeded in propagating it among the Muslim majority. The ascendancy of 'Abdul Hamid to the sultanate in 1876 caused political reforms to come to a halt.[6] In 1878 he suspended the newly born Ottoman constitution and dissolved the assembly. Instead of political liberalization, he raised the slogan of pan-Islamism and cracked down on the empire's proliferating ethnonationalisms. 'Abdul Hamid's religious approach appealed to most Muslims and allowed him to maintain political control for a few years. It did not however stop the further disintegration of the empire. The sultan was fighting for time that eventually conspired against him. His repressive policies backfired and sealed the future of the empire. The only surviving legacy of that period pertains to the image of the police state terrorizing its populations. 'Abdul Hamid had originally set up the agencies of official repression nowadays dominant in Middle Eastern societies. The following excerpt, from a major work by William L. Cleveland, which describes 'Abdul Hamid's draconianism, applies as well to most present-day Arab regimes:

> . . . ['Abdul Hamid had] tried to impose total control over the information available to his subjects and the activities in which they could engage. The press was tightly censored, the school curricula were subjected to close scrutiny, and the public discussion of politics was forbidden. An internal network of government spies and informants, aided by the new telegraph system, infiltrated all levels of the administration; its reports led to the imprisonment and exile, often on the most dubious evidence, of many loyal Ottoman officials and intellectuals. Others escaped the tyranny by voluntary exile or immigration. Away from the reach of Abdul Hamid's police in Paris and Berlin, they formed protest groups and published pamphlets, which were smuggled into Istanbul, denouncing the sultan and his autocracy.[7]

It is in this repressive atmosphere that ideological change took place among Ottoman Arabs in the nineteenth century. Arab national governments apply similar coercive and mental framing techniques, especially since the defeat of Arab liberalism following the establishment of the state of Israel in 1948.

The period of 'Abdul Hamid's reign exposed the Ottoman empire's ethnic and religious contradictions and placed them on a collision course. Yet the seeds of ideological rift took root in the East many years earlier. Napoleon Bonaparte's Egyptian expedition in 1798 had staggering repercussions on the ideological development of Arabs and Muslims in the Near East. This was the first time in some six hundred years that a European army had come to the heart of the world of Islam. The French army—a symbol of European modernity and rationalism—brought with it not just sophisticated weaponry but liberal ideas and modern organizational techniques as well. The French devastated the Mamluks in a grossly uneven confrontation that underscored the greatness of European achievements and the magnitude of Muslim decay. The failure of traditional Islam to confront the challenges of modernity became all too obvious, and the need for change seemed dire. An intense debate on the course of reform ensued. Its substance dealt with issues relating to Islam's compatibility with the spirit of the age, identity redefinition in view of rising nationalism, perceptions of desired linkages to the Ottoman empire, modern state legislation, and economic rejuvenation. This process occurred in an atmosphere of increased uncertainty, as well as a steady shift from moderation to radicalism.

The Direction of Change

The surge in Ottoman despotism coincided with the expansion of European colonialism. Muslims had apparently missed, or did not fully understand the implications of, French occupation of Algeria which occurred in 1830. It surely was not a repetition of Napoleon's invasion of Egypt a generation earlier. In the case of Egypt, French occupation lasted only three years—before their expulsion by the British—after which it returned to the world of Islam, even under the rule of a new line of elites. As for Algeria, the French came in and stayed for 132 years. If the Muslims had absorbed the shock of the fall of Algeria, they could not swallow the loss of Tunisia to France in 1881, nor the takeover of Egypt by England the year after. Near Easterners did not see Cairo and Tunis just as two Muslim cities but rather as two major centers of Muslim learning and Arab-Islamic civilization. Their loss seemed nonredeemable. In that era of despair, the call for change came from a new educated class that made daring reform propositions. Islam still provided the starting point for all reformers; it did not seem to matter if they were Muslims, Christians, Arabs, secular, or religious. However, the centuries-old intellectual stagnation seemed to loosen by the third quarter of the nineteenth century.

Confusion marred from the beginning the search for a plausible identity that could stop the erosion of the Muslim state. Thus, Jamal al-Din al-Afghani vacillated between Islamic solidarity, the unity of the Nile Valley and North Africa, and Arab identity. From his initial slogan which focused on Islam as a source of solidarity, al-Afghani concluded his cross-country preaching by settling for Arab nationalism.[8] Al-Afghani even entertained the notion of Egyptian nationalism when he established in 1877—during his stay in Egypt—the Misr al-Fatat (Young Egypt) society. However, al-Afghani's greatest contributions to Arab-Islamic thought lay in advocating nationalism and in his reform propositions that go to the extent of encouraging a comprehensive intellectual revolution. Other Muslim reformers such as Muhammad 'Abdu and 'Abd al-Rahman al-Kawakibi concurred with al-Afghani's central views. They realized the need for advancing reason at the expense of the poorly researched and superficially understood religious code. Of equal importance was their approval of al-Afghani's call upon Arabs to develop a nationalistic alternative to Ottoman pan-Islamism. Thus pleas for reforming Islam went hand in hand with the rise of Arab national consciousness. Islam continued to provide legitimacy for political action, but its glory, as most reformers insisted, rested with the Arab race. The secular appeal of Christian reformers of the caliber of Butrus al-Bustani, Nasif al-Yazigi, and Najib 'Azuri had little impact then on the minds and souls of Arab Muslims. The idea of the state, along Western legal and rational terms, was nebulous, to say the least.

The Arabs definitely wanted political change and adjustments, not outright departure from the past to their Islamic identity. Their options were murky, however. While Europe's notions of liberalism and humanism inspired them, its military juggernaut and proneness to colonialism outraged them and exposed the magnitude of their decline. Europe's onslaught on Muhammad 'Ali's efforts to modernize Egypt and French occupation of Algeria only confused the Arabs by adding the slogans of struggle and resistance to the terminology of modern Arab thought. Arab reformers operated in an awkward period that featured an organic attachment to Islam, an increase in Ottoman despotism and rise of Turkification policies, and contradictory European signals of colonialism and prodding of Arab nationalism.

Islamic revivalists in Arab-Islamic lands carried the banner of reform against religious laxity and European domination throughout the nineteenth century. Even Sultan 'Abdul Hamid found it expedient to use religious symbols to unify his subjects and as a last resort to check the further disintegration of the Ottoman empire. All of these efforts met with failure and suffered defeat one after another. During the period of 1810–19, Muhammad 'Ali's campaign in Najd, at the instigation of the Ottoman sultan, put an end to the Wahabiyya movement's ambitions outside Arabia. In Algeria, the French defeated prince 'Abdul Qadir's religiously inspired insurrection by 1847 and banished him to Damascus. By quelling the rebellion of the Rahmaniyya Order in 1871, the French pacified Algeria and neutralized Islam as an oppositional force. In Cyrenaica, the Sannusia remained a local movement and failed to stop Italian expansionism. Most dramatic was the fate of the Mahdiyya movement in the Sudan. The Mahdis scored spectacular success against Turco-Egyptian troops and threatened Egypt itself. In 1885 they routed the British-led Egyptian garrison in Khartoum and executed General Charles Gordon. Thirteen years later an Anglo-Egyptian army under General Kitchener reentered Khartoum. In an unusual expression of anger over the death of Gordon, he ordered the disinterment of Mahdi's remains, a gesture that also reflected Britain's aversion to militant Islam, as well as a commitment to defeat its objectives. Last vestiges of nineteenth-century Islamic revivalism, represented by Sultan

'Abdul Hamid's doctrine of pan-Islamism, succumbed to the Young Turks' military coup in 1908. The triumph of pan-Tauranism put Ottoman Arabs on the track of ethnonationalism almost by default. From that date until the Arab-Israeli Six Day War in June 1967, it was nationalism, especially Arab nationalism, that captured the souls and minds of the vast majority of the speakers of Arabic. The devastating Arab defeat finally awakened the masses to the limitations of Arab socialism, the ineptitude of the military ruling elite, and the inadequacy of a Western developmental approach and the liberal political foundation upon which it rests. Mobilized sectors of Arab populations gradually shifted to Islam, sometimes in its pristine form, until Islamic groups finally loomed as the only probable inheritors of political authority both to the ailing secular leaderships and to traditional political systems.

The Content of Change

The triumph of Arab nationalism against pan-Islamism on the eve of World War I was probably fortuitous. Arabs in the Fertile Crescent, especially in Syria, accepted the hastily contrived tenets of pan-Arabism almost by default following the rise of pan-Tauranism among Turkish army officers. By and large, Muslim Arab thinkers had a strongly expressed commitment to Islam as they sought to reform the Ottoman empire. Despite the relentless efforts of Anglo-French missionaries who propagated secular and ethno-national ideas, their impact remained minimal and limited to a few Christian Arab converts such as Nasif al-Yazigi, Butrus al-Bustani, and Najib 'Azuri.[9] Joel Carmichael interpreted the pioneering role of the Christian elite in the Levant in championing the cause of Arab nationalism as an effort "to burst out of its ghetto."[10] Understandably, Christians advocated Arabism in the hope that it would redeem them politically and put them on a par with Muslim Arabs.

Lebanese-born Najib 'Azuri, who in 1905 founded Jam'iyyat al-Jami'a al-'Arabiyya (the Arab League Association), called for establishing a decentralized and secular Arab empire in West Asia. He tried to solve the issue of linkage to Islam, a sine qua non for Muslims, by advocating a compromise arrangement calling for the installation of an Arab caliph in Mecca that commanded political sovereignty over Hijaz and charged with universal Islamic matters.[11]

Most Egyptians reacted negatively to the rise of Arab nationalist tendencies in West Asia. Some considered it an act of perfidy against the Ottoman empire whose maintenance, they insisted, constituted the third obligation after belief in God and Prophet Muhammad.[12] To be sure, Sharif Husayn's

Arab revolt against the Ottoman empire, in collaboration with the British, invited angry condemnations among Egyptians. Egyptian poet Ahmad Muharram scorned Sharif Husayn and stigmatized him as the enemy of "God and the Prophet."[13] Sati' al-Husry, the shaykh of Arab nationalism in the twentieth century, expressed his disappointment about Egyptian aversion to pan-Arabism:

> We considered Egypt as part of the greater Arab homeland. . . . But when we sought refuge in Egypt—after the collapse of the Arab state in Damascus—we were shocked to realize that the Egyptians—including most men and leaders of the revolution—did not feel the same way towards us. . . . They did not accept that Egypt was part of the Arab countries, nor recognize the Egyptian people as part of the Arab nation.[14]

The views of Egyptians toward pan-Arabism became somewhat more favorable beginning in the 1930s. This issue will receive more attention in chapter 3. Perceptions of the scope of Arab nationalism underwent significant changes elsewhere in the Near East. A new universalist approach to Arab nationalism received impetus from the works of thinkers such as Shakib Arslan, Rashid Rida, and George Antonius. The disillusionment of early Arab nationalists with France and Britain, mainly as a result of their occupation of most parts of the Arab East, put them in a similar situation with other speakers of Arabic in North Africa. This seemed to have broadened the scope of Arab nationalism and allowed the incorporation of Egypt and North Africa under its umbrella. Majid Khadduri recognized that the Arabs' negative experience with Britain and France had "widened the horizon of the [nationalist] movement"[15] and conferred on it a "negative character."[16] By the late 1930s, verses applauding Arab nationalism pervaded the Levant and provided the essentials of political socialization into Arabism among schoolchildren. Consider, for example, the following few lines:

> The Arab land is my homeland
> From Damascus to Baghdad
> From Egypt to Yemen
> From Najd to Tetuan
> No religion separates us
> The Arabic tongue unites us.

The following three themes emerge from the previous lines: First is the expanded version of the Arab nation, in which it is no longer confined to

West Asia but now includes all the countries from the Atlantic Ocean to the Persian Gulf. Second, the Arabic language is taken as the most important bond in the new version of pan-Arabism. Third, one discerns the rudiments of secular orientation as manifested by toning down the importance of religion. The third theme is further pursued by another famous set of nationalistic verses characterizing the period:

> Ye the soil of my nation
> And my ancestors' resting place
> We came when becked and called to
> To defend us the nation from
> The firm and determined enemy
> Paving a new road to glory.

These verses emphasize the role of Arab nationalism in supplanting Islam in the search for a new road to glory. This was in fact a revolutionary change of heart that symbolized the rise of the short-lived secular liberalism in the Arab East.

Even as political affection shifted from Islam to Arab nationalism, it was virtually impossible to dissociate from Islam as a belief system. Arab nationalists such as Qustantin Zurayq, Edmond Rabbat, and 'Abdul Rahman al-Bazzaz sought to establish a rapport between Islam and Arab nationalism. In fact, al-Bazzaz resurrected the notion that Islam first appeared as a national religion.[17] Intense religious feeling failed to check the march of Arab nationalism thanks to two major events: the creation of the Middle Eastern state system and the establishment of the state of Israel.

The Tenuous Creations

Prodded by the British, Sharif Husayn raised on 16 June 1916 the flag of the Arab revolt against the Ottomans. The Arabs felt optimistic about carving out a state of their own and seemed on the verge of making a successful ideological transition from Islamism to Arabism. They also expressed readiness to cooperate with the West and bury centuries of confrontation and animosity with Christian Europe. However, the disclosure of the contents of the Sykes-Picot Agreement of May 1916, which partitioned the Levant between Britain and France, shocked the Arabs and revived their legacy of distrust toward Europe. They saw an act of deception in the British urging the Arabs to rebellion against the Turks, and only a replacement of one master by another. Arabs who thought that their destiny would be better than that of Egypt, which the British designated as a protectorate following the termination of Ottoman sovereignty over it in 1914, got a major disillusionment. To make things even worse for the Arabs, the British government issued on 2 November 1917 the Balfour Declaration that favored establishment of a Jewish national home in Palestine.[18] The completion of the final touches to Western domination and Arab subservience occurred on 20 July when French troops, marching from Lebanon, defeated the Syrian army in Maysalun near Damascus and overthrew the Arab government of King Faysal I.

The collapse of the Arab kingdom in Syria set the stage for the final phase of Anglo-French control of the Fertile Crescent, which lasted until the end of World War II. North Africa and the Nile Valley had been conquered years earlier. During the occupation period Britain and France laid the foundations of the Middle Eastern and North African state system. The West finished the territorial reorganization of the speakers of Arabic in the aftermath of the war, completing it in the Mashriq faster than in the Maghrib. Today, the Arab League—founded in 1945 to coordinate political, cultural, and economic activities of its then seven founding countries—boasts twenty-one full-member states.

The process of territorial and political reorganization of the Arab components of the Ottoman empire began shortly after the conclusion of the Paris peace conference in 1919. Only a few weeks after he had entered Damascus and aborted the Arab state dream, General Gouraud announced the creation of Greater Lebanon that gave the Maronite Christians a preeminent role in running its domestic affairs. This was immediately followed by the institution of French mandate over Syria, and similar British actions regarding Iraq, Palestine, and the hastily carved emirate of Transjordan.[19] The Council of the League of Nations validated these mandates in July 1922.[20] These were truly artificial creations since they had no historical roots, or even a semblance of ideological content. Arabs in the Fertile Crescent were denied the opportunity to live under the umbrella of an Islamic political entity or to try to elaborate the crude tenets of emerging pan-Arabism. Instead, the West created faceless and uninspiring political entities.

In Egypt the overall political picture differed from its counterparts in the Fertile Crescent and the Arabian peninsula. Egyptian nationalism grew during the years of British occupation; its ultimate objective of achieving independence was reinforced by the recent discovery of dazzling pharaonic civilizational legacy. Peter Mansfield illustrated the point in the following manner: "In Egypt, Britain had already been effectively governing the country for nearly forty years, but it was there dealing with a people who had constituted a nation for some 5,000 years, even while under the rule of a series of empires. In the rest of the former Ottoman provinces . . . there were no nation-states."[21] The Egyptian people's distinct national consciousness, which caused widespread disturbances against the colonial power, finally compelled Britain to recognize the independence and sovereignty of Egypt on 28 February 1922. A decade later the British proclaimed the independence of Iraq and facilitated its membership in the League of Nations. Constitutional law and parliamentary life sprang up in Egypt, Iraq, Syria, and Lebanon but failed to take root anywhere. The heavy weight of Western imperialism and the absence of secular antecedents doomed the transition to participatory government.

The historical experience of North Africa differed sharply from that of the Arab East. Although thoroughly Islamized, Arab control of the Maghrib, which started in 710 A.D., ended toward the end of the eighth century. With the exception of the Almohads period (1147–1269) that saw the unification of the entire Maghrib from Morocco to Libya, Algeria, Tunisia, and Morocco were ruled by local Berber dynasties until the middle of the sixteenth century when the Ottomans established themselves along much of the North African Mediterranean coast. Morocco maintained its independence, although it suffered from the same political stagnation that beset its Algerian and Tunisian brethren.[22] Soon they fell, although at different times, to the French imperial juggernaut. The French occupied Algeria from 1830 until 1962, Tunisia from 1881 until 1956, and lastly Morocco from 1912 until 1956.

The territorial fragmentation of the Arabic-speaking world covered every corner of this vast geographical area. The Italians took Libya from Ottoman hands in 1911 and lost it to Britain in 1942 during World War II, but Libya was proclaimed independent in 1952. In the Sudan, the British-led Egyptian troops defeated the Mahdist movement in Khartoum in 1899 and launched the condominium rule. The Sudan declared its independence in January 1956. In the Arabian peninsula the British had long since controlled Arabia's outlets to the Persian Gulf and Aden at the southern tip of the Red Sea. In the hinterland, Ibn Saud forged the Kingdom of Hijaz and Najd in 1932 after finally defeating the Hashemites in Hijaz.

In most places Western ideas penetrated the Arab-Islamic mind and reshaped political thinking, especially in North Africa where a clear mass-elite cultural dichotomy dominated society. Western notions of liberalism, democracy, secularism, and nationalism became hot issues in the Arab political discourse, although they did not transcend the level of an intellectual veneer. In the meantime the crisis of identity and legitimacy persisted while the Arabs pondered their future as they woke up to the bitter reality of the collapse—if only symbolic—of the Islamic state, the overwhelming power of the West, and inter-Arab factiousness.

The Dashing of Hopes

The creation of Israel and the political inadequacies of the traditional ruling elites destroyed fragile Arab liberalism and nascent secularism. Young and politically inexperienced army officers launched successful military coups in key Arab states such as Egypt, Syria, and Iraq and promised to promote Arab unity, achieve economic and political development, and destroy the Jewish state. Debilitating as it was to the Arab psyche, the loss of Palestine raised new hopes, nevertheless. Arab nationalism surged; ironically, the dazzling successes of the Zionist movement stimulated its revival. The new version of Arab nationalism was radical, that is, anti-Western (for betraying the Arabs and planting Israel in their midst), anti-Zionist (for taking Palestine and revealing to the Arabs the extent of their incompetence), and at odds with Arab traditionalists (for the warmth of their relations with the West and their lukewarm concern for the plight of the displaced Palestinians).

The Damascus-based Arab Socialist Ba'th Party championed the cause of Arab unity with its expanded boundaries which encompassed all countries between the Atlantic Ocean and the Persian Gulf. However, the banner of Arabism soon went to Egypt's charismatic president, Gamal 'Abdul Nasser, who, as of the mid-1950s, expressed great interest in Arab affairs. His defiant interaction with the West endeared him to the Arab masses who saw their salvation and redemption in his person.[23] But Nasser's forthright approach and heavy dependence on rhetoric aggravated Arab divisiveness and fell short of achieving the elusive dream of Arab unity. On 28 September 1961 a military coup in Damascus by a group of discontented army officers terminated Syria's three-year union with Egypt.

Inter-Arab hostility gained momentum in the aftermath of the republican coup in Yemen on 26 September 1962. Egypt sent a large contingent of its army to support the beleaguered republicans in San'a', while Saudi Arabia sponsored the royalists operating against Egyptian troops from Yemen's impregnable mountains. Unification talks between Egypt and the new Ba'thist regimes in Damascus and Baghdad collapsed in the spring of 1963, leading to a heavy exchange of propaganda warfare between the two sides. The Arab summit held in Cairo in January 1964 did little to alleviate political strife among Arabs. If anything, the decision of the conferees to divert the tributaries of the Jordan River provided the major impetus for the Six Day War in 1967, which resulted in an unprecedented military defeat to the armies of Egypt, Syria, and Jordan and put an effective end to hopes of recovering Palestine and bringing about Arab unity. Instead, the Arab countries, especially the confrontation states, concentrated their efforts on retrieving the land Israel occupied in June 1967.

The Arabs' prewar mood of confidence in their military might, particularly in the Egyptian armed forces, changed to disgrace and loss of faith in their elites including the so-called progressives. The influence and prestige of al-'Asifa forces, the military wing of Yasser 'Arafat's Fat'h movement—on the defensive since they launched their first attack in northern Israel in January 1965—increased rapidly after the war. In the eyes of Arab publics, these irregular fighters were doing a better job in fighting Israel than the combined armed forces of Egypt, Syria, and Jordan. Before long, the number of guerrilla movements launching raids against Israel mushroomed as radical political movements (Arab nationalists and communists) and embarrassed states (such as Syria and Iraq) followed the example of 'Arafat and established their own. Even Egypt, which was lukewarm to the Fat'h movement before the Six Day War, found it difficult to stay out of the race.[24] In 1969 Munazzamat Tahrir Sina' al-'Arabiyya (the Arab front for the liberation of Sinai), an extension of the Egyptian army, announced a series of military operations against Israeli forces on the eastern bank of the Suez Canal. The rise of guerrilla organizations, the demise of radical pan-Arabism, and the ascendancy of territorial nationalism failed to bring about balance and a sense of direction to Arab politics. The malaise caused by the ideological retreat of Islam in the nineteenth century, the collapse of the Islamic state, the coming of Europe, and the planting of Israel proved too deep to overcome, as proved by subsequent events.

The Years of Misdirection

Recovering the territory lost to Israel proved to be the most divisive issue for the Arabs in the years that followed the June 1967 war. The first reaction to the consequences of the war was rejection and a pledge not to give in to Israel. Thus Arab heads of states convened in Khartoum in September 1967 and issued their three famous "no's" vis-à-vis Israel: no reconciliation, no recognition, and no negotiations. However, the realization that their armies were too weak to take on the Israeli army prompted Egypt and Jordan in November 1967 to accept British-proposed U.N. Security Council Resolution 242. The resolution, which called for returning lost Arab territory in exchange for Arab recognition of the Hebrew state, was immediately rejected by Syria and the PLO. The Palestinians increased the pace of their raids against Israel, but the latter responded heavy-handedly. Palestinian use of Jordanian and Lebanese territories as staging grounds drew these two Arab countries reluctantly into the fray. Israel continued to demonstrate its military superiority as Egypt's war of attrition along the Suez Canal proved counterproductive. In view of the pessimistic military situation, especially after Israel started a series of in-depth air raids in Egypt, Nasser announced on 23 July 1970 his acceptance of U.S. Secretary of State William Rogers's peace initiative.

To show their displeasure with the Rogers Plan, which they regarded as a betrayal to the Palestinian cause, members of the Popular Front for the Liberation of Palestine hijacked three Western passenger airplanes to northern Jordan and blew them up after releasing the passengers. The incident provided the direct cause for King Husayn's all-out war against the Palestinian movements in September 1970, which effectively ended their presence in Jordanian territory. With Syrian help, the defeated Palestinians crossed to Lebanon, where they established a defacto mini-state in this politically and religiously divided country.

Even though the Lebanese factions did not lack the motive for feuding among themselves, the influx of armed Palestinians upset the country's fragile sectarian balance and surely slipped it into the throes of civil war. The civil war not only exposed the tenuousness of Lebanon's liberalism and its mode of religious coexistence, but it also revealed the frailty of the Middle East's state system. Arab money and scheming helped keep the civil war alive for fifteen years. For neighboring Arab countries Lebanon provided a forward battleground and a first line of defense for their illegitimate regimes. The Lebanese war, a microcosm of Arab vulnerabilities, foretold what would become of the Arab world within a few years. Michael Hudson predicted an era of turbulence in the Arab world in the 1990s. He suggested, in response to the rapid expansion of the machinery of the state between the 1960s and 1980s, that the enlargement of the government did not necessarily imply its becoming stronger.[25] Hudson's premonition successfully grasped the domestic determinants of Arab politics as they actually transpired with the opening of the last decade of the twentieth century. He said: "Indeed, the growth of the state itself, in its bureaucratic dimension, is responsible for a growing estrangement. Burgeoning bureaucracy breeds frustration; lack of access breeds resentment; ubiquitous repression breeds subversion; ineffective policy exacerbates discontent, bruises interests, and generates protest. Politicized elements in a society increasingly educated and yet excluded from access to power incessantly challenge the right of regimes to rule. Moreover, the extent to which incumbent regimes are perceived as 'clients' of external powers pursuing 'neo-imperialist' policies will also weaken their legitimacy."[26]

The oil boom in the early 1970s both delayed the onset of widespread opposition in the Arab world and set the stage for its violent eruption in the 1990s. The huge oil revenues of Arab states in the Persian Gulf area paved the way for launching gigantic and unparalleled development projects. Structurally, the area leaped from the medieval age into the fourth quarter of the twentieth century almost overnight. Lavish government spending transformed the Gulf states into oases of welfare, thus preempting the development of demand groups outside the ruling establishment.

Oil money trickled into neighboring Arab countries and gave a semblance of normality to their weak economies. Most funds took the form of foreign aid and financial transfers by the millions of expatriate workers to their countries of origin, namely Egypt, Sudan, Yemen, Syria, and Lebanon. Everywhere in the Arab world development eluded the leaders. Simplistic plans, widespread corruption and nepotism, and concentration on the economic aspect of development, to the detriment of its political counterpart, doomed the process. The advent of the oil glut in 1980 lowered the price per barrel and decreased market demand. The reduction of oil revenues forced the Gulf states to curtail their development and welfare programs. It also led them to send back large numbers of Arab workers to their countries of origin, which had little employment opportunities to offer.

Outside the Arabian peninsula, Iraq, Sudan, and Algeria missed a unique opportunity to modernize their countries. Endowed with plentiful natural resources and able workforces, these countries had the opportunity to provide models for Third World development. But factionalism, ideological myopia, and personal politics reduced them to civil war (Algeria), ignominiousness and defeat (Iraq), and sectarian strife (Sudan). The failures of modern Arab politics, at all levels of operation, produced a political vacuum and resulted in the current mood of gloom.

The State of Oblivion

Two centuries of successive setbacks and frustrations finally have had their toll on the Arab mind. The first wave of European colonialism put an end to the Islamic reform movement of Afghani, 'Abdu, and their likes. Western-friendly Arab nationalism of the last quarter of the nineteenth century and the first two decades of the twentieth, the offspring of missionary effort in the Levant, was devastated by the introduction of Anglo-French mandate in the Fertile Crescent. The issuance of the Balfour Declaration and the subsequent creation of the state of Israel had the impact of radicalizing Arab nationalism by giving it a fascistic demeanor. Arab unity sentiments reached a peak during the 1950s and 1960 yet achieved little in terms of actual unions. The brief merger between Egypt and Syria ended in acrimony that revealed the elusiveness of the concept of Arab unity, and the magnitude of Arab unreadiness for it. Apart from paying lip service, Arab leaders neither showed genuine interest in unity nor demonstrated willingness to pursue it diligently. Even the 1990 union between the northern and southern parts of Yemen is not a cause for celebration by Arab nationalists. Heavy tribal infighting in the fall of 1990 raised a serious question about the tenability of the union. The answer came in May 1994 when war broke out between the two Yemeni parts. Although the north prevailed and restored the union, the staggering human and material cost of the war makes the question about the viability of mergers in tribal settings more compelling.[27]

The Yemeni War succeeded the Gulf War launched by the United States and its hastily assembled coalition against Iraq, following the latter's invasion of Kuwait on 2 August 1990. The war created a major schism in the Arab world as most ruling elites sided with the United States while the masses supported Iraq. The rallying of Arab troops, especially from Saudi Arabia, Egypt, and Syria, to fight alongside the Americans, British, and French shocked the Arab publics everywhere. It was particularly agonizing for the Arabs to see their leading armies show unusual vigor in fighting Iraq, none of which they had ever shown in dealing with Israel. Most Arabs perceived the U.S. move against Iraq as a deliberate act to destroy Iraq's significant military, scientific, and economic potential. In this connection, Muhammad Hallaj insisted that the administration of U.S. President George Bush, despite its public proclamations to the contrary, ". . . was in fact going the extra mile for war."[28]

Earlier, Iraq fought Iran for eight years from 1980 until 1988 in a war that drained the two countries' resources and split the Arabs between the two foes. For many years Arab masses hoped, in vain, that their elites would mobilize all available resources to contain Israel and reinstate the Palestinian refugees. Instead, Iraq launched a senseless, and practically unwinnable war against the new Islamic republic in Iran and received full financial support from the Gulf Cooperation Council states and significant military assistance from Egypt. On the other hand, Syria and Libya transferred valuable military hardware to Iran, namely surface-to-surface missiles.

Previous developments pointed to intense fragmentation in the Arab political order. These included the inception of the civil war in Lebanon in

1975 and Egypt's defection from the Arab camp by signing two frameworks for peace with Israel toward the end of 1978. Israel's invasion of Lebanon in June 1982, eviction of the PLO, and entry of Beirut three months later all signified the extent of Arab disarray and lack of resolve. In this seemingly dead-end situation, the Arabs opted for peace with Israel; nevertheless, the Jewish state proved to be an exceptionally tough negotiator and less than forthcoming on the idea of land for peace.

It is in this atmosphere of defeat, lack of leadership, and loss of direction that Islamic groups surged powerfully in many Arab lands. In Egypt, Lebanon, Algeria, the Sudan, Bahrain, and eventually Saudi Arabia, the Islamists emerged as the new definer of identity, and a major contender for political authority. The ideological vacuum caused by the retreat of Arab nationalism has been compensated for by Islamic identity. The result is that today the Arabs find themselves at the crossroads as they try to determine who they are, what they aspire to, and how to locate their place on the map of a rapidly changing world. In view of this, chapter 2 will focus its attention on the components of identity. This is very important since the examination of the theoretical underpinnings of identity will place the forthcoming discussion of Arab nationalism and Islamic revival in proper perspective.

2

Identity and Political Entity

Identity is an inherent property of mankind. It would not be an exaggeration to say that it forms the raison d'être of human earthly being. Loss of identity leads to social marginalization, and to political ineptitude in open and competitive societies. Apart from the great impact of identity on political behavior, it has an unsurpassed influence on interpersonal relationships including socialization, the vehicle for cultural dissemination. The formation of identity normally corresponds to the patterns of population distribution. Living together eventually generates distinct group values; also, individuals of similar persuasions may choose to relocate to a new territory so that they can immerse themselves in shared values. Identities are dynamic phenomena constantly influenced by social space, geopolitics, fresh ideas, and changes in the mode of production. Identities evolve to the extent that culture permits, the latter itself being subject to complex environmental changes. Mach Zdzislaw recognizes identity as a complex whole that ". . . represents the multidimensional, integrated human personality and cannot be reduced to a series of separate roles which an individual plays in various social groups and situations."[1] They are true representations of cognitive realities at certain points in time. Hence they are authentic replications of group experiences, achievements, and aspirations; they often express themselves in terms of specific social organization.

Political anthropologists generally distinguish between two types of social organization, which inevitably lead to varying forms of political structure and behavior. Essentially, these are segmentary (decentralized) and inclusive (centralized) systems. Segmentary systems include simple egalitarian, rank, and stratified societies, whereas inclusive societies produce the modern state.[2] The concept of the state as we know it today has deep European roots going back to the Treaty of Westphalia in 1648, which dealt a heavy blow to medieval universalism and introduced etatism, the precursor of nationalism.[3] The following section will explore the development of nationalism to the extent that it gave birth to the nation-state.

The Birth of the Nation-State in the West

In Europe, land, language, culture, and ethnic differentiation—the products of prolonged historical interactions—finally enabled the monarchs, who provided the symbols of national unification, to centralize and rationalize political authority and forge new bonds of identification that gave birth to the nation-state. Political development (assessed in terms of institutionalization and broad participation) and changes in the mode of production appear to have ensured the concretization of the nationalistic idea and its embodiment in statehood. This process entailed a steady decline in the political imperatives of religion and the symmetrical upsurge of secularism. The transformation involved a shift in the origin of sovereignty from the divine to the state; by inference, the people became the source of legislation.

The great social, political, and economic implications of the nationalistic phenomenon in Europe have intrigued many social scientists and enticed them to explore its complex dimensions. Hans Kohn, who saw a connection between the emergence of nationalism and broad integration of the masses in the political system, dismissed the universal utility of the doctrine. He emphasized that ". . . nationalism is not a natural phenomenon, not a product of 'eternal' or 'natural' laws; it is a product of the growth of social and intellectual factors at a certain stage of history."[4] Kohn insisted that its development largely depends on the fulfillment of "certain objective bonds."[5] Similarly, an approving Eugene Kamenka advanced the theory that "nations arise by historical accident, that is as the result of various factors not linked to each other by iron necessity."[6] The triumph of the nationalist drive results in heightening the status of the state at the expense of the individual, who now assumes a subservient role. This happens only when the individual accepts that ". . . he and the state are one,"[7] as Elie Kedourie has commented.

The literature on nationalism points to the primacy of the political and economic variables in the formation of new European societies, namely the latter's impact on the division of labor, and hence on social stratification. According to Karl Deutsch, a modern nationalistic society ". . . is a group of individuals connected by an intense division of labor, and separated from other societies by a marked drop in this intensity."[8] Ernest Gellner, who attributed political legitimacy to nationalism and drew a parallel between ethnic and political boundaries, proposed that it is a certain form of homogeneity (not the other way around) dictated by changes in the mode of production that "eventually appears on the surface in the form of nationalism."[9] Since Gellner's nationalistic model hinged on industrialization and a standardized educational system based on communication, he quickly precluded its proliferation successfully in agrarian societies. Gellner expressed his reservations in the following manner: "The social organization of agrarian society . . . is not at all favorable to the nationalist principle, to the convergence of political and cultural units, and to the homogeneity and school-transmitted nature of culture within each political unit. . . . [N]ationalism is, essentially, the general imposition of a high culture on society, where previously low cultures had taken up the lives of the majority, and in some cases of the totality, of the population."[10]

Anthony Smith shared Gellner's thoughts regarding the connection between culture and identity. Smith understood a community's national ideal in relation to its "vision of the world and a certain type of culture."[11] His emphasis on historical experience in shaping culture is especially important for understanding the dilemma of Arab nationalism, as well as the ease with which Islam is currently reasserting its influence in Arab and Muslim lands. The last section in this chapter treats the influence of religion as an alternative to ethnonationalism more closely.

Joseph Strayer considered the period of the collapse of the Roman empire as the starting point for Europe's march toward nation building. The fall of Rome facilitated the emergence of the barbarian regna and the demographic reshaping of the continent.[12] These two changes constituted the initial building blocks for the emergence of present European ethnonational states. Deeper societal interactions occurred that made possible the breakup of medieval universalism in the interest of centralized state authority. The church propagated the idea of monarchical justice and lent support for its administration. Similarly, the monarchs realized that the maintenance of their power required the fulfillment of public demands for law and order.[13] The synthesis of complex social, political, cultural, and economic variables finally transformed nationalism in Europe into a state of mind. In the nation-state setup, Tamotsu Shibutani and Kian Kwan argued, a citizen "owes his supreme loyalty to his nation, and children are taught to place love of country above all else."[14] Loyalty and love have political implications since they confer legitimacy to the system of governance, which is needed for managing an organized society. Equally important, the ensuing affinity endows the members of an ethnonational state what Talcott Parsons has termed a "diffuse enduring solidarity."[15] The rise of national consciousness and the concretization of the idea of the nation-state in Europe proceeded solely between the fourteenth and eighteenth centuries. Kamenka noted that economic development augmented the transition into the age of nationalism by "transforming the domestic economy of the rural manor and the urban guild into a national economy."[16]

It makes no difference whether it was the economic variable that launched the nationalistic vehicle in Europe, or whether it was just one important variable which, along with others, had the combined effect of producing the European nationalisms we know today. No matter how one looks at the origins of European nationalisms, the end result is that they are there, most probably the outcome of a multivariable historical interaction. The salient consequences of the advent of European nationalisms included the formation of a new political consciousness based on anonymous membership in a national community in which the participants achieve a fairly high level of mobilization resting on solidarity and an accepted political program.

The march of nationalism in Europe did not stop at the walls of the continent; instead, it swept throughout the world causing reverberations in countries as distant as China and Japan. The pervasiveness of the nationalistic doctrine has invited a pertinent comment from Smith: "No other vision has set its stamp so thoroughly on the map of the world, and on our sense of identity."[17] The next section discusses how nationalism found its way outside Europe, namely in Africa and Asia.

The Universalization of the Nation-State Phenomenon

Nationalism spread beyond Europe in the early years of the nineteenth century, first to the Ottoman empire's Christian peripheries, then into the Near East, until it eventually reached the most remote areas of Asia and Africa by the 1950s. It is not easy to account for everything that caused the tide of nationalism, but it is safe to make a case for some generally agreed upon contributing factors. The list includes Western liberal ideas, Europe's dazzling industrial achievements, colonialism, and the standardization of the nation-state concept in international relations. There is little doubt about the range and reach of European impact on the dormant ethnicities in Asia and Africa; everywhere, it awakened ethnic consciousness and gave it a seemingly permanent political charge. Hans Kohn, who dealt with this matter in the 1920s, brilliantly explained the Western-inspired transformation of the non-European races. He said:

> By the end of the nineteenth century it seemed assured that, with negligible exceptions, Asia and Africa were to fall under the dominion of the White race. Christian missionaries brought not only the religious conceptions of the West to the Orient, but wherever they succeeded in establishing schools they brought European political and social doctrines. And this fresh contact between East and West

brought new life to the East, as centuries before Arabian influences had helped shape modern Europe. . . . Europe became not merely the adversary but the schoolmaster. Western ideas concerning manners and customs, the principles of statecraft, religion, democracy, and industry began slowly to penetrate to the East.[18]

In areas where Western ideas advanced ahead of colonialism, the latter tarnished the transformation to nationalism, often radicalizing it. In Africa, colonialism preceded Western ideas and disturbed tribalism (the dominant social form of organization) without eliminating it. In this context African nationalism, and many other nationalisms in the Third World, thrived on anticolonialism instead of reflecting genuine societal change. For example, social science analysts expressed utter disbelief when, in Morocco, traditional Berbers joined the ranks of Arab insurgents against French Protectorate officials.[19] The trajectory of events in the Third World (and in Arab countries for our purposes) since the 1950s explains why nationalism seemed appropriate at the time. Put simply, nationalism was in vogue; Asian and African peoples aspiring for an identity to keep up with changing times hastily wore the loose robe of nationalism. In due time it got too tight for the expression of their genuine needs, not to mention airing unresolved grievances. Rupert Emerson realized the inherent problems in African nationalisms south of the Sahara where "the basic foundations for national communities still remained to be achieved after the nationalists had been called into action."[20]

Aspiring national movements and rising charismatic leaders such as Sukarno in Indonesia, Nasser in Egypt, Nkrumah in Ghana, and Nyerere in Tanzania sought to develop their countries by grounding their efforts in nation and citizen building. They all failed. The euphoria generated by the proliferation of national movements, which became powerful after the end of World War II, and the crumbling of French and British colonial empires did not last long. They soon had to reckon with the realities imposed by their countries' social structures deeply embedded in wholesale inner divisions. Involvement in the East-West superpower rivalry, even as they preached the principle of nonalignment, and tinkering in regional politics sidetracked them from their primary objectives. The neat division of the world into a community of interactive nation-states under the umbrella of the United Nations gave in to the intricacies of international relations and tangles of domestic politics. Before the end of the 1960s, domestic tensions in many Third World countries reached a peak and threatened the fiber of their fragile societies. Economic development was bogged down, and the fuzzy notion of the state showed signs of fatigue; simultaneously, political opposition mounted and separatist ethnic groups took up arms to plead their cases. In less than a quarter of a century, the upbeat mood of national self-determination and nation building in the Third World gave way to pessimism as Western-injected nationalism stumbled over the persistence of historical and cultural constraints.

The Limits of the Western Nationalistic Model

The initial appeal of nationalism, which proved highly successful in launching politically modern and economically developed nation-states in Europe, quickly regressed into aversion as primordial forms of identification reasserted themselves in many African and Asian countries. Political nationalism proved maladaptive to non-Western cultures, perhaps except in Confucian and Buddhist environments where a self-contained version of protonationalism existed for centuries in most societies there. The concept of the modern nation-state rests on the premise of an organic relationship between the wielder of power and the governed. The essentials of this relationship includes the public responsibility of the governor and the civic responsibility of the governed. The political system must possess, according to Joel Migdal, sufficient capabilities that include "the capacities to penetrate society, regulate social relationships, extract resources, and appropriate or use resources in determined ways."[21] The fact that political and cultural evolution in most non-Western societies has not fulfilled the essential prerequisites of state nationalism implies systemic malfunctioning—when Western concepts are applied—in terms of political performance.

The intrusion of the concept of the nation-state on African and Asian peoples has created far more tensions than resolved problems. Under the guise of centralizing and rationalizing authority, the Western colonial powers have established states without foundations and constructed artificial boundaries for them. The new system of governance ignored village and regional particularism, which was not conspicuously injurious under a loose federation system, and became particularly damaging in the imposed nation-state context.[22] One of the main liabilities of particularism on state functioning relates to the nature of interpersonal relationships. Reflecting personal experience as an educator in Syria during the 1950s, Alford Carleton summed up his impressions as follows: "The basic problem of the integrated Arab [in society] is that he needs to work through the question of his social culture. The basic problems of the area are not technological. They are not even, at heart, economic but sociological. . . . They are the problems of human inter-relationships."[23] Carleton noticed the absence, among Syrian college students with whom he dealt in Aleppo, of social responsibility and coordinated thinking.[24] By the latter he meant the ability of an individual to work in a group on an anonymous basis. At the root of the problem of political integration is the issue of the kinship groups which existed in the region long before the coming of Islam. The new religion did not challenge the kinship groups—with their emphasis on personal relationships—as long as they defended the caliph and paid tribute to Islam, even if nominally.[25] Although by the late eighteenth century traditional Islam seemed no longer capable of controlling social tensions and maintaining the apparent unity of the community, state nationalism of the twentieth century hardly provided a viable alternative.

Emerson has defined the nation as a community of people brought together by past experiences and future expectations.[26] If this is the case, and there is no reason to assume otherwise, then the majority of Third World states would amount to little more than inappropriate structural transplants. An evident weakness of the state system outside Western societies is the tendency among many populations to eschew interaction with the state in terms of impersonal rules. Robert Presthus said that abiding by established rules of the game is a characteristic of nationally oriented and self-conscious groups.[27] The political dilemma in most Third World societies glaringly presents itself in the weakness of identification with the modern state, purportedly the inheritor of traditional forms of organization and association.

Religion as a Competing Form of Identity

If Western publics could not be free without a nation-state of their own, the opposite holds true for many other peoples. Ethnonationalism has located earthly sources for fraternity, equality, and justice, its most cherished mottoes. Conversely, religious nationalism seeks a divine path for the attainment of mundane needs, and by mixing the temporal with the spiritual it gives the upper hand to the latter. It is the content of a group's collective consciousness that determines whether it is predisposed to a distinct and secular form of ethnonationalism, religious nationalism, or some inconclusive form of interaction between ethnicity and religion. In Asian and African societies, namely among Muslims, the clash between ethnonationalism and religion seems to resolve itself to the detriment of the former, without the latter emerging as a clear victor. This indicates the presence of a serious consciousness problem in which faith, personality structure, and national identity manage to interact but fail to interlock. Out of this convolution of ideas certain periods witness a surge in ethnonationalism which, in the absence of grassroots social transformation and robust economic activity, eventually recedes against the onslaught of stand-by religious ideas, and vice versa. In the absence of a societal breakthrough whose ideas successfully penetrate the collective consciousness of the masses, the vicious cycle of doctrinal wandering goes on indefinitely.

Religion has always played a momentous role in the lives of both individuals and collectivities, no matter how they viewed the relationship between religion and politics. The supremacy of the nationalistic doctrine in the modern history of Western societies has not done away with religion. Nationalism only privatized faith through a lengthy, but partially incomplete, process. To be sure, religion continues to play a variable role in the polities of Western societies. For example, Hugh Seton-Watson recognized the impact of religion on the development of certain nationalistic movements in Europe and North America. He cited the influence of Catholic priests on the development of national feelings among the Basques, the Bretons, the Croatians, and the Quebecois. He credited the Catholic church in Poland for standing up against Soviet penetration, and gaining the confidence of the vast majority of Poles.[28]

In the United States, religion asserted itself in political affairs as early as the colonial period. After independence, the churches played a major role in establishing the Indian territories and championing the abolition movement. Other important politically relevant functions assumed by churches included the socialization of new immigrants into U.S. institutions and way of life and participation in the civil rights, anti-Vietnam war, labor, and woman suffrage movements. More recently, Catholic bishops opposed U.S. policy in Central America and advocated the introduction of democratic rule into its political systems.[29] Chief executives have not antagonized mainstream religious movements and leaders. In fact, religion played a role in presidential campaigns at least for the Richard Nixon, Jimmy Carter, and Ronald Reagan campaigns. Nixon adopted a "Southern Strategy" in order to gain support from southern Evangelicals who traditionally identified with the Democrats. Jim Castelli revealed that "for years it was almost impossible to go to the White House without tripping over Billy Graham."[30] Carter, who pursued an active and well-publicized church attendance, urged federal civil servants to get married so that they would not live in sin. Reagan's 1980 presidential campaign focused on the silent majority, an allusion to the rise of the radical right. Preoccupation with a possible change in the political mood of Anglo-America has alarmed many politicians and academicians about the reshaping of American society into radicalism.[31]

Even though religion has not ceased to exercise some influence on political matters in Western countries, it remains, nevertheless, subservient to the authority of the secular state. There, the fundamental change in power relationships saw a shift in the locus of earthly sovereignty from God and his papal intermediary to the state. The church could not stem the tide of the centralized state; instead, it chose ". . . to transform itself to accommodate these challenges from the state."[32] In spite of the agility of American religious groups and spokespersons, the strength of the secular political system obtained constitutional legitimacy when the First Amendment to the U.S. Constitution put a "wall of separation" between religion and politics by prohibiting ". . . the government from establishing a state religion or interfering with religious affairs."[33] The institutionalization of the idea of the secular state in the West and its faltering in the Third World keeps religious activity bounded by agreed upon rules of the political game in the former, and beyond the control of the weak state in the latter.

In developing countries, religious movements do not just discuss the moral dimension of public issues—as most of their Western counterparts normally do—but they employ doctrine to advance their case against the state. In doing so, they resort to religious authority which they delegate to themselves. The surge of religious groups, while itself a universal phenomenon, made a forceful showing in Hindu and Muslim societies.[34] Peter Van Der Veer observed that the failure of secularization in India and the increase in the pace of politically oriented religious activism instead occur ". . . despite rapid industrialization and urbanization and the spread of educational institutions—all aspects of 'modernization.'"[35] The overlap between politics and religion among India's Hindus and Muslims characterizes Middle Eastern societies where, in recent years, Islam has surfaced as a serious contender for political influence in most countries. Writers on Arab affairs currently appear more appreciative of the political weight of Islam, among other things, than in previous decades. Writing in 1990, Issa Boullata successfully outlined the significance of Islam on different aspects of the Arabs' way of life. The following excerpt summarizes his strong argument: "That Islam is an inalienable component of Arab culture is not only a historical fact of the greatest significance, but it is also a socio-psychological factor that continues to this very day to be of the utmost importance on the existential level. Secularistic Arab modernists who have ignored this truth or made light of it have continuously seen their projects dashed on its reality."[36] Historical developments in the world of Islam did not produce Europe's processes that led to the emergence of the nation, the state, and the modern national economy which in due time eroded the political power of the church. Thus faith persists not only as a belief system but also as a protest movement and as a vehicle for profound political change.

The contemporary strength of religious movements in the Arab world by no means indicates the absence of doctrinal change in modern history, rather its intensity. The recent surge of Islamic fundamentalism occurred at the expense of other doctrines such as pan-Arabism, territorial nationalism, and regional cooperation councils. Western ideas of nationalism, market economy, secularism, and liberal democracy have surely influenced Arab thinking since the nineteenth century without dislodging the spiritual power of Islam, nor its underlying political potential. The arrest of religious reform in Islam by the advent of Western colonialism in the Nile Valley and North Africa, and the early defeat of nascent Arab nationalism by the introduction of Anglo-French mandate in the Fertile Crescent, have complicated resolution of the emerging identity crisis among the speakers of Arabic.

Militant religious groups attempting to create Islamic political orders in the Middle East only complicate events in a volatile and conflict-ridden region. Even though active Islamic groups agree on the fundamentals of religion, they articulate competing religious persuasions, pertaining to Islamic jurisprudence, that impose limitations on the scope of their cooperation.

Present Arab governments operate in an atmosphere of ideological loss, marginality in regional and international affairs, social unrest masquerading in Islamic revival, and an uncertain political future. The next chapters deal with these issues, but chapter 3 will focus on the long journey of Arab nationalism from its genesis in the 1870s until its decline in the late 1960s.

The Case for Arab Nationalism

Arab ethnicity wielded substantial influence in the tribal politics of Arabia and the fringes of Byzantium and Persia, long before the appearance of Islam in the beginning of the seventh century. The amazing triumph of Islam and its brilliant expansion (in Syria, Egypt, North Africa, Iraq, Persia, and the Caucasus) extended the domain of Arab influence beyond the wildest imagination on the eve of Arab advances, best referred to as the Muslim conquests. The glory of the Arab race reached its peak during the years of the Umayyad empire (660–750), thanks to Mu'awiya, its first caliph, who introduced a dynasty and stood accused of changing Islam's prophetic caliphate into the temporal sovereignty of kingship.[1] 'Abdul Malak and 'Abdul Walid, Mu'awiya's successors, Arabized the administration and introduced the Arab dinar and dirham as standard currency to replace widely used Persian and Byzantine coins.[2] The Arab character of the Umayyad empire rested on an elitist social caste of peninsular conquerors who maintained themselves by eschewing close interaction with the indigenous population.[3]

The Arabs who built an impressive empire had failed, mainly due to their inner divisions, to endow it with longevity. Bernard Lewis emphasized that "the main internal weakness of the Umayyad order and that on which it ultimately fell was the recurrent feuds of the Arab tribes themselves."[4] Islam had apparently not succeeded in reconciling the differences between the northern (Qaysi) and southern (Yemeni) tribes. Following a brief remission in tribal hostility in the early phase of Islam, conflict regained its full intensity after the death of the resourceful caliph Mu'awiya, whom historians consider as probably the most influential Arab statesman of all times. Prophet Muhammad seemed less interested in undermining the political relevance of the tribes than in uniting them in a community of believers (*Ummat al-Muslimin*). Thus the Constitution of Medina of A.D. 622 introduced the concept of *ummah* as a means to bring the Arab tribes together in a conciliatory state. Wilson Bishai saw the move as a step toward instilling an Arab national character.[5]

Islam's sanctioning of tribal authority eventually gave birth to a multi-layered community of believers that included familial, clannish, tribal, regional, and ethnic elements. Abid al-Marayati felt that this arrangement yielded a traditional Middle Eastern society composed "of relatively closed but interlocking ethnic groups, religious sects, craft organizations . . . [and] village-nomad-urban complexes. . . ."[6] By necessity, the emerging political system—the precursor of modern Arab systems—adopted accommodation as a means for resolving tensions and sought to maintain the status quo. Instead of integrating the different groups in the political program of a responsive government, the ruling elite encouraged the development of a closed and anti-change system. Manfred Halpern appreciated traditional Islam's ability to transform tensions into balances ". . . for more than a millennium in a harsh and uncertain environment."[7] But he concluded that Islam fell short of meeting the challenges of modernity and that, hence, tensions went out of control and expedited the collapse of the Islamic state.

The fall of the Umayyad empire and the rise of Persians, Seljuks, and Mamluks to the pinnacle of royal power in the Islamic state forced ethnic Arabs to redefine their notion of the Arab race. During the Abbasid period "an important change was taking place in the meaning of the word Arab itself. . . . [T]he Arabs ceased to be a closed hereditary caste and became a people, ready to accept . . . any Muslim speaking Arabic as one of themselves."[8] The emergence of the Shu'ubi movement among Persians, who demanded political recognition and built their case on a rich culture, awakened a certain Arab feeling that did not develop into nationalism proper. Nationalism had not yet made its appearance anywhere in the world. Furthermore, ethnic tendencies in the Islamic state remained subject to Islam's still useful method of accommodation, which precluded the possibility of open interethnic conflict. Islam still provided political identity even for decades after it became evident that the Ottoman empire, languishing from a combination of domestic decay and Western intrigue, seemed doomed to collapse.

The Beginnings: Nationalism without Consciousness

Ibrahim Pasha, who led the Egyptian army into Syria in 1830, introduced the concept of Arab nationalism for the first time in front of an assembly of Western consuls in Egypt. He talked to them about his political agenda which included the creation of a distinct nationalistic identity for the speakers of Arabic.[9] Ibrahim Pasha's dynastic ambitions encouraged him to pursue far-fetched territorial objectives that hinged on a false nationalistic consciousness. True, from the early sixteenth century the Islamic world had broken up into two disparate Iranian and Arab components, as Charles Issawi has correctly noted.[10] The breakup influenced the Arabs far more culturally than politically, as events in the nineteenth century had clearly demonstrated. At the time of the Egyptian expedition, Arabs in West Asia had not yet become conscious of themselves as a distinct ethnic group. The Arabization of the Fertile Crescent is a better example of cultural, rather than ethnic, transformation. In fact, the failure of the Egyptian campaign in Syria attested—in addition to the forbidding role of England—to the total absence of Arab national consciousness. George Antonius fully understood the sociopolitical dynamics of the area when he said that ". . . the ambitious plan of an Arab empire, conceived by Mehemed 'Ali and nurtured by Ibrahim, failed to find in Syria the sustenance it needed and was more easily stifled by England's hostility. Its great weakness was that it was formed out of time, in advance of the birth of Arab national consciousness."[11]

Europe's abortion of state-sponsored Arab nationalism (Muhammad 'Ali's Egypt) effectively ended the possibility of uniting the Arabs in an ethnonational state. One can accept the dynastic charge against the efforts of Muhammad 'Ali and Ibrahim Pasha to create an Arab kingdom. Centuries earlier, European monarchs propagated nationalistic slogans that had dynastic aims as well. In due time however, the personal components of European nationalisms gained broad popular legitimacy and acquired an institutional status. But the major powers in Europe denied the Arabs such a historic opportunity when they decided to defeat the territorial objectives of Ibrahim Pasha's army. Subsequently, the elimination of a territorial base for the spread of Arab nationalism and the termination of ruling elite support for its cause reduced the pan-Arab drive to a theoretical exercise by intellectuals of limited political influence.

Distinct Arab associations of some political import made their first appearance at the onset of the second half of the nineteenth century. It would be a gross exaggeration to infer from the proliferation of literary, scientific, and occasionally political societies a rise in Arab national consciousness. Nothing comparable to what had previously occurred in Europe as its peoples branched out nationalistically appeared in Syria.[12] Religion-focused Arab culture had already for many centuries swayed the souls and minds of ethnic and hybrid Arabs and provided, during the Ottoman period, one of the two mainstays of the empire (the other being Turkish), the bearer of the caliphate. Ethnic and religious differentiation prevailed in the Ottoman empire and was officially sanctioned by the *millet* system that recognized a separate civic status for Christians and Jews.

What actually happened during the second half of the nineteenth century was that sustained European military activity further weakened the Ottoman empire, a process that seemed irreversible after the end of the Crimean War in 1856. Anglo-French pressure finally compelled the Ottoman leadership to unleash political liberalization which, in addition to the continued subversive impact of Europe, finally sealed the fate of the empire. Liberalization resulted in the issuance of the Hatt-i Humayun (a civil code which, in addition to introducing Western-type legal processes, put Christians and Jews on a par with Muslims as far as inclusion in the political affairs of the state). It is in this environment of Ottoman weakness, Western penetration, and local Christian immersion in public life that the first cries of Arab nationalism fell on deaf ears.

Modern Arab writers disagree on the impact and motives of early pan-Arab associations. Arab nationalists herald them as the resuscitators of ancient Arab glory and affinity, whereas their Islamic-oriented counterparts dismiss them as Western ploys designed to divide Arab and Turk Muslims. Thus, 'Imad 'Abdul Salam Ra'uf regarded the establishment of al-Jam'iyya al-'ilmiyya al-Suriyya (the Syrian scientific association) in 1857 and Jam'iyyat Hifz Huquq al-Milla al-'Arabiyya (the association for the preservation of the rights of the Arab ethnic group) in 1881 as landmarks in the evolution of Arab nationalism.[13] Conversely, Taqiy al-Din al-Nabahani deplored the emergence of pan-Arab associations as part of Europe's evangelical invasion that took place "under the guise of science and humanity."[14] It is correct that the spread of Jesuit missionaries preceded by a few years the formation of Arab associations. The American evangelists' decision to relocate their printing press in Malta to Beirut proved exceptionally useful in the dissemination of knowledge, notably Western ideas on liberalism and nationalism. But there is no irrefutable evidence to support the Islamists' implication of the West in promoting Arab nationalism for the purpose of destroying the Ottoman empire, which was dying anyway.

An ostentatiously proud West sought—apart from displaying military prowess, as well as appetite for colonizing African and Asian peoples and securing their raw materials and markets—to export its ideas on culture, politics, and society. Unpretentious but sometimes condescending missionaries led the drive of introducing Asians, Africans, and Near Easterners to the West's ways. In the Near East, initial missionary work made little headway as the futile experience of Jam'iyyat al-Funun wal 'Ulum (the society of arts and sciences) had shown. After five years of relentless work throughout Syria by Eli Smith and Cornelius van Dyke, the society—which attempted to spread scientific knowledge among adults and school children—failed to recruit more than fifty active members, all Christians and mostly Beirut residents.[15] Western ideas on liberal thought did not seem to interest skeptic traditional Muslims whose collective consciousness and nurtured negative images about Europe went back to the epoch of the Crusades. Recent European assumption of overwhelming military and economic power relative to the world of Islam only rekindled Muslim fears, causing them to shun the ideas of the Christian West.

Paranoia and the Islamic modus vivendi coalesced to bar the influx of the European-inspired tide of nationalism among Muslim Near Easterners. Thus, other associations, such as al-Jam'iyya al-Sharqiyya (the Oriental society) founded by the Jesuits in 1850, met doom since it attracted only a handful of all-Christian members. Even the founding in 1857 of al-Jam'iyya al-'Ilmiyya al-Suriyya (the Syrian scientific association), whose success in recruiting Muslims and Druze has led observers to credit the association with achieving an important ideological penetration in the Levant, had little impact on the mainstream of society. Its 150 members adopted a program for reconciling Syria's sectarian divisions and socializing the masses into Arab nationalism. For the Muslim majority, the pan-Islamic policies of Sultan 'Abdul Hamid had a decisive influence on their thinking and aspirations. The faint secular and nationalistic propositions went unnoticed by the rank and file. The novice doctrine of Arab nationalism attracted only a few Muslim and Druze members from notable families such as Husayn Bayham and Muhammad Arslan, and Christians who saw in Arab nationalism a lesser evil than Islam.

The formation in 1875 of al-Jam'iyya al-Sirriyya (the secret society) whose approach to Arab nationalism centered on taking religion out of politics had no impact on a population shaped by religious doctrine. Exhorting the Arabs of Syria to rise against the Turks, "who usurped the Islamic Caliphate from the Arabs and abandoned shari'a,"[16] proved equally unsuccessful. The Arabs, who generally assumed important functions in Ottoman politics and administration, found the content of Arab ethnonationalism totally indecipherable. For the most part, Arab nationalism remained an elitist slogan that did not ring a bell among the masses until subsequent developments, which included the emergence of the Young Turk movement, had shocked the Arabs and lured them to identify with a nationalism they knew little about.

Anti-Turkism: Nationalism by Default

The last decade of the nineteenth century portended the change of heart among Levantine Arabs from pan-Ottomanism to Arab nationalism. Cognizant of the difficulty that confronted Sultan 'Abdul Hamid in keeping his faltering empire together, the Khedive of Egypt, ʿAbbas Hilmi II, entertained the thought of becoming the Muslim caliph. James Jankowski traced the origin of the Khedive's fleeting idea to his meeting in 1895 with Jamal al-Din al-Afghani in Istanbul.[17] Al-Afghani must have grasped the full meaning of the profound changes that were beginning to occur inside the Turkish component of the empire. Six years earlier, a group of Turkish cadets of Istanbul's medical military academy formed the pan-Tauran Young Turk movement. The ideas of the French Revolution had a great influence on the movement, especially on its leader Ahmad Rida, who wished to transplant the civilization of the West into Turkey.[18] The Young Turks (some refer to them as the Unionists) conspicuously practiced an anti-Arab policy, especially in the military, and sought to resolve the Eastern Question by Turkification.[19] In a book entitled *Tarikh al-Mustaqbal* (History of the future), Jalal Nuri, a famed Turkish author, proposed forcing the Arabs of Syria to emigrate and urged ". . . transforming Yemen and Iraq into Turkish settlements to facilitate the propagation of the Turkish language that must become the language of religion."[20]

In the aftermath of their successful coup in 1908 against the Hamidian rule, the Unionists adopted a systematic policy of evicting Arabs from key official positions. For example, they assigned to a Turk the ministerial portfolio of religious endowment (traditionally reserved for Arabs) and deliberately excluded Arabs from assuming the top position in the ministry of foreign affairs. And to make an already tense situation even worse, the Unionists chose to appoint Turkish governors who did not speak Arabic for Arab regions; previously, Ottoman sultans committed to compromise and accommodation normally commissioned native speakers in Arab areas.[21] It appears that part of the Unionists' actions against the Arabs emanated from fears of further dismemberment of the Ottoman empire. They grew wary of secessionist tendencies, which many active Arabs tended to articulate as demands for decentralization and more political participation, and pledged to stem them.

Even before the 1908 coup, Christian Arabs, such as Najib ʿAzuri, called for establishing a secular Arab empire, headed by a prince from the Egyptian royal family, in West Asia. Given his stated intention, it remains unclear why ʿAzuri proposed autonomy for Yemen, Najd, and Iraq! It looks as if the formation of a Syrian homeland had preoccupied the thinking of ʿAzuri, which he could not contemplate without the extension of legitimacy by the dominant Muslim majority. For this reason, he produced an arrangement that considered, in addition to the secular entity, a spiritual leadership in Mecca whose political domain he limited to Hijaz.[22]

As early-twentieth-century Arab intellectuals—be they Muslims or Christians—envisaged a conceptual framework and an operational mechanism for Arab nationalism, their worldview bound them to reconcile it with Islam. Ethnonationalism was encroaching upon faith; therefore, disregarding religion would have discredited Arab nationalism in the public view. In addition, the intellectuals themselves were the product of a culture heavily influenced by Islam. It is worthwhile to restate that Arab nationalism prior to World War I acquired a following as a symbol of resistance to the pan-Tauran Unionists, not to the Islamic tenets or way of life. Muhammad al-Jabiri gave serious thought to this important issue which signified—and continues to do so in the present—the intertwinement of Arab nationalism with Islam. He said: "The beginnings of the formation of the content of modern Arab nationalism saw no contradiction between Arabism and Islamism, neither at the level of discourse nor consciousness. . . . It was not conflict with Islam as a religion and culture that determined the rise of Arab nationalism, but the . . . despotic Turkish ruler."[23]

Arab nationalism brewed as a negative movement because antagonism, rather than a doctrine of beliefs and shared values, shaped its course from the very beginning.[24] The Syrian Arab Congress which convened in Paris in 1913 did not consider the elements of Arab nationalism, not to mention defining them. Anti-Turkism constituted the sole ingredient of the un-wrapped package of Arab nationalism. Ra'uf noticed that the delegates made no reference whatsoever to the idea of merging the Arab regions of the Ottoman empire in a unitary state. Surprisingly, they accepted Ottoman administrative divisions of Arab lands as unalterable entities.[25] Consequently, they settled for Syria to embody the undefined Arab national dream.

The concoction of Arab nationalism and Islam presented itself in the first communiqué of the revolution distributed by Sharif Husayn on 26 June 1916. The communiqué described the revolution as Arab-Islamic and saw Islam as a source of strength for Arab national identity. Reciprocally, it found in the surge of Arabism glory for Islam and a way to return to shari'a.[26] The Arab masses would not have been expected to articulate national identity without reference to Islam. Mustafa 'Abdul Qadir Al-Najjar asserted (though without substantiation) that the Arab rebellion ". . . constituted a true revolution in Arab political thought."[27] However, he correctly observed that the rebellion took place "due to the bitter experience of Arab nationalists and intellectuals resulting from the Turks' racist policy."[28]

Fanned by European influence, Arab grievances against the Turkification policies of the Unionists finally took their toll on the last bonds that nominally held the Ottoman empire together.[29] After the Arab rebellion and the final defeat of Ottoman troops at the hands of the Allies, Arabs waited for the Anglo-French alliance to redeem their prewar promises.[30] Soon they came to realize that the Allies had a postwar agenda that did not include setting up an independent Arab kingdom. Waking up to the new reality, in which Britain and France had direct military control of most Arab lands, the Arabs shifted the thrust of Arab nationalism from a movement favorably disposed to the West to one bitterly anti-Western.

Anti-Westernism: Bitter Nationalism

The Sykes-Picot Agreement of May 1916 (which involved Britain, France, and tsarist Russia in a conspiracy to divide among themselves the remnants of the Ottoman empire at the end of the war) constituted the first—of many more to come—jolt for Arabs in the twentieth century. The agreement deeply shook west Asian Arabs, no matter what territorial arrangements they had cherished for the future. It denied the Hashemites in Hijaz the opportunity to establish an Arab dynasty incorporating, in addition to Arabia, the lands of the Fertile Crescent. Sykes-Picot also stifled the high-profile Arab nationalists of Damascus who aspired to establish an Arab kingdom in Syria, legitimated by some form of political linkage, either with Arabia or Egypt. The agreement represented one of the hallmarks used by Daniel Pipes to propound his ideas on Arab fears of Western conspiracy. He wrote that the Sykes-Picot Agreement ". . . remains the archetype of European perfidy . . . and is still vividly remembered and resented."[31]

Britain's issuance of the Balfour Declaration on 2 November 1917, which viewed with favor the formation of a Jewish national home in Palestine, occurred before the Arabs knew about the Sykes-Picot Agreement. Soviet disclosure of the terms of the agreement in the aftermath of the communist revolution angered the Arabs and overwhelmed them by feelings of betrayal. This episode, in addition to the Balfour Declaration and the French army's destruction of Arab rule in Damascus in July 1920, diverted the attention of Arab nationalists from struggle against former Turkish partners in the Ottoman empire to outright European colonizers. The inception of European colonialism had transformed pan-Arab nationalists from seekers of unity into activists merely preoccupied with the pursuit of independence for the territorial units created by the architects of Sykes-Picot. Al-Jabiri noticed that the achievement of independence for colonized Arab areas only formalized the division of Arab lands according to the interests of European colonial powers; Europe had not weakened but, quite to the contrary, developed indirect techniques for exercising greater influence.[32] Martin Kramer commented on Arab reaction to Western policies as follows: "Arab nationalism, once inspired by the West's liberalism, began to redefine itself as a negation of its imperialism."[33]

The main center of Arab nationalism shifted from Syria to Iraq during the interwar period, especially after the latter's independence in 1931. Led by the pan-Arab ideologue Sati' al-Husry, Syrian émigrés propagated among Iraqis the idea of Arab nationalism, ultimately convincing Nuri al-Sa'id to sponsor the project of merging the countries of the Fertile Crescent (Iraq, Syria, Lebanon, Transjordan, and Palestine) into a single state.[34] Iraq offered the only possible grounds for advocating pan-Arab doctrines since most Egyptian leaders and intellectuals showed little interest in it. Sati' al-Husry, considered by many nationalists as the father of Arab nationalism, reflected on his personally unfavorable experience in Egypt where he sought refuge after the fall of the Arab state in Syria. Recollecting how most Egyptians felt toward the events in Syria, al-Husry said: "The Egyptians showed little concern for the situation in Syria. The collapse of the Arab state there had no impact on them. We noticed that, among those who followed the news on Syria, they did not just lack in positive affective evaluation of the situation, but even condemned the Arab rebellion [against the Ottoman empire]."[35] Communist influence on al-Husry's thinking is evident in his belief in historical determinism. He took Arab nationalism, as well as its social and economic underpinnings, for granted. Al-Husry, obviously impressed by Europe's political organization along ethnonational lines, assumed it was only natural to group peoples in nationalistic states. Perceiving the embodiment of nationalism in statehood as the source of ultimate happiness, he implored Arabs to work for unity and to treat other issues as secondary.[36] He called for the formation of political movements to participate in the struggle for achieving Arab unity but neglected the mighty obstacles that stood in front of this improbable objective.

The loss of Palestine in 1948 caused severe repercussions among Arab nationalists. They blamed the defeat of the seven armies of the Arab League on a Western conspiracy and Arab official collusion. The triumph of political Zionism, the rival of Arab nationalism, further radicalized Arab nationalists in the 1950s. Immediately after the Arab debacle in Palestine, a previously unheard of militant Arab nationalist movement named Kata'ib al-Fida' al-'Arabi (Arab martyrdom units) launched a series of attacks against Western and Jewish targets in Syria and Lebanon. It dynamited the only synagogue in Damascus, and in Beirut the movement destroyed the Jewish Alliance School. Other attacks aimed at Western personnel included the attempted assassinations of the *Times'* correspondent and a British diplomat.[37] George Habash, a Palestinian medical doctor, established a movement which he called al-ʿUrwa al-Wuthqa (the close-knit association), which advocated "political struggle to eliminate Zionism and imperialism from the Arab homeland, and to create an Arab state extending from the [Persian] Gulf to the Atlantic Ocean."[38] After 1948 Palestinian activists stood in the forefront of a vibrant Arab nationalist movement that saw in Arab unity the only hope for recovering Palestine. Besides Israel and the West, they identified an Arab enemy in the form of the traditional ruling elite, whom they branded as reactionary Western proxies. In 1951 Habash renamed the movement Harakat al-Qawmiyyin al-ʿArab (movement of Arab nationalists). Apparently influenced by Soviet openness in the early 1950s to the nationalist liberation movements in Asia and Africa, he incorporated the notion of Arab socialism—a non-Marxian adaptation of communist tenets—in the movement's program of action. ʿAbdallah Sallum al-Samirraʾi, who wrote favorably on the impact of Harakat al-Qawmiyyin al-ʿArab on increasing Arab national consciousness, agreed that the movement had endorsed ". . . ideal assumptions that did not lend themselves to the formation of an integrated theory."[39]

Negativism assumed theoretical proportions as evinced by the hastily contrived tenets of the Baʿth, the leading pan-Arab political party. The Baʿth, embittered by the consequences of European colonialism, rejected the liberal ideas of the West. In their lieu, the party improvised a three-dimensional doctrine of secular Arab nationalism that integrated fascist, communist, and Islamic components. Baʿthist ideologues such as Salah al-Bitar and Michel ʿAflaq combined the radical aspect of fascist nationalism with a nonscientific version of communist socialism and garnished them with cultural Islam. The Baʿth vehemently opposed the existing system of Middle Eastern states, including the formation of Israel, and defied the logic of Marxian internationalism. Conversely, the party emphasized the historicity of the Arab nation.[40]

Before the new Arab Socialist Baʿth Party could establish itself inside Syria, let alone in neighboring Arab countries, new developments in Egypt quickly shifted the locus of Arab nationalism from the Fertile Crescent to Cairo. The Baʿth articulated a secular program of action that failed to appeal to Syria's heavily religious Muslim population. Spearheaded by members of Syria's minority groups (Greek Orthodox, Druze, and ʿAlawis)—in a country plagued by sectarianism, regionalism, and urban-rural divisions—the party could hardly present itself as a conveyor of the majority's nationalistic aspirations. The Baʿth enjoyed most of its support in the country's politicized army where, along with other factions (mainly communists and Syrian nationalists), it competed for political influence. Syria's intense political instability, caused by ideological polarization and wholesale outside intervention in its domestic affairs, further weakened the ability of the Ba'th Party to carry the banner of Arab nationalism. Gamal 'Abdul Nasser, the rising star in Cairo immediately captured the hearts of Arabs and quickly became the uncontested champion of Arab nationalism.

The Nasser Years: Unconsummated Nationalism

The Free Officers who toppled King Faruq in a bloodless coup on 23 July 1952 acted for purely Egyptian reasons. These junior army officers, mainly from lower-middle-class backgrounds, succeeded in joining the military academy as a result of the British-influenced Egyptian government's decision to expand the army after the rise of Nazism in Germany and Fascism in Italy. The primary objectives of the republican regime in Cairo focused on ending British control of the Suez Canal Zone, agrarian reform, constructing a solid industrial base, and building a strong national army. Shortly after the revolution, Nasser outlined the Free Officers' agenda in a pamphlet entitled *Falsafat al-Thawra* (The philosophy of the revolution).

Nasser foresaw in Falsafat al-Thawrra a prominent role for Egypt in inter-Arab affairs. He recognized three circles for the operation of Egyptian foreign policy: Arab, Muslim, and African. Although the Arab circle presented itself as the closest and most important, the fact that Nasser did not overlook the Islamic aspect of his country's foreign policy, something that the Ba'th had neglected, must have assured most Arabs about his good intentions. By criticizing the failure of Sa'd Zaghlul's 1919 revolution to establish bridges with West Asian Arabs, Nasser thought that an important organic link beyond Sinai had been sundered. He seemed determined to reestablish the historical contacts with Arab Asia; now that Islam had lost its driving political force, Arab nationalism supplied Nasser with the legitimacy needed for his momentous undertaking.

Arab leaders had already sought to establish a basis for cooperation among their countries from as early as 1945. A new world order began to take shape as the end of World War II seemed imminent. Most Arab publics considered the establishment in March 1945 of the Arab League, consisting of seven founding member states (Egypt, Iraq, Syria, Saudi Arabia, Lebanon, Yemen, and Transjordan), as the first step toward the concretization of the Arab nationalist dream. But personal grudges among Arab statesmen meant that the league, only a token of Arab solidarity, could not grow into a more serious form of interstate cooperation, not to mention unity. In 1949 King Faruq proposed the formation of an Arab Collective Security Pact only to thwart the possibility of a merger between Iraq and Syria. Tension between Iraq and Egypt grew under the new republican regime in Cairo and developed into a bitter hostility between Gamal ʿAbdul Nasser and Nuri al-Saʿid for power and hegemony in the Arab world.

Security alliances and territorial mergers in the 1950s highlighted the political tensions of the period. The phenomenon of political coups and the concomitant emergence of the military as another class of ruling elite confounded the political spectrum of Arab societies. Young and ambitious, but politically inexperienced, Arab politicians in Egypt and Syria struggled with the pro-Western traditional elites in Iraq, Jordan, and Saudi Arabia thus heralding an era of cold war, extinguished only by the eruption of an Arab-Israeli war in 1967. In February 1955 Iraq and Turkey signed a military agreement that formed the nucleus of the Baghdad Pact. In retaliation, Egypt concluded its own military agreement with Syria, and both countries signed a defense pact in October 1955. A few days later, Egypt reached a similar agreement with Saudi Arabia. By 1956 five Arab countries (Egypt, Syria, Saudi Arabia, Yemen, and Jordan) operated an Arab defense system that opposed the Baghdad Pact.[41] Nasser certainly wanted to involve Egypt in Arab affairs far more than had any of his predecessors since Muhammad ʿAli. Egyptian nationalism, to the extent that it resulted from Anglo-French influence on the development of political thought among the country's intellectual class, seemed abhorrent to the extremely proud young Egyptian leader. In addition, as R. Hrair Dekmejian has argued in a brilliant study on Egypt under Nasser, ". . . anchoring modern [Egyptian] nationalism on the Pharaonic period had a ring of unreality, especially to Muslim Egyptians."[42] In a major political move, Nasser ensured that the constitution of January 1956 recognized the Arab character of Egypt. The preamble of the constitution stated that the Egyptian people ". . . consciously perceives of its existence as a part of the great Arab whole, and correctly acknowledges its responsibility and duty within the common Arab struggle for the victory and glory of the Arab nation."[43]

There is absolutely no doubt about Nasser's stature as the most influential pan-Arab figure in the twentieth century. His sweeping popularity among the masses in all Arabic-speaking countries, as well as his prominent position in the Movement of Nonaligned Countries, placed him in a position of high political esteem throughout the Arab world. Notwithstanding Nasser's embodiment of the ethos of Arab nationalism in the eyes of the masses, he shrouded his pronouncements on it in enigma and ambivalence. He never expressed a pan-Arab doctrine, nor a plan for achieving unity. Even ardent admirers of Nasser admit this. In assessing his impact on Arab nationalism,

Nejla Abu Izzeddin noticed that "until the union of Egypt and Syria was decided upon in January 1958, president Nasser had thought of Arab unity in terms of coordination and consolidation of Arab effort in all spheres of activity."[44]

Nasser learned to appreciate the advantages of Arab nationalism to which he developed a realistic, as opposed to emotional, attachment. Himself an outcome of Egypt's religious environment, severe socioeconomic disparities, and British occupation, Nasser evolved into a very pragmatic politician. Derek Hopwood suggested that he succeeded in assimilating the currents characteristic of the Egyptian sociopolitical scene, believing he had the "ability to chart the correct path for Egypt without relying exclusively on a pre-formulated framework."[45] He probably accepted Arab nationalism thinking it would benefit Egypt, and not necessarily the other way around. One must not forget that the Free Officers launched the 1952 revolution, in which Nasser assumed a key function, for completely domestic reasons. Even though this is hardly a revelation to students of Egyptian politics, its enunciation by Khaled Mohi El Din, a member of the Free Officers and the Revolutionary Command Council, convinces the skeptic. He said: "In fact, the very reason for the Free Officers organization and the revolution was to liberate Egypt from the clutches of British occupation. The evacuation issue became our main preoccupation and prime concern. Should evacuation not be fully and totally realized, then the revolution would have been diverted from its original goals and would have lost the rationale for its existence."[46] Nasser, having achieved British evacuation from the Suez Canal Zone and consolidated the country's political power in his hands, turned his attention to the Arab world. His versatility and pragmatism enabled the young Egyptian leader not just to perceive the natural links (historical, cultural, linguistic, economic, and religious) with West Asia but also provided him with the stamina to pursue them. Arab publics most welcomed Nasser's openness toward them, and in an extremely short period they crowned him as their most beloved leader.

Nasser implemented a vigorous Arab policy; he generously supported the Algerian revolution, opposed the Baghdad Pact, sent token troops to Syria to help in defending it against a possible Turkish invasion, and in 1958 merged Egypt and Syria in a unitary state under the name of the United Arab Republic (UAR). Nevertheless, his actions fell far short of the expectations of pan-Arab activists in the Fertile Crescent. In a speech before the National Union Congress, Nasser spelled out a three-tier policy for realizing Arab unity. He proposed that:

1. The path of any Arab people to unity should be one of free and independent choice.

2. This people should first achieve internal unity before attempting to unite with others outside their border.

3. The desire for unity should represent the unanimous will of the people concerned.[47]

In retrospect, Nasser's second and third stipulations for expanding the UAR seem unrealistic, for he emphasized internal unity and unanimity. Given that most Western-created political entities in the Middle East lacked solid foundations and legitimacy, it is difficult to understand how Nasser expected them to achieve internal unity. Furthermore, his insistence on unanimity, not simple majority, is in itself undemocratic. Nasser believed that the individual Arab states ought to solve their political development problems before thinking about unity. Would not it have been possible for successful development to introduce a new basis of legitimacy that discarded Arab unity? Unlike the Ba'th whose political agenda gave unity the utmost priority (followed by liberty and socialism), Nasser's ranking of his objectives placed socialism first and unity last. One of the compelling reasons for Arabs in the Fertile Crescent to push for prompt unity stemmed from the conviction that it offered the only hope to defeat Israel and reinstate the displaced Palestinians to their homeland. Conversely, Nasser insisted that Arab solidarity and strategic cooperation sufficed to neutralize Israel; his thoughts on unity seemed far more cautious than west Asian Arabs.

Nasser never abandoned the Arab region as an arena of vital interest to Egypt, even after a military coup in Damascus on 28 September 1961 withdrew Syria from the UAR. In a speech one day after the secession he responded defiantly: ". . . [T]his republic will always be the fortress of Arab nationalism; it will always uphold Arab freedom and sustain Arab evolution toward prosperity and justice."[48] After two military coups in February and March 1963 brought the Ba'th Party to the helm of power in Iraq and Syria successively, Nasser agreed to discuss unity with them. The three countries concluded a federation plan on 17 April 1963, but it soon collapsed as the Ba'th leaders accused Nasser of trying to dominate the federation by treating Egypt as the nucleus state. Muta' Safadi wrote in defense of Nasser; he explained how the young Egyptian leader eventually understood the complexities of the Middle Eastern system of states. Realizing that the West and its local proxies vehemently stood against Arab unity, he came to believe that Arab nationalism could not be attained without overthrowing the existing ruling elites. Nasser determined that this change required direct action by the Arab masses against their own elites.[49]

Instead of coming closer to achieving their objective of unity, the 1950s witnessed a bitter Arab cold war which eventually turned hot in the early 1960s. On 26 September 1962 a military coup occurred in Yemen. The new republican regime in San'a' appealed to Egypt for military assistance against the Saudi-supported royalist forces of Imam al-Badr. Nasser, who expected an easy victory that would help restore his tarnished image after the Syrian coup of 1961, committed 70,000 troops in Yemen in an inconclusive war that drained Egypt's economy and tied up more than one-fourth of its armed forces in a rugged terrain two thousand kilometers away from the Israeli borders. While war in Yemen preoccupied Egypt and Saudi Arabia, political instability plagued both Iraq and Syria as Algeria tried to chart a new system of governance after the overthrow of Ahmad Ben Bella in 1965. In this convoluted Arab order an unexpected Arab-Israeli war erupted on 5 June 1967 following false reports disseminated by Soviet intelligence about massive Israeli military concentrations along the borders with Syria.[50] The war which Israel decisively won against the combined armies of its Arab neighbors effectively sealed discussion of Arab unity, and official concern and public attention shifted to efforts to liberate Sinai, the West Bank, and the Golan Heights. Nasser vowed to eliminate "the consequences of Israeli aggression" and raised the famous slogan "what is taken by force can only be retrieved by force." The staggering defeat in 1967 caused many Arab nationalists to distance themselves from the Egyptian leader, calling for the creation of a new pan-Arab leadership to replace Nasser's.[51] Arab nationalism now lay to rest without scoring any lasting victory since its revival in the mid-1950s.

Nationalism in Coma

It is undoubtedly true that the spasmodic surges of Arab nationalism since the third quarter of the nineteenth century have produced little concrete results. Among the countless hurdles that prevented its materialization into a pan-Arab political entity (some of them pertain to colonialism, regionalism, tribalism, Zionism, and the competing identities of Islam and territorial nationalism), the idea of Arab nationalism stood on thin conceptual grounds. Like other malfunctioning conceptual transplants (such as bureaucratic organization and the unilinear approaches to development), all of which reflected Western developmental patterns, Arab nationalism failed to enlist uninterrupted grassroots support in Arab societies. Unlike its European counterparts where the monarchs (who controlled the machinery of the state) committed themselves to nationalism and functioned as its role models, Arab nationalism—being a movement from below—commanded much less proselytizing capacity. From rise to eclipse, intellectuals without political decision-making prerogatives, and themselves disunited on tactics and strategy, preached in vain Arab nationalism to masses and elites.

Having said this by no means denies the development, over the years, of a consciousness that makes the speakers of Arabic a solidary people, at least sentimentally. In attestation of this, al-Jabiri made the following perceptive remark: "Arab existence is present and alive; the recent war waged by the allies against Iraq has demonstrated the vitality of Arab tendency and its penetration of the souls of Arab masses from the [Atlantic] Ocean to the [Persian] Gulf when they took the side of Iraq, in many cases against the policies of their own governments. Particularly significant was the pan-Arab position of the French-educated intellectuals in the Greater Maghrib, many of whom were deprived of Arab education in their youth. They sided with Iraq and bitterly expressed their feelings of disappointment and frustration towards the position of Europeans in support of the aggression against Iraq."[52]

Arab publics outside the states of the Gulf Cooperation Council expressed firm support for Iraq against the forces of the coalition led by the United States. In Syria, for example, where the government condemned Iraq's invasion of Kuwait and contributed a sizable military contingent to the anti-Iraq campaign, the street belonged to Saddam Husayn. Pro-Iraq demonstrations broke out in the governorate of al-Jazira; in Beirut where Syria keeps a military brigade to maintain stability, Beirut residents could easily notice how angry and frustrated these troops were when the coalition forces launched their destructive air campaign against Baghdad.

Sentiment aside, most Arabs seem politically disoriented and ideologically at loss. A long series of military defeats and political setbacks finally have taken their toll on the Arab mind. Sa'dun Hamadi lamented the confused Arab personality as he unduly reported in the mid-1980s signs of pan-Arab revival. He attributed the condition of the Arab state of mind to two factors: weakness of political thought and incompatible ideologies that have disoriented the thinking of Arabs in rapid succession (such as Arab nationalism, Western liberalism and constitutionalism, socialism, territorial nationalism, and finally Islamism).[53] Hamadi judged that Arab experience with civil societies has failed. His substantiating remarks focused on the weakness of the concept of citizenship and the predominance of tribal, kinship, sectarian, and regional loyalties everywhere in the Arab world.[54]

The sense of Arabness (measured by shared characteristics drawn from history, culture, language, a predominant religion, and a legacy of colonialism) has not diminished since the peak of Arab nationalism in the 1950s. The main casualty nevertheless has been the decline of political movements fostering Arab nationalism and unity. The impracticability of the idea—in view of official lukewarm enthusiasm, absence of economic integration, geopolitical reality, preoccupation with internal security, and local challenges to ruling elite authority—resulted, from the early 1970s onward, in its virtual absence from Arab political discourse. One would have expected the Arab-Israeli conflict and the burden of economic and political development to have invigorated the growth of Arab nationalism. To the contrary, both factors have served in a way that ensured its atrophy. These issues will be expounded in the next two chapters.

4

War and Peace with Israel

The conflict over land, natural resources, and political influence, which is characteristic of the contemporary relations between Arabs and Jews, has completed its first century without signs of imminent cessation. Since the Crusades, this evolving conflict has had more impact on the psyche of the Arab populations of the Middle East than any other issue, including the official abrogation of the Islamic caliphate in 1924. Early Arab nationalists were not oblivious to the challenge which Zionism posed to the embryonic notion of Arab nationalism. The vigor with which political Zionism has presented itself in pursuing its own nationalistic objectives put the Arabs on the defensive and mightily contributed to the latter's political radicalization. Zionism provided a main tributary to anti-Western Arab nationalism of the post–World War I period and the decisive element in focusing it on the Hebrew state in the aftermath of Israel's creation. Arab confrontation with Israel boosted pan-Arabism, insofar as their repeated defeats at Israel's hands finally laid the ailing idea to rest. Its supplantation by Islamism, itself a phenomenon of complex underlying factors, has strong roots linking it to the Arab-Israeli conflict. It is sufficient to mention that all Islamic revival movements in the Arab world commit themselves to the continuation of armed struggle against Israel, ostensibly until its liquidation.

The currently prevailing mood of despair—and the concomitant political impasse—in the Arab East cannot be objectively explained without making reference to the far-reaching consequences of the protracted conflict with Israel on Arab publics and ruling elites. Ambitious army officers used the Palestinian cause as a pretext for launching numerous military coups and mobilized their countries' scarce resources for the day of liberation that never came. The masses tolerated excessive human rights violations and material deprivations for the sake of reinstating the displaced Palestinians to their homeland, as well as redeeming Arab military honor. The ruling elites, having debilitated the masses by the humiliation of defeat, finally declared Israel unconquerable and resigned themselves to a peace with the Jewish state which their populations interpreted as an instrument of surrender. The enduring conflict, which lingers in the shadow of fragile peace, requires revisiting in order to determine its influence on the Arabs. This is an absolute necessity as they ponder their uncertain future in the turbulent present.

Initiation and Progression of the Conflict: The Role of the West

The West neither planted the thought of Jewish return to Palestine nor sowed the idea of Zionism; yet Western countries, namely Britain and the United States, made the dream of establishing a Jewish homeland in Palestine come true. Even though Napoleon called upon the world Jewry—upon his occupation of Egypt in 1798—to return to Palestine and rebuild their civilization there, his proclamation rang hollow as the scope of Jewish interest in the Holy Land did not exceed religious and humanitarian activities. But the resurgence of nationalistic movements in Europe, and more specifically the resumption of pogroms in Russia in 1881, altered Jewish interest in Palestine altogether. As a few fleeing Jews found their way to Palestine (most others made it to North America and Western Europe), a Russian Jew named Leon Pinsker proposed for the first time the concept of a Jewish nation.[1] In the course of the Berlin Conference in 1884 the British government, apparently persuaded by Pinsker's suggestion, recommended statehood as a means of resolving the Jewish question, but fierce German opposition prevented its endorsement.[2] But Theodor Herzl, an Austrian Jewish journalist, pursued the matter with determination, and in 1897 he succeeded in convening the first Zionist Congress in Basel. The participants resolved themselves to the establishment of a Jewish home in Palestine, and Herzl pledged to seek British support, which he attained with remarkable success.

In November 1917, just five weeks before General Edmund Allenby's forces occupied Jerusalem, the foreign secretary issued the Balfour Declaration in which His Majesty's Government pledged to support the establishment of a Jewish National Home in Palestine. British policy, including the secret Sykes-Picot Agreement to partition the Fertile Crescent between Britain and France, ushered in the plight of the Palestinians, frustrated Arab political aspirations, and profoundly upset the sociocultural aspects of their lives. S. A. Haqqi, who contended that there was no Palestinian problem prior to the Balfour Declaration, summed up the feelings of Arabs in West Asia at that time. He stated that ". . . although Palestine formed a province of the Ottoman Empire it was very much a part of the Arab homeland, being under the uninterrupted occupation of the Arabs for more than 1,300 years, and sharing the hopes and aspirations of the rest of the Arab world.

These were now based on the promise of immediate independence to the Arabs made by the British Government in 1916, in return for the Arab revolt against the Turkish rulers and significant role played by them in the ultimate defeat of the Ottoman Empire."[3]

The traditionally structured and politically unmobilized Palestinians dealt ineptly, joined by the less than enthusiastic Anglo-French elites in neighboring Arab countries, with the burgeoning Zionist domination of their ancestral land. The Arabs welcomed U.S. President Woodrow Wilson's declaration concerning the right of the peoples of the non-Turkish provinces of the defunct Ottoman empire to self-determination, and they reacted enthusiastically to his King-Crane Commission on Syria and Palestine. Wilson's initiative, which Arab nationalists interpreted as a positive American gesture toward them, was scrapped shortly afterwards as the United States isolated itself from the world's affairs and decided against joining the League of Nations. The recommendations of the King-Crane Commission, although they encouraged the creation of an Arab state in Syria and advised against setting up a Jewish state in Palestine, had little impact on Western foreign policy makers. In July 1922 the League of Nations approved British mandate in Palestine and authorized the implementation of the Balfour Declaration. Less than two months later, the U.S. Congress endorsed the declaration, thus paving the way for unwavering commitment to the welfare of the Jewish state in Palestine that emerged a quarter of century later.[4]

The nationalistic zeal of the Zionist movement and its ambitious agenda for territorial acquisition in Palestine alarmed the Arab population, leading to spates of poorly coordinated attacks against the rapidly expanding Jewish community. The British, torn between their desire to mollify local Arabs without reneging their promise to establish a Jewish National Home in Palestine, reacted halfheartedly to the deteriorating situation. In 1922 they issued the Churchill White Paper to emphasize that British commitments to the Jews did not aim to jeopardize the Arab identity of the indigenous population. It seemed unrealistic for the British to try to safeguard the interests of the Palestinians in view of the continuing growth of the Jewish community, both numerically and organizationally. Thus the Peel Commission of 1937, realizing the impossibility of integrating the conflicting nationalistic interests of Arabs and Jews in a joint political entity, solemnly pronounced the failure of British administration in Palestine and proposed partitioning the country.

War in Europe and the salience of the Nazi threat tilted the official British position to the Arab side. Stunning German military successes made

Britain vulnerable and drove it to find allies and mend matters with disgruntled peoples in Asia and Africa. The strategic location of Arab lands and their oil riches—both of paramount importance to subsequent Allied campaigns—necessitated a new policy on Palestine. The exigencies of war dictated the promulgation, in May 1939, of the White Paper that favored the creation of a predominantly Arab state in Palestine within ten years, provided that constitutional guarantees protected vital Jewish interests there. Curbs on Jewish immigration and the dimming of hopes for creating a national home in Palestine caused the Zionist movement to focus its attention on obtaining American support, now that British commitment had begun to waver. The Zionist response came, in collaboration with American Jewry, from the Biltmore Hotel in New York in May 1942. The Extraordinary Zionist Conference adopted the Biltmore Program for implementing the Balfour Declaration and urged the creation of a Jewish Commonwealth in Palestine. Bernard Reich thought that Biltmore reflected the plight of the Jews in Europe, and the ". . . urgency of the situation in which the Jewish leadership found itself as a consequence of the Holocaust and the need to provide for the displaced Jews. . . ."[5]

No matter how one looks at British policy in Palestine during the interwar period, the obvious conclusion is that London used its mandatory power in the Holy Land to bolster Jewish presence there. While official declarations legitimized Zionist claims to the land, law enforcement officers tolerated Jewish militant activities. Whether tolerance resulted from tacit approval or sheer indecisiveness, the fact remains that it lent credence to the Zionists' tactics and put them in an advantageous position vis-à-vis the Arabs when London suddenly terminated its mandate in Palestine. British resolve to manage the conflict in Palestine waned after World War II. Emboldened by triumph in the war, an ever-more-confident United States immediately filled in the vacuum and assumed a vigorous pro-Zionist policy. This became apparent as the Anglo-American Committee of Inquiry deliberated the Palestinian problem in January 1946. Although neither the United States nor Britain formally endorsed the committee's report, President Truman readily welcomed the recommendation for admitting 100,000 Jewish immigrants from Europe.[6] The significance of the Anglo-American Committee lay in associating the future of European Jewry with Palestine, and in setting the stage for future U.N. involvement in resolving the crisis in Palestine.

Soon came Britain's disengagement from the conflict immediately after the failure of two last-minute initiatives. Both Arabs and Jews rejected Herbert Morrison's plan of July 1946, which suggested the cantonization of

Palestine and placing Jerusalem under direct British administration. Similarly, the London conference failed to reconcile the antagonists' differences; thus to justify turning the Palestine problem over to the United Nations, British Foreign Secretary Ernest Bevin announced on 18 February 1947 his government's inability to bridge the gap between Arabs and Jews. On 29 November 1947, the U.N. General Assembly—where the United States enjoyed tremendous influence at that time—adopted Resolution 181 for partitioning Palestine. The United States had brought to fruition the idea of a Jewish national home in Palestine which the British put on track in 1917. Palestinian resistance and Arab League opposition did not deter David Ben-Gurion from announcing the birth of the state of Israel on 14 May 1948.

Defeat in War

Arab countries neighboring Palestine immediately declared war against Israel, and by doing so they launched a series of ill-fated military encounters with the Hebrew state. In evaluating Arab reactions to the main events connected with the Palestinian issue since 1948, Israel's constant victories would seem only logical. Concerned Arabs, their political entities themselves being Western creations, responded lukewarmly to the determined Zionist program endowed with Anglo-American encouragement and support. Surely the Arabs did not do their best in reacting to the Zionist threat facing their brethren in Palestine. Muhammad Haj Hamad accounted for the generally unsatisfactory Arab showing in wars with Israel in a most brilliant analysis. His analysis concentrated on the tribal dimensions of Arab social and political organization, a reality recognized by the Qur'an and sanctioned by Prophet Muhammad. The following Qur'anic verse encourages peoples and tribes (alluded to as separate entities) to interact among themselves under the guidance of faith: "We have indeed created you of a male and a female, and have made you know one another. Surely the most gracious one amongst you is he who is godfearing. Indeed God is Omniscient, Cognizant."[7] It sets fear of God as the ultimate human achievement; hence belief—consolidated by interaction—suffices as a common bond among disparate tribes and peoples. The Prophet accepted in the Constitution of Medina in 622 the tribe as an autonomous social unit subsumed in an all-encompassing Islamic confederation.

Haj Hamad's interpretation of the weak Arab commitment to Palestine rested on grounds that Islam did not promote a sense of nationalism among the community of believers. Tribes emigrating from Arabia—to the areas presently known as the Arab world—after the Islamization of the peninsula embraced two behavioral qualities: the concept of *al-Diyar* (the abode) as opposed to *al-Watan* (the homeland), and the centrality of Mecca—in whose direction the faithful turn for prayer—in the development of attachment and personality, both at the individual and collective levels.[8] Therefore, the inviolability of Mecca concerns all Muslim Arabs, whereas the fate of Palestine is strictly the business of its local Arabs. According to Haj Hamad, Arab believers do not turn to Jerusalem for prayer; moreover, Palestine is just the abode of its local Arabs. In effect, the Arabs could not go beyond expressing solidarity with the Palestinian cause, viewing the conflict with Israel as peripheral to their own well-being.[9]

The nature of Arab countries' involvement in wars with Israel confirms the view of Haj Hamad. The Egyptian political elite stayed unmoved by the events in Palestine. During an Arab League meeting in Cairo during October 1947, Egyptian Prime Minister Nuqrashi Pasha informed Arab delegates that his government had decided against committing its army in the Palestine conflict.[10] Except for the Muslim Brethren who donated generously to the anti-Zionist campaign and dispatched volunteers to fight against it, the Egyptian public reacted indifferently to the plight of the Palestinians, even after the Dayr Yasin massacre in which the Irgun slaughtered 254 villagers. King Faruq's sudden decision to commit the Egyptian army to the war in Palestine surprised his country's political and military establishment, the latter worrying about the combat unreadiness of their units. The king, who contemplated becoming the Muslim caliph (the post being vacant since the abrogation of the Ottoman empire in 1924), thought that a victory in Palestine would improve his chances. However, the Hashemite monarchs of Iraq and Jordan, themselves politically and territorially ambitious, were intent on thwarting King Faruq's objectives.

Eager to expand his nonviable desert kingdom, King 'Abdullah of Jordan—the staunchest Arab ally of Britain, whose assassination in 1951 by an angry Palestinian invited a mournful Winston Churchill to acknowledge losing "a faithful comrade and ally"[11]—did not hesitate to cooperate with the leaders of the Zionist movement to partition Palestine.[12] John Glubb, the British commander of the Arab Legion, surrendered the towns of Lydda and Ramlah to the Haganah in compliance with a prior political agreement between King 'Abdullah and David Ben-Gurion, who became Israel's first prime minister. The Jordanian move exposed the flank of the Egyptian contingent in Faluga, leading to its encirclement by the Israelis. Similarly, the Iraqis who committed a token force of 2,000 troops to the Arab war effort in Palestine (out of a total fighting force of 26,000 men), suddenly pulled out from the coastal town of Naharia, thus freeing the movement of the Israeli army against the Egyptians in Ascalon. The Hashemites had indeed compromised the position of their fellow Arabs in Palestine, and in the process, they sealed the fate of the Egyptian monarch's pan-Islamist ambitions.

By July 1948 the Israelis had soundly defeated the Jordanians and Egyptians and easily intimidated the rudimentary Syrian and Lebanese armies into retreat. Israel's Arab neighbors leaned toward peace; they signed armistice agreements with the Jewish state and accepted U.N. General Assembly Resolution 194 (11 December 1948), which called for repatriating the displaced Palestinians or compensating those unwilling to return. Within a few months, and under the auspices of the Conciliation Commission (composed of the United States, France, and Turkey), Arabs and Israelis signed a protocol in which the former literally recognized the Jewish entity in Palestine and rescinded their opposition to the 1947 partition plan. Arab acquiescence and willingness to resettle hundreds of thousands of refugees, if Israel reciprocated in a likewise manner, invited a nonchalant response from David Ben-Gurion, who said: "Peace is vital—but not at any price."[13] With the Zionist plan of establishing a Jewish national home in Palestine becoming a reality, Ben-Gurion and subsequent Israeli policy makers saw no compelling need to compromise with the Arabs, especially if it meant undermining the Zionist claim to Palestine. Confronting militarily weak and politically disunited neighbors, Ben-Gurion charted a belligerent policy toward the Arabs, one that his successors have guarded with zeal.

In an important policy statement, Israel's first prime minister summarized his government's foreign policy objectives as follows: "Israel, preeminently, needs and longs for closer fraternity and true co-operation between peoples. On her land borders, she is surrounded by hostility. She will be safe as long as her army is strong enough to deter her neighbors. . . . The surest way of arriving at peace and cooperation with our neighbors is not by proclaiming and preaching peace to the people of Israel . . . but by making the largest possible numbers of friends in Asia and Africa and elsewhere . . . [without] lessen[ing] our striving for cooperation and friendship with the peoples of Europe and America, where over 90 per cent of the Diaspora dwells."[14] In a nutshell, Israeli foreign policy strategy rested on maintaining overwhelming military superiority against the combined Arab armies and aggressiveness in seeking friendships elsewhere. This approach continued even after the peace talks had progressed in the early 1990s. Immediately after signing the Declaration of Principles with PLO Chairman Yasser 'Arafat in Washington (on 13 September 1993), Israeli Prime Minister Yitzhak

Rabin flew to Djakarta. He probably hoped that peace in the Middle East would improve his country's relations with the Islamic world, especially its economically prosperous countries such as Indonesia and Malaysia.

The signatories (the United States, Britain, and France) to the Tripartite Declaration of 25 May 1950 pledged to preserve the existing Middle Eastern system of states, a tacit reference to the territorial integrity of the new state of Israel. To keep the peace, the three Western countries committed themselves to the maintenance of military balance between Israel and neighboring Arab countries, which in spirit meant Israel's ability to defeat the armies of all contiguous Arab states. Western interest in the security of Israel and Arab regimes' focus on domestic issues and preoccupation with inter-Arab conflicts convinced them to avoid disturbing the de facto peace along the armistice lines. On the eve of Israel's Sinai campaign—launched on 29 October 1956—French Foreign Minister Christian Pineau relayed a message of peace from Nasser to Ben-Gurion. The Egyptian president expressed his belief that the Arabs and Israelis would, in due time, resolve their outstanding problems. Until such a time came, Nasser would focus his energies on bringing about the modernization of his country.[15] Fully dedicated to development, he sought to de-emphasize military spending, but Israeli provocations injured his pride and alerted him to the reality of its impending threat. In February 1955 Israel attacked an Egyptian police station in Gaza and killed dozens of its occupants. The incident compelled the Egyptian president to seek military hardware from the Soviet Union (after the United States and Britain declined his request), and on 27 September 1955 Nasser announced the famous Czech arms deal.

Nasser's military strategy with regard to Israel was essentially defensive. He hoped to contain the Jewish state and to that effect he concluded military treaties with Syria and Jordan, which in turn sparked Israel's preemptive campaign in 1956. Israel has made it clear that Arab military coordination—even for defensive purposes—is totally unacceptable. Since the end of the 1956 war and until the June War of 1967, Nasser repeatedly stated that he did not have a military plan to attack Israel and saw the resolution of the Arab-Israeli conflict in the context of U.N. resolutions. Arab leaders used the Palestine question as a slogan for political legitimization, and apart from paying a lip service to the matter, they did little to cope with the Israeli menace. In February 1966, a military coup in Damascus brought one Druze and two 'Alawi army officers (Salim Hatum, Hafiz al-Asad, and Salah Jadid respectively) to power in Syrian politics. Resented by the country's Sunni majority and alienated in the Arab world, the new regime in Damascus raised the slogan of the popular war for the liberation of Palestine.[16] Syria provided training and logistic support to the Fat'h movement's raids against targets in Israel; simultaneously, its artillery in the Golan Heights engaged Israeli farmers in the demilitarized zone. Syrian escalation of tensions with Israel occurred when the former's army seemed unprepared for war.[17]

The larger and better-equipped Egyptian army—whose government signed, at Moscow's insistence, a mutual defense treaty with Syria in November 1966—suffered from serious problems that reduced its military capability as well. Marshal 'Abdul Hakim 'Amir controlled the armed forces and made it loyal to his person. His patronage of the officer corps, through the extension of special material and symbolic privileges, transformed the army into a hotbed of corruption and lowered the morale of the enlisted men. The war in Yemen against the Saudi-supported royalist tribes, which bogged down one-third of the Egyptian army in a costly war of attrition, depleted the country's meager resources and, still worse, gave its command a false sense of combat readiness.[18] Nasser, who had no illusions about the ability of his armed forces to defeat Israel's, nevertheless believed they could repel an attack, even after sustaining heavy casualties. This mindset affected the Egyptian president's miscalculation in responding to incorrect Soviet intelligence reports—communicated by the Kremlin—about an Israeli military buildup near the Syrian borders.

Despite evidence to the contrary, Nasser treated the Soviet reports as genuine and set out to reap political gains by creating an atmosphere of war in the region. His brinkmanship backfired. By closing the Tiran passes to Israeli navigation in the Red Sea, a decision that restored Nasser's popularity among the Arab masses to the mid-1950s level, he thought the then two superpowers would prevent the eruption of all-out hostilities in the Middle East. In retrospect, it seems that the Egyptian president did not understand how Israel decides to go to war. Egypt's military cooperation with Syria and Jordan in the 1950s prompted Israel to invade Sinai in 1956. In May 1967, after Nasser mobilized his army and sent it to the borders with Israel, Jordan and Iraq concluded defense treaties with Egypt, thus restoring the military situation that existed on the eve of the 1956 war. On 5 June 1967 Israel struck with precision and determination, deploying its entire military reserves in the throes of battle. By 10 June its forces occupied the West Bank of Jordan, Sinai peninsula, and the impregnable Golan Heights, thus emerging as the uncontested military superpower of the Middle East. Defeat in war, Arab public repudiation, and a lack of superpower concern for their debacle finally compelled Arab leaders to aim for peace with Israel, even when they clamored that "what is taken by force can only be retrieved by force."[19]

Disgrace in Peace

At first, Arab statesmen rejected the consequences of the Six Day War and swore not to compromise with triumphant Israel. On 1 September 1967, the extraordinary Arab Summit in Khartoum issued a defiant resolution denying the existence of the state of Israel and refusing reconciliation and negotiation with it. But the magnitude of the defeat and realization that they had no means to recover the lost land by force had a quick sobering effect. Therefore, in November 1967, Egypt and Jordan readily accepted U.N. Resolution 242, which called for Israel's withdrawal from the occupied Arab land in exchange for ending the state of belligerency with it and recognizing its existence as a sovereign entity. In the absence of U.S. pressure on Israel to return land in exchange for peace, the militarily supreme Jewish state declined to make significant concessions and foiled all peace initiatives. The Arabs clung to U.N. resolutions on the Palestine issue and demanded Israel's withdrawal to the borders of 4 June 1967, but in defeat they were not in a position to set the rules. For years, the dialogue of the deaf concerning the resolution of the conflict bore no results because Israeli negotiators assumed that dead men (in reference to the vulnerable Arabs) do not bargain. Thus the efforts of the Big Four (the United States, the former Soviet Union, Britain, and France), the Superpower discussions, and the mission of U.N. envoy Gunnar Jarring all ended in failure because of Israeli intransigence.

The PLO, which in 1975 U.S. Secretary of State Henry Kissinger branded as a terrorist organization, actively sought a rapprochement with Israel.[20] In 1968 the organization raised the slogan of establishing a democratic state in Palestine in which Muslims, Christians, and Jews could live in peace. The inadmissibility of the proposal convinced the PLO leadership, especially after its ouster from Jordan and relocation to Lebanon, to settle for the creation of a Palestinian state in the West Bank and Gaza Strip.[21] Obsessed with security, claustrophobic Israelis shrugged off the idea and adamantly denied the existence of a Palestinian people.[22] Israel manifested little enthusiasm for communicating with the Arabs beyond tranquilizing the cease-fire lines. With this in view, it accepted the Rogers Plan which ended the War of Attrition on 7 August 1970. Although William Rogers's initiative, better known as the "stop shooting, start talking"[23] proposal, revived the Jarring talks, the Swedish envoy—frustrated by Israeli intransigence—gave up his mission a year later. In the wake of the 1973 October War, Israel cooperated with Henry Kissinger's shuttle diplomacy because it resulted in the disengagement of the belligerents' troops. Israel signed the first disengagement of troops agreement with Egypt in January 1974 and withdrew its forces from the West Bank of the Suez Canal. The more difficult disengagement agreement with Syria, which involved Israel's relinquishment of the city of Qunaytira, took place four months later.

Subsequent shuttle diplomacy efforts by Kissinger succeeded in the conclusion of the Sinai II Accords between Egypt and Israel on 1 September 1975. According to the terms of the agreement, Israeli troops pulled back from the strategic Mitla and Gidi Passes and surrendered the Abu Rudeis oil fields. In return, Egyptian President Anwar al-Sadat prematurely agreed to renounce the use of military force to resolve his country's conflict with Israel.[24] Sadat's decision weakened Egypt's bargaining position vis-à-vis Israel, which felt that Sinai II had achieved its security needs with the largest Arab country and effectively neutralized it in the still ongoing conflict.[25] Exasperated and driven into despair by Israeli reluctance on the issue of full withdrawal, the Egyptian president did the unthinkable. In November 1977 Sadat said he would do anything for the sake of peace, even if it meant going to Jerusalem. Before the month ended, he stood at the podium of the Israeli Knesset offering peace after three decades of formal hostility. The visit, which violated a taboo and brought ineffable condemnation from countries throughout the Arab world, also made a celebrity of Sadat in Western, especially U.S., media. In all other respects, the visit had negligible impact on the strategic outlook of Israeli Likud Prime Minister Menachem Begin.

The futility of the Jerusalem visit became evident with the collapse of the Joint Political Committee, as well as the failure of the Sadat-Begin meeting in Isma'ilia to amend the hard-line stance of the Israeli prime minister. Even the rescue visit of U.S. President Jimmy Carter to Aswan in January 1978 fell short of creating an atmosphere conducive to fair negotiations, since Israel insisted on treating Egypt as a defeated country. At the conclusion of a quick meeting with Sadat, Carter announced the stillborn Aswan formula which stressed U.S. commitment to achieve a just and comprehensive peace in the Middle East. Ostracized in the Arab world and ridiculed by many fellow countrymen, Sadat promptly accepted Carter's invitation to negotiate peace with Begin at Camp David, the presidential retreat in Maryland. After twelve days of grueling talks, Egyptian and Israeli negotiators—aided by U.S. mediators—reached, on 17 September 1978, a general principles agreement that provided the basis for continuing negotiations. Impatient to recover Sinai and desperate for a face-saving agreement, Sadat gave in to Begin's conditions. He rashly dropped the principle of a comprehensive settlement, thus immeasurably undermining the negotiating position of other Arabs, namely the PLO and Syria.[26] The exit of Egypt from the arena of the Arab-Israeli conflict unleashed Israeli military might against its much weaker northern neighbors. The personal feud between Syrian President Hafiz al-Asad and his Iraqi counterpart Saddam Husayn doomed the resolutions of the Baghdad Arab Summit, held on 5 November 1978, to counteract the implications of the Camp David Accords. Thus faded away the Arab dream of establishing an eastern military front incorporating the armies of Syria, Iraq, and Jordan. In the new regional environment of Egyptian neutrality and intense Arab bickering, Israel struck again, asserting its military superiority and setting the rules of the game.

In June 1981 Israeli jets flying through Saudi Arabian air space bombed and destroyed Iraqi nuclear installations near Baghdad. Six weeks later, the Israeli air force attacked PLO positions in Beirut and killed more than 200 people, mostly civilians. Arab officials protested feebly and perfunctorily. Having transgressed against Arabs with impunity, Israel decided to invade Lebanon and evict the PLO from its stronghold there. In June 1982, it launched Operation Peace for the Galilee and besieged Beirut; in September of the same year, the Israeli army entered the city, violating the first Arab capital. As the Arab world winked at the developments in Lebanon, exhaustion and rout forced the PLO leadership to abandon Lebanon where, for more than a decade, they had established a state within a state. Israel's victory in Lebanon voided peace gestures from substance; militarily, Israel proved more than a match for the Arabs, whereas politically it could count on the United States as a shield against world condemnation. In May 1980 the Knesset adopted a Basic Law concerning the status of Jerusalem as the capital of the Jewish state, and in December 1981 the Israeli government virtually annexed the Golan Heights by extending its laws and jurisdiction over that area. Getting away with its actions, Israel, not surprisingly, dismissed all peace initiatives as deficient in providing for its security needs.

After signing the peace treaty with Egypt on 26 March 1979, Israel seemed reluctant to proceed with peace on the Palestinian, Syrian, Jordanian, and Lebanese tracks. Achievement of its strategic objectives and unwillingness to make commitments for additional territorial withdrawals, a matter opposed by a broad cross-section of the country's population, influenced the decision of Israel's ruling elite to stall the drive toward peace. Thus a litany of peace endeavors, based on U.N. Security Council Resolutions 242 and 338 and the principle of exchanging land for peace, collapsed simply because Israel found them superfluous. The main initiatives included the Venice Declaration (July 1980), the Prince Fahd Plan (August 1981),[27] and in the aftermath of Israel's invasion of Lebanon, Fez and Brezhnev Peace Plans and Reagan's Fresh Start Initiative (September 1982). A period of relative inaction followed the post–Camp David diplomatic flurry that lasted until the eruption of the *intifada* in December 1987, which led, in March 1988, U.S. Secretary of State George Shultz to propose convening an international conference to bridge the gap between Arab and Israeli attitudes toward peace, but prime minister Yitzhak Shamir vehemently opposed the idea, arguing that it ran "contrary to Camp David."[28]

The intensification of the intifada spurred Swedish Foreign Minister Sten Anderson to arrange a meeting between PLO Chairman 'Arafat and a group of five American Jews in his country's capital. It accomplished the Stockholm Declaration on 7 December 1988, in which the PLO renounced violence as a means to achieve Palestinian national objectives and accepted Resolution 242. As a result, the U.S. government agreed to engage in a dialogue with the PLO in Tunis to determine if the organization met the prerequisites for involving it in the peace process. The United States failed the PLO and discontinued the dialogue; thus two important Palestinian concessions went into the gutter. An intercontinental rush to stimulate the stagnant status of peace in the Middle East, extinguish the intifada, and capitalize on recent PLO concessions produced—to no avail—the European Community's Madrid Declaration (June 1989), Mubarak's Ten Point Plan (July 1989), and U.S. Secretary of State James Baker's Five Point Plan (October 1989). In the comfort of military preponderance, unequivocal American support, and inter-Arab discord, Israel insisted on getting all or not dealing at all. Its golden opportunity to get all soon came.

On 2 August 1990 the Iraqi army invaded Kuwait, inviting a crisis of the greatest magnitude with the U.S. government. President Saddam Husayn's unprecedented move translated his frustration with Kuwait's leaders over the issues of border demarcation and Iraq's multibillion-dollar debt to al-Sabbah rulers (this topic is treated in chapter 6). Iraq's defeat in the ensuing war was in fact a general Arab defeat, be it for those who actively supported the U.S. military effort (Egypt, Syria, and Saudi Arabia), or those who took Iraq's side (Jordan and the PLO). Very little came from President Bush's pledge to turn his attention to settling the Arab-Israeli conflict, once the liberation of Kuwait was achieved.[29] The much-publicized three-day Madrid Peace Conference convened on 30 October 1991 but proved to be nothing more than a grandiose ceremonial activity. With Bush's loss in the 1992 U.S. presidential elections, the march for Middle Eastern peace returned to the starting point. The only tangible outcome of the Madrid Conference occurred on 16 December 1991, when the U.N. General Assembly passed Resolution 3379 which repealed a 1975 resolution considering Zionism a form of racism.

The PLO, isolated by Israel and the United States and outcast by most Arab leaders for siding with Iraq during the Gulf Crisis, turned to secret negotiations with Israel under the auspices of the Norwegian government. The Oslo talks paved the way for Israel-PLO mutual recognition on 9 September 1993, making it possible for both parties to sign in Washington, four days later, a declaration on the principles of peace. In a bitter response to the agreement that articulated the true feelings of most Arabs, Palestinian intellectual Edward Said strongly condemned it. He stated that: "[a]ll secret deals between a very strong and a very weak partner necessarily involve concessions hidden in embarrassment by the latter. It's true there are still lots of details to be negotiated, as there are many imponderables to be made clear, and even some hopes either to be fulfilled or dashed. Still, the deal before us smacks of the PLO leadership's exhaustion and isolation, and of Israel's shrewdness."[30] On 4 May 1994 the two sides signed the Cairo Agreement, which called for Israel's military withdrawal from the areas of Gaza and Jericho and the extension of a modicum of self-rule to the Palestinian Authority. Cautiously, the Labor government of Rabin-Peres proceeded with peace talks with Arabs from an advantageous position, despite fierce opposition from Israel's increasingly strong religious groups. On 26 October 1994 the Hebrew state signed a peace treaty with Jordan that legitimated Israeli territorial expansion and control of the contested sources of fresh water.

Syrian-Israeli peace talks, which culminated in meetings between the chiefs of staff of the two countries at the Wye Plantation near Washington, never went beyond the preliminary and exploratory stage. Israel, believing that peace with Syria had little impact on its relations with economically important Arab and Islamic states, saw no need to return the strategically important and water-rich Golan Heights to Damascus. Although Syria dropped its earlier preconditions for negotiating with Israel, three years of talks revealed that the Jewish state was not quite ready for peace with its northern neighbor.[31] The Syrian regime took pains to prepare the population for the possibility of peace with Israel, often describing it as an achievement of Syrian national objectives.[32] After decades of preparing the masses for an inevitable military confrontation with Israel to reinstate the Palestinians into their homeland, the Syrian ruling elite abruptly raised the slogan of a just and comprehensive peace with their former enemy. But peace did not arrive; instead, the Israelis steadily chose to retract the option of peace.

The assassination, on 4 November 1995, of Israeli Prime Minister Yitzhak Rabin by a fellow Jew opposed to peace demonstrated the deep divisions within Israeli society on the matter of relinquishing occupied lands to the Arabs. Less than seven months later, Israeli voters ousted the pro-peace Labor government of Shimon Peres and elected Benjamin Netanyahu, the uncompromising Likud leader, as their new prime minister. The peace talks hit a snag, and Arab pleas for their resumption neither impressed the new Israeli leader nor sufficiently influenced the United States to pressure Netanyahu to modify his unyielding stance on peace. Encouraged by Arab divisions and preoccupation with other security concerns, as well as an unusually supportive administration in Washington, Israel accelerated its efforts to complete its control of Jerusalem. In October 1996, it opened a controversial archaeological tunnel close to al-Aqsa mosque, touching off Muslim feelings in the West Bank and Gaza and causing a bloody confrontation in which more than seventy people were killed, mostly Palestinians. In March 1997 Israel precipitated a crisis with the Palestinian Authority by launching a major housing project on Arab land on the outskirts of Jerusalem. Some Arab countries threatened to halt all steps toward normalization with Israel if it did not shelve its settlement plans. However, the failure of Arab countries to agree on excluding Israel from the fourth economic summit in Doha, Qatar, illustrated the fragility of Arab resolve to stand up to Israel. Acquiescence to defeat in war seems to have made Arab ruling elites amenable to disgrace in peace.

The Conflict Goes On

As the invitees to the White House ceremony celebrated the signing of the Israel-PLO declaration of principles, climaxed by the Rabin-'Arafat hand-shake, voices of opposition roared at both ends of the historic conflict. Polar Muslim and Jewish religious extremists vowed to fight all peace drives until the fulfillment of their messianic visions on the outcome of the Arab-Israeli conflict. The Islamists armed themselves with Qur'anic verses to express disapproval of peace and to justify launching terrorist attacks against civilian targets in Israel. Verses such as the one that follows provided them with the religious legitimacy they needed for militant activities: "So, do not lose spirit nor call for peace, for you are the supreme. And God is ever with you, and He shall not render your deeds in vain."[33] Islamists involved in suicide attacks sought divine reward, for the Qur'an said: ". . . And those who are slain in the cause of God, their deeds will not be in vain."[34] Having identified scriptural support for a stand against Israel, Islamist writers articulated an uncompromising, and apparently unrealistic, stance on peace. For example, Hamad al-Farhan, a member of the Muslim Brotherhood and former minister without portfolio, said that resolving the Arab-Israeli conflict was not an urgent matter. This is the explanation he gave: "The present condition of the Arab world necessitates [merely] containing this danger. First, by freezing steps toward recognition, reconciliation, and interaction [with Israel]. . . . The final solution is the destruction of Israel, once and for all, when the [Arab] nation forms."[35] Farah Musa, another Islamist, argued that reconciliation with Israel cannot occur "if Palestine remains a Jewish state. . . . Peace means the return of the Jews to where they originally came from."[36] Shaykh Muhammad Husayn Fadlallah, Hizbullah's spiritual leader, opined that the "Koran-based Islamic culture . . . may be one of the active ingredients in consolidating the already strong barriers against Israeli expansion in the region."[37]

The strength of the Islamists' opposition to peace with the Jewish state seems to have had a restraining effect on the pro-peace attitudes and behaviors of moderate religious clerics. One of the best examples of this was Shaykh 'Abdul 'Aziz Ibn Baz, the grand mufti of Saudi Arabia, who issued a *fatwa* (religious edict) in December 1994 that legitimized "establishing lasting or temporary peace with Israel."[38] This aroused a firestorm of protest from Islamists and leftists that swayed the mufti to issue a reinterpretation of his previous statement, which he claimed was warranted by Arab weaknesses. He went on to say that "peace with the Jews does not require liking them, [and that] as soon as the Muslims acquire the means to reverse the situation, they must fight the Jews who occupy Muslim lands."[39]

Thus the 1993–96 period, during which Israel concluded significant peace accords with the PLO and Jordan, witnessed an unprecedented escalation in Hamas and al-Jihad al-Islami's terrorist activities in major Israeli cities, while Hizbullah's operations in southern Lebanon—including occasional firing of Katuysha missiles at the northern Galilee—continued unabated.

If the Islamists deny Israel's right of existence, their Jewish counterparts reciprocate by articulating equally strong attitudes against the Arabs, particularly the Palestinians. For example, Kahane Chai and Moredet, two right-wing religious nationalist parties, call for the establishment of a Torah state and the expulsion of all Arabs from Israel and the territories. Similarly, the political programs of Gush Emunim and Tehiya, two other extreme religious groups, emphasize the construction of illegal settlements in the West Bank and Gaza until they are completely Judaized. Jewish religious militants themselves took part in several atrocities against Palestinians, notably the killing of dozens of Muslim worshipers in a Hebron mosque in February 1994. Needless to say, the presence of foolhardy armed Jewish settlers in the midst of Arabs in the territories serves as a constant reminder that conflict in the Holy Land is far from over.

Recent public opinion polls showed that Arabs were not quite ready for peace. They distrusted Israeli intentions toward them, and even though respondents tended to resign themselves to the signing of peace treaties with Israel, they expressed strong opposition to any type of normalization with the Jewish state. Dismayed by the magnitude of Arab concessions to Israel, most respondents viewed peace with Israel as a truce in a long historical conflict.[40] Obviously, Arab publics considered the terms of peace agreements with Israel as unacceptable. To signify disapproval, Mohamed Heikal attached to the negotiations the label of "flags of fantasy"[41] that gave birth to a "violent peace."[42]

The march toward peace deterred neither the militants (both Muslim and Jewish) nor the Israeli government from military escalation. The two heaviest Israeli onslaughts against Lebanon since the 1982 invasion took place in the shadow of peace: Operation Accountability in July 1993 and the Grapes of Wrath in April 1996. In spite of a combination of Arab publics' aversion to and aloofness from the issue of peace with Israel, their ruling elites pursued the matter diligently. But the political and military vulnerability of Arab political orders—caused by a new unipolar international system and aggravated by incompetent domestic politics, heightened by inter-Arab rivalries, as well as the decline of their overall regional influence in comparison with the non-Arab countries of the Middle East—excluded the possibility of reaching balanced peace deals with Israel. Arabs demanded just and comprehensive peace settlements, but militarily preponderant Israel insisted on treating them as defeated countries. Raymond Cohen presented an interesting argument asserting that cultural differences—revealing disparate historical experiences—have stood in the way of negotiations, especially between Israel and Syria. Shame and guilt, which respectively preoccupy salient positions in Arab and Israeli cultures, tended to bog down negotiations in a "dialogue of the deaf."[43]

The existing political environment in the Middle East (reflecting the influence of military, cultural, social, and economic variables) suggests that the Arab-Israeli conflict is bound to continue in the twenty-first century. Political uncertainty obsesses the power elite in every country in the region, Arab and non-Arab. As opposition grows in many countries, mostly taking the form of religious extremism, one expects the pace of political tension to increase, including the revitalization of the Arab-Israeli conflict. In this part of the world where Middle Easterners seem thoroughly absorbed in the historicity of the region's social, cultural, and political setting, consequential conflicts do not die away but instead enter deep into the consciousness of affected people.

5

The Failure of Development

The topic of modernity has preoccupied laypersons, reformers, and political elites of the Middle East since the beginning of the nineteenth century. Perplexing issues pertaining to modernity such as the political and economic halves of development, cultural regeneration, and identity have come to pervade the political space in the region for the past two centuries. Failure was the common denominator that doomed the fervent activities of state builders (such as Muhammad 'Ali), religious reformers ('Abdu and al-Afghani), and the assortment of Levantine Arab nationalists. Arab and Muslim Middle Easterners could not stand up to the West militarily, economically, or even spiritually. The centuries of stagnation and deterioration finally took their toll on the ancient peoples of the region. The eventual collapse of the Ottoman empire did not gratify the ambitions of pan-Arabists or territorial nationalists but instead introduced Britain and France as liberalizing powers in the Middle East and North Africa. They created a strange amalgam of states in West Asia, rendered Sudan ungovernable, and brought about ethnic and cultural tensions in North Africa.

It was with this background that Arabs—now a widely usable nationalistic concept from the North African shores of the Atlantic Ocean to the marshlands of the Persian Gulf—societally reorganized along an arbitrary Western nation-state model and began the journey toward modernity under the watchful eyes of their colonial overseers. 'Abdullah al-Shahir grieved over the problematic essence of Arab renaissance, finding it appropriate to implicate the West. He blamed European colonialism for breaking the territorial unity of the Arab world and for meddling with Arab thinking by transplanting contradictory thoughts in it.[1] Arab modernizing elites, especially those considering themselves progressive, have generally tended to function under the assumption of Western hostility and the stated objective of undermining the legacy of colonialism.

Western countries have certainly interfered with the social, political, and economic evolution of the Arabs, but wholesale criticism of them misses the point. Arab weaknesses are essentially the result of their own evolutionary processes, mostly unrelated to Western influence. Charles Issawi identified two major reasons for Arab decline: (a) the prevalence of religious mysticism at the expense of "the objective criteria of Orthodox reasoning and Hellenistic science";[2] and (b) steady economic decline, accompanied by intellectual and cultural stagnation, from the thirteenth century until the end of the eighteenth.[3]

Needless to say, the West has capitalized on Arab weaknesses and aggravated them. It can be reasonably advanced that the existing Middle Eastern state system is not conducive to optimal modernization. Still, saying this should not obscure a compelling question. Would the ruling elite of an all-encompassing Arab political entity have performed better in terms of economic achievement and interaction with the population? The forthcoming discussion on Arab development may give clues for answering this question. More specifically, it will demonstrate the maladjustment of Arab political systems to the requirements of modernity.

Blunted Liberalism

In the wake of World War I, victorious Britain and France helped establish liberal political systems in countries such as Egypt, Iraq, Syria, and Morocco. Only Morocco, in North Africa, has survived the onslaught of the military which toppled political liberalism in the Arab East as early as the mid-1930s but especially after the creation of the state of Israel.[4] John S. Badeau wrote on Arab nationalist leaders' preference for Western liberalism as an option to pursue modernization. Although they dreaded the military prowess of Europe, they still believed that "salvation will come by a wedding between the forms of nineteenth century Middle East society and liberal Western institutions."[5] Badeau discussed the rationale for, and the procedure of, founding sociopolitical mechanisms in the Arab world deriving from the West's distinct experience in modernization.

> Seeking to explain why Europe was able to overrun and control so much of the East, nationalist leaders of the late nineteenth and early twentieth centuries concluded that the answer was to be found in the constitutions, parliaments and social organizations of the European state. They therefore sought to introduce these institutions into their own societies. At the end of the First World War, in the fluid aftermath left by the collapse of the Ottoman Empire, the Mandatory European Powers in the Middle East were able to find wide support for the introduction of many features copying current political and social

organization of Europe. Constitutional monarchies were created, the party system appeared, government services of education, public health and agricultural reform were started or expanded.[6]

The main political actors during the liberal period were essentially landed aristocrats, merchants from the major urban centers, and tribal leaders.[7] They demonstrated inability to establish harmonious working relationships among themselves and failed to recognize public needs, let alone commitment to achieving them. They discredited themselves in the eyes of the population by acting as Western lackeys, whose main concern seemed focused on staying in office and accomplishing other personal gains.

In Iraq, for example, fifty-nine cabinets administered the country between 1921 and 1958. The Constitution of 1924 was never implemented in spirit and proved to be nothing more than a cloak camouflaging personal feuds and scheming. The independence of Iraq in 1932 added to instability, and the army stepped into the political struggle, taking advantage of the institutional vacuum caused by excessive civilian bickering in the political field. In 1936 General Bakr Sidqi staged the first military coup in modern Arab politics and overthrew the government of Yasin al-Hashimi. Several other coups rocked Iraqi politics, thus transforming the country's experience with liberalism into a mockery. The Iraqi army, of which a high proportion of its officer corps had served in the defunct Ottoman army at the time of polarization between Arabs and Turks, exhibited a strong pan-Arab sentiment and conversely an acute resentment of British domination of their country. The army supported the anti-British camp among Iraqi politicians, and in 1941 it staged a coup that briefly overthrew the pro-British regime of 'Abdul Ilah and Nuri al-Sa'id.[8] The anti-Western orientation of the Iraqi army, as well as a similar disposition among a number of Egyptian and Syrian officers, partly explains the ease with which Arab liberalism gave way to radical military intervention. They abhorred the West for occupying Arab lands, aborting the hope of creating an Arab kingdom in West Asia, and injuring Egyptian national pride. Army officers, especially younger ones, regarded their countries' ruling elites as Western pawns who cared little about the well-being of the people.

The wedding of Western democratic trappings (constitutionalism, party competition, and representative government) to the local aristocracy proved counterproductive in the Arab world's segmentary societies, which contradicted the West's inclusiveness. Societal organization heavily influenced by tribalism, clannishness, and regionalism created an inhospitable milieu for the propagation of liberal trends, be they in culture or politics. Elite preference of co-optation and patronage to mollify the opposition, or crude force to suppress it, predominated in systemic transactions much to the detriment of participation, the hallmark of liberal democracy. Members of the traditional aristocracy, politically empowered by the mandatory, had not adequately understood the universalistic dimensions of national politics. They busied themselves in petty jealousy and sought cooperation with the colonial power as subservient collaborators, which often implied sacrificing the interests of the population.

In Egypt, for example, the Constitution of 1923, which provided for the introduction of a representative government, soon caused the working relationship between King Fu'ad and the parliament to develop into a bumpy one causing the former to recant the country's commitment to political liberalism. He introduced a measure that made the cabinet members responsible to him, and another that disenfranchised many Egyptian voters.[9] Similarly, Egypt's experience with political parties was not pleasant either. Al-Wafd, the leading nationalist party in the land, showed signs of strains, eventually giving rise to a number of splinter groups such as the People's Party, the Liberal Constitutionalist Party, the Union Party, the Sa'dist Party, and the independent Wafd of Makram 'Ubayd.[10] Factiousness among leaders destabilized the Egyptian political system and enabled the king to manipulate the parties, thus further weakening the country's incipient liberal apparatus. As in the case of Iraq, Egypt suffered from frequent cabinet turnovers totaling thirty-two between 1922 and 1952.

The consequences of introducing Western liberalism in the Arab world did not seem to vary considerably. The French mandate extended a semblance of their democratic procedures in the countries they administered more slowly than did the British. This is evident in Syria where the National Bloc, a loose affiliation of Sunni aristocrats, came into existence in the early 1930s. Its composition reflected Syrian regionalism and the ideological crosscurrents that prevailed in the country. Shortly after Syria's independence, the bloc gave way to the emergence of two urban political groupings, the National Party and the People's Party. Infighting among the aristocratic elite, neglect of the rules of orderly political exchange, and bureaucratic corruption resulted in a highly volatile situation in Syria that eventually compelled the government to request army intervention to restore domestic peace. This period saw the rise of other parties, namely the Syrian Social Nationalist Party, the Communist Party, the Muslim Brethren, the Ba'th Party, and the Socialist Party. Unlike their Egyptian and Iraqi counterparts,

Syrian politicians mainly looked toward their Arab neighbors for affiliation and identification. They seemed obsessed with the idea that the geographical boundaries of post-independence Syria were artificial, and they aspired to fit Syria in a redrawn political map of the Middle East.

In this context of extreme instability and deep elite divisions, the army struck in 1949 and put an effective end to Syria's stillborn liberalism. Before the year ended, two other military coups rocked Damascus, ushering in an era of army assumption of political power, not just in Syria but in Egypt, Iraq, Sudan, and Libya. Even in countries that eluded the coup phenomenon, the army emerged as the defender of the status quo, be it in Saudi Arabia, Jordan, or Algeria.

The political evolution of Morocco after it seceded from the 'Abbasid empire in the eighth century facilitated the development of an institutionalized monarchy there. Religious homogeneity (Maliki Sunnism), absence of ethnic tensions (between Arabs and Berbers), war against Christians in Muslim Spain, and conquest in Sudan in the name of Islam extended religious legitimacy to the king, who won the title of Amir al-Mu'minin (the commander of the faithful), which has been preserved intact until now.[11] In due time, religious legitimacy gained political dimensions that survived the period of French protectorship in the twentieth century. The rise of political parties in Morocco in recent decades did not erode the authority of the king, complementing it instead, though from a fragile power base.

Although it has survived the demise of the liberal trend elsewhere in the Arab world, Moroccan liberalism has not led to the transformation of the political system into a democracy. Al-Jabiri complained about the backwardness of Moroccan political thought, which has not been successful in transcending the obsoleteness of past habits and ways of doing things.[12] Intellectual stagnation and two abortive military coups in the early 1970s set back Moroccan liberalism, until it bounced back in recent years. Despite the rejuvenation of this North African country's liberalism, it does not challenge or present a countervailing force to the king's authority. Mark Tessler ascribes this to the preponderance of the king's prerogatives: he ". . . commands Morocco's economy and distributes patronage, which sustains the king's clientele and builds alliances. Indeed, these commercial and patronage resources are probably the king's most effective levers of political control. Through the use of royal patronage, [he] balances and dominates the political elite."[13] Even though Morocco's political conversion process allows for input from, and participation by, the active political parties and interest groups, in an atmosphere of fairly open mass media system, the king does not accommodate them in a way that undermines his authority. The use of coercion and intimidation to tame the opposition, which is widespread in the Arab East, is applicable in Morocco and tarnishes its liberal orientation.[14]

By and large, the short-lived Arab liberal period collapsed because the narrowly based political elite refused to expand the arena of politics, let alone the rotation of incumbents. Captives of their own nobility class, they jealously guarded their economic and political achievements and, in connection with that, they subserviently cooperated with the mandatory powers, to the intense resentment of the masses. They abused the Western-provided parliamentary systems by transforming them into assemblies for ratifying, instead of legislating, policy.[15] The creation of the state of Israel provided the final blow that brought down a severely malfunctioning liberal order. Watching the triumph of political Zionism in carving out a Jewish state in the heart of the Arab world, Arab publics interpreted this occurrence as an anti-liberal upheaval, for which they implicated the West and their own leaders. They became ready for an illiberal period. The moment of army officers had come.

The Officers as Modernizers: Mission Impossible

If the Syrian military coups of 1949 onward had introduced radicalism into Arab politics, the Egyptian revolution had legitimized it in public eyes. The charismatic leadership of President Gamal 'Abdul Nasser, the young army officer who led the Free Officers on the morning of 23 July 1952 in a bloodless coup that dethroned King Faruq, had survived the military disaster of 1967. The Sudanese and Libyan army officers who staged successful coups in their countries in 1969—latecomers to the club of Arab military rulers—admitted the great influence of Nasser on their political views and actions. Even though Nasser retained most of his popularity (although his credibility diminished somewhat), he was not oblivious to the implications of the defeat, which underscored the unworkability of his political and economic policies. But there was little that he could do to rectify Egyptian developmental policy before first getting the Israelis to relinquish their recent territorial gains. Nasser died on 28 September 1970, broken by defeat and frustrated by the seeming incapacity of fellow Arab leaders at cooperation to confront Israel. Arab military elites apparently had not grasped the lessons learned by the Egyptian leader. They had to learn on their own, the hard way.

The masses welcomed the arrival of army officers to political power but did very little for them by way of mobilizational support. Two major reasons explain an important part of this deficiency. First, the politically inexperienced officers did not know how to create a political apparatus (political parties and voluntary associations) capable of enlisting public support and channeling their demands. Second, the masses were unfamiliar with the process of group organization. Their social evolution produced particularistic tendencies, with emphasis on provincialism and clannishness, and precluded the possibility of effective group action. The ruling military elites, impressed with army organization and discipline (made possible by use of physical coercion), sought to extend their control in the military to the public field. The result was the introduction of extreme measures of coercion in society, reminiscent of the last decades of Ottoman rule. Arab populations, not unaccustomed to repression and intimidation, disengaged themselves from interaction with the state, for them a nebulous concept of political interaction and popular identification. They tended to believe the promises of the military, acquiesce to their authority, and tolerate their repression, but they expected them to produce results. Arab publics exhibited mixed economic and political demands. In Egypt, the pressing issue centered on improving the quality of life for the impoverished population; in Syria and Iraq, although economic needs were important, the most articulated demand was political, its salient aspects pertaining to the achievement of Arab unity, the elimination of Western influence, and the destruction of the state of Israel.

Less than two years after the revolution, Nasser in Egypt set the pace of social and economic change in the Arab Middle East; simultaneously, the Ba'th Party in Syria patterned political debate on the rhythm of Arab nationalism. The dominant themes of Arab unity, modernity, and confrontation with Israel overshadowed the potentially destructive ethnic and religious problems which incubated almost unnoticeably everywhere in West Asia and the Nile Valley. The Arab military elites performed dismally on all fronts of politically relevant activities, domestic or foreign. Every country they ruled was eventually battered either by regional and international wars, civil strife, U.N. sanctions, or isolation.

The army officers entered the arena of politics intent on political reform and economic development. From the beginning, Nasser outlined the six objectives of the 1952 revolution as follows:

(1) eliminating imperialism and its agents, namely Egyptian traitors,

(2) eliminating feudalism,

(3) eliminating monopoly and capitalist control of the political system,

(4) instituting social justice,

(5) building a strong national army,

(6) introducing sound democracy.[16]

These objectives invariably appealed to the Arab publics to the extent that they were adopted as the blueprint for change wherever the army took over the political system in an Arab country, even when the interests of the new military elites clashed with those of the Egyptian president. These objectives were embraced by the masses because of their negative tone toward the West, considered by the majority of Arabs as the major reason for the region's backwardness. While the forces contributing to modernity are complex and cannot possibly be reduced to one variable or another, it would not be unfair to assert that Arab political and economic decay—previously facilitated by centuries of unenlightened Ottoman despotism—suffered enormously from Anglo-French military occupation. Western colonial powers created arbitrary political entities, restructured Arab economies, and decimated long-established patterns of politico-economic continuity in order to serve their own imperial interests.[17]

The world order that took shape after the end of World War II boded well for the national liberation movements in Asia and Africa. Army officers in core Arab countries (Egypt, Syria, and Iraq) saw themselves as part of a broader movement in the Third World that resented the colonial legacy of Britain and France and were spirited by their quick decline in the postwar period. Soviet tactical ideological retreats, dictated by the inception of the Cold War between the capitalist and socialist blocs, encouraged Asians and Africans (Arabs included) to chart a developmental course that parted from the colonial period. Profound change took place. Thus socialism and nationalization measures aimed at remedying social injustice. Agrarian reform liquidated feudalism through the distribution of agricultural land among the peasants. State control of the means of economic production put an end to the monopolies that prevailed in the private sector. Finally, the new ruling elites introduced the single-party system, which in their view offered a viable alternative to the abuses of Arab liberal democracy. The exigencies of defense warranted by conflict with Western-supported Israel justified heavy military spending and exacerbated Arab grievances against the West. Coming from lower social and economic classes, Arab military rulers introduced an extreme version of modernization symbolizing resentment against the concentration of economic power and political prerogatives in their countries' small aristocratic class.[18] The entry of the officers into the political arena signaled the retreat of the historical role of the city in Arab politics, heralding the era of agropolitics.

Nasser in Egypt (as of 1954) and the Ba'th in Syria and Iraq (about ten years later) sought to transform the structure of society in order to bring about modernity to their countries. Their immediate concern was to concentrate political authority and eliminate opposition. In doing so, they abolished the political parties, obliterated the interest groups, and silenced public opinion, three precious achievements of the liberal period. Heavy use of the secret police to suppress political expression and violate elementary human rights traumatized the intelligentsia, as well as the independently mobilized sectors of society. The new ruling elites depended exclusively on the army to stay in power, and to that end they purged it of disloyal officers. The army became the de facto parliament for the officers who used it as a jumping-off point to capture political control; in exchange it received disproportionately generous budgetary allocations from economies gripped with poverty and mismanagement. Full dependence on military support for regime survival, first begun in revolutionary Egypt, enabled the military rulers to consolidate the powers of the chief executive at the expense of the legislature. On three occasions Nasser unsuccessfully experimented with political party organization. In 1953 he created the Liberation Rally to muster public support for his regime, but three years later the Egyptian president introduced the National Union in its stead. Previous failure in enlisting broad mass support for the regime did not deter Nasser, who in 1962 announced the establishment of the Arab Socialist Union (ASU), which he fashioned somewhat after the Communist Party of the former Soviet Union. Plagued with widespread corruption and nepotism, the ASU nevertheless provided a cloak of institutional legitimacy for Egypt's populist political system, although it did not survive the death of Nasser in 1970.

Other ruling military elites in the Arab world, who labeled their countries as politically progressive, entered an alley similar to Egypt's institutional wandering. Notable has been the experience of the Ba'th Party in Syria and Iraq, where military partisans transformed a theoretically democratic party organization into an instrument of authoritarianism, and a bloody one at that. Within a few weeks after the coup of 8 March 1963 in which a combination of Ba'thist and Nasserite officers assumed political power in Syria, the Ba'thists consolidated their gains and pursued sectarian politics that undermined the traditional authority of the Sunni community.[19] In fact the secular tenets of the Ba'th Party provided an ideological camouflage for religious minorities to control Syria (especially after the coup of 23 February 1966) and Iraq (after the coups of 17 and 30 July 1968). In the first instance, the impoverished 'Alawi peasants from the downtrodden Nusayriyyah Mountains produced a class of political bosses in Damascus, whereas the Sunni clans of Takrit prevailed in Baghdad. Political emphasis shifted in the two countries from pan-Arabism to territorial nationalism, a sharp ideological departure which signaled the need for locating local sources of regime legitimacy. The drive for the consolidation of authority, which required pacifying the masses, depended on increasing physical coercion and accelerating economic transformation. The new rulers were able to cow the population, but they mismanaged the economy and undid the meager achievements of previous administrations.

The collapse of economic development projects in Arab countries ruled by army officers has been striking. However, their failure should not be attributed to lack of sincerity or commitment to modernization. The officers, influenced by their humble socioeconomic origins and then-in-vogue slogans of national liberation movements, behaved in accordance with their worldview. They perceived modernity—to be administered by a large public sector—in terms of industrialization, economic self-sufficiency, and land grants to peasants. Huge lots of lands were confiscated from the aristocracy and redistributed in the form of several-acre parcels to landless peasants. This policy had a devastating effect on agricultural output as well as on the quality of crops. The agricultural sector of the economy suffered immediately because of the peasants' lack of entrepreneurial skills and dependence on the state's inefficient system for providing assistance (seeds, fertilizers, fuel, tractors, and so forth) and for marketing the produce. Searching for better employment opportunities and dreaming of a higher standard of living, many peasants chose to abandon agriculture and seek life in the major urban centers. Within a few years, the inhabitants of historical cities such as Cairo, Baghdad, and Damascus more than doubled in proportion to their countries' total population, effectively ruralizing them. The construction of the High Dam in Aswan, perceived in the mid-1950s as the key to Egypt's modernization, did little to alter the country's economic situation given the rapid increase in the size of the population. Syrian hydroelectric and irrigation projects connected with the completion of the dam on the Euphrates were seriously hampered by Turkey's water diversion plans. Although Iraq has the potential (given its adequate water supplies and abundance of cultivatable lands) to fulfill most of its population's food needs, two costly Gulf Wars, burdensome U.N. sanctions, and fluid domestic conditions seem to have curtailed Iraq's agricultural prospects for many years to come.

Of all the Arab countries ruled by the military, the agricultural policies of republican Libya—under Colonel Mu'ammar al-Qadhafi—have been most controversial. The Libyan leader ordered the launching of extravagant wheat cultivation and oasis agriculture projects fed by nonrenewable sources of fossil water. Agricultural expansion along the coast depended on irrigation schemes whose rate of extraction from the local aquifers exceeded the rate of recharge by six times, causing serious water salinity.[20] The regime invested heavily in a wasteful project to transport water from aquifers of undetermined reserves in the southernmost part of the country to promote agriculture in the coastal plain. Al-Qadhafi adopted the price-regulation policies of his Egyptian, Syrian, and Iraqi counterparts and obtained the same bad results. His endorsement of the failing policies of the Arab socialist countries made agriculture an unappealing enterprise to many Libyan farmers.[21] Agricultural setbacks aside, industrial ventures never achieved the stated objective of stimulating the economy and generating revenues for real growth. Arab army officers, having used sophisticated military hardware and experienced the difficulty of getting it from the international market, appreciated the importance of industrialization—the symbol of European might—and became obsessed with it; hence it occupied the inner core of their developmental strategy. They hastily nationalized their countries' small but potentially promising production sectors and entrusted their administration to inept and corrupt bureaucracies. Again, Egypt led the way (and was quickly followed by Iraq and Syria) of industrial expansion but realized the consequences of injudicious planning sooner than the rest. With the help of Eastern European countries, hundreds of factories were built whose products included ironworks, electrical appliances, textiles, processed food, kitchenware, and so forth. Low-quality products ruled out the possibility of competing in the international market, thus necessitating the continuation of government subsidies to meet local consumption needs at reduced prices.

Military and political tensions in the Middle East obscured the need for economic and political reform. Only a few months after Nasser had proclaimed in the spring of 1962 his preference for a guided economy, he committed the Egyptian army to the civil war in Yemen on the side of the beleaguered republican forces. Quagmired in a costly civil war that became his Vietnam, the Egyptian president found himself compelled to reroute scarce material resources from domestic development to war in the rugged Yemeni mountains. Five years later, miscalculation led him to plunge Egypt in a disastrous war with Israel that resulted in the loss of Sinai, the defeat of his vaunted army, and the shattering of the precarious Egyptian economy.

The new priorities dictated by the emerging politico-military reality connected with the course of the Arab-Israeli conflict not only put an effective
end to modernization, but they also prevented an evaluation of the socialist
experience. Similarly the republican regime in Baghdad had to cope with
the eruption of the long-abated Kurdish insurgency in the north.[22] Iraq's
preoccupation with the military aspect of the Kurdish question coincided
with 'Abdul Karim Qasim's action to modernize the economy. It is worth
mentioning in this regard that President Saddam Husayn launched serious
modernization only after signing the Algiers Agreement (which ended
Teheran's support for the Kurds) with the Shah of Iran.[23] While Iraq's prospects for modernization seemed fairly good by regional standards, despite
mediocre performance—mainly because generous spending was matched
by the acquisition of Western technology and the absorption in production
of the large local workforce—the catastrophic consequences of two wars in
the Gulf devastated the country and raised questions about its survival as a
nation-state (the question of Iraq lends itself to discussion in chapter 6).

Immediately after the coup of 1 September 1969 which toppled the
Sanusi monarchy in Libya, al-Qadhafi promised his countrymen to elevate
their standard of living to international levels. In an interview on Egyptian
television in which he oddly looked to the dying Nasserite model for modernizing Libya, he complained against the adverse effects of Western cultural imperialism on his country and pledged to take all necessary steps to
undo them.[24] For the Libyan leader, the most appropriate way to get even
with the West was to show the world that his people were capable of rep-
licating the West's industrial achievements. This explains the fervor with
which he undertook the inordinate task of industrializing a country without
previous exposure to any form of technical know how, and whose very
small and traditional population could not sustain modern industrial activity. Allan Findlay wrote on al-Qadhafi's involvement in prestige industrial
projects: "An iron and steel complex was built with Western technological
assistance on the coast of Misurata. This was ill-conceived, requiring im-
ports of iron ore and of foreign skilled staff, yet needing foreign markets to
achieve efficient production levels. A similarly ill-founded project was the
scheme for an aluminum smelter near Tripoli. Prestige projects such as these
boosted the country's already soaring import bill for equipment, manufac-
tured goods and foreign services."[25]

In the industrial domain of development, al-Qadhafi repeated the mis-
takes committed by the ruling officers in the Arab East. The detrimental
effects of his faulty policies on the modernization of Libya were greater
however, essentially because he introduced them into a thinly populated

and tribal society. The Libyan case smoothens the shift from the experience of the army officers (to whom al-Qadhafi belongs) to that of the conservative monarchies (with whom Libya shares the two important characteristics of oil wealth and tribal organization). In fact, the repercussions of many of al-Qadhafi's policies echo their counterparts in the Gulf area.

The Conservative States: A Veneer of Modernization

Arab oil-producing states on the western shores of the Persian Gulf, which constitute the Gulf Cooperation Council (GCC), best describe the conservatives' approach to modernization. The six members of the GCC, Saudi Arabia, Kuwait, the United Arab Emirates, Qatar, Bahrain, and Oman, all qualify as rentier states. They derive almost all of their material resources from oil revenues as opposed to the economic cycle; hence, they are not considered production states. Furthermore, each of them depends almost entirely on an expatriate workforce to run the economy and to provide the amenities of civilized living. It would not be an exaggeration to say that without expatriate workers in the GCC countries, all manifestations of modern life would come to an immediate halt.

The oil boom generated by the consequences of the October War in 1973—when the Egyptian and Syrian armies simultaneously struck against Israeli positions along the Suez Canal and the Golan Heights—during which Arab oil-producing countries imposed an embargo against many Western countries for siding with Israel, caused prices to quadruple as soon as oil deliveries resumed four months later. Instantaneous wealth triggered crash development projects. In the absence of indigenous workforces capable of handling the requirements of extensive economic development, the Gulf states launched major activities that relied in their entirety on Eastern labor and Western technology. Investment in gigantic projects of uncertain economic feasibility (such as al-Jubayl and Yunbuʿ petrochemical installations in Saudi Arabia) consumed hundreds of billions of dollars. Instead of coordinating the activities of their similar environmental conditions including total dependence on oil for revenues, the Gulf countries duplicated the enterprises of one another rather than integrating them. Elite prestige and tribal pride, as well as the requirements of domestic legitimacy, impelled the rulers to invest large sums of money in unsustainable undertakings. Saudi Arabia's effort to become self-sufficient in the production of staple foods (wheat, corn, dairy products, and so forth) is a case in point and deserves elaboration.

The Saudi political elite, wishing to ensure for the kingdom a large degree of political autonomy in regional and international affairs, decided to depoliticize the question of food supplies and achieve alimentation security. In view of this, Saudi five-year development plans, especially the second and third plans implemented during the period of 1975–84, stressed the importance of expanding the agricultural sector, in addition to building the infrastructure of development. In terms of quantitative figures, Saudi achievements have been impressive. In 1990 the wheat crop yielded more than four million tons, exceeding domestic requirements by at least three times.[26] In fact, Saudi Arabia boosted its ability to export (at subsidized prices) high-quality products among which were wheat, fresh milk, corn oil, and confectioneries to neighboring countries.

Experts have questioned the soundness of Saudi Arabian agricultural policy on several grounds. Saudi wheat cultivation, especially in al-Qasim north of Riyadh, depends on drilling deep wells, which has caused the water table to drop seriously. It is believed that at the current rate of attrition, the wells will dry up in less than twenty-five years. Saudi vigor in exporting wheat has spurred Allan Findlay to say that the policy is "no more sensible than Saudi Arabia exporting water."[27] The same argument has been used against the kingdom's exportation of dairy products, since about 1,500 gallons of water are needed to produce fodder crops for cattle to yield one liter of milk.

Equally disturbing is the lack of institutionalizing the modern agricultural technologies used in farming. Saudi farm owners take advantage of generous government subsidies but defeat their objectives by treating agriculture as a trade. While the government seeks to help basic agriculture to eventually stand on its own, Saudi farm owners seem interested in it as long as they continue to get state support, including guaranteed purchase of their crops. Perceived as such, there is little evidence that agricultural domestication is taking place in Saudi Arabia. Saudi farm owners employ Egyptian and Pakistani agricultural engineers and Bengali peasants in a production cycle that limits the role of Saudis to the entrepreneurial aspect. While Saudi farm owners are naturally interested in maximizing their financial gains, it would be unfair to blame them alone for the travails of their country's agriculture. The simple fact is that most Saudi people, and as a matter of fact their GCC brethren, resist involving themselves in economic production.

The main predicament of economic development for the GCC states lies in the failure of the ruling elites to recruit their nationals in the workforce. Culturally unacceptable occupations that involve economic production are shunned in the region's tribal and primarily egalitarian societies. Even though the development plans of all GCC states have made it clear that their ultimate goal is to involve the indigenous populations in all aspects of modernization (by encouraging vocational training and giving lucrative monetary incentives), the results have been invariably meager. Slogans calling for Saudization, Qatarization, Kuwaitization, and Bahrainization present theoretical elements for elusive development. The rulers, obsessed with the maintenance of traditional political legitimacy in a threateningly changing regional environment, choose not to press the issue of inducing cultural change. To the contrary, the elites have seen fit to prevent the erosion of traditional values, fearing that they might bring about demands for elite accountability and popular representation. The third development plan made it clear that the kingdom of Saudi Arabia's pursuit of modernity should occur in accordance with the tenets of shari'a, and without altering the existing values of society.[28] Instead of benefiting from the presence of large numbers of expatriates to help propagate work-related values among traditional Saudis, the government did everything to prevent their interaction with the population. It is in this connection that one understands why Saudi officials preferred Asiatic to Arab workers. Fouad Al-Farsy praised the success of Saudi officials in segregating expatriates from Saudis. He commented on this matter, saying: "It is an extraordinary tribute to the self-confidence and resilience of Saudi society that it has been able to face the challenges posed by such a large, albeit temporary, immigration—without any weakening of its religious, moral and social convictions."[29] The instinct for political survival has apparently dissuaded them from coercing their populations—hence possibly antagonizing them—to immerse themselves in the cycle of economic production. Thus most of the duties in running the greatly expanding industry and services fell on the shoulders of expatriates.

In appearance the Gulf states, especially Saudi Arabia, have witnessed remarkable industrial expansion, ostensibly of miraculous proportions.[30] In 1974 King Faysal translated his determination to industrialize his country by ordering the establishment of the Saudi Industrial Development Fund (SIDF) to promote the activities of the private sector and public utility companies. His successor, King Khalid, issued in 1976 a Royal Decree creating the Saudi Arabian Basic Industries Corporation (SABIC) to handle the country's hydrocarbon and mineral-based industries.[31] Industrialization efforts went hand in hand with massive infrastructural expansion that included the construction of highways, airports, harbors, power and water desalination plants, warehouses, schools, hospitals, and a modern bureaucratic structure. The expansion relied exclusively on the efforts of foreign workers, which official statistics tend to grossly underestimate.[32] An oversensitive government finds it politically unacceptable to reveal to the population, who does not seem alarmed by the fact, that the entire economic system depends on expatriate operation. Saudi officials note with satisfaction that the total number of foreign workers has declined since the completion of the infrastructure for development by the mid-1980s. The number of residence permits has declined from more than 950,000 in 1984 to less than 600,000 in 1987.[33] The reduction in the number of expatriates in Saudi Arabia, and as a matter of fact in other GCC states, does not mean that nationals are taking over the vacated posts; it simply indicates that fewer projects are under way. Although the rulers insist that the expatriates are working in the kingdom on a temporary basis, until such time comes when Saudis assume full control in running their country's economy, evidence suggests that expatriates have become a permanent component of the job market.

The GCC states focused their attention on the material manifestations of development and the extension of comprehensive social welfare services. The publics reacted passively as idle recipients of government allocations, the latter acting as both extractor of oil revenues and disburser of the national wealth. Thus government programs in the Gulf continued to rely on revenues from plunging oil prices which eventually forced GCC states to resort to deficit spending. Sobering figures about the worsening financial situation of Saudi Arabia are stated in a study by Eliyahu Kanovsky. The report said that "Saudi Arabia's gross domestic product (GDP) has declined from a peak of $156 billion in 1980 (and about the same in 1981) to $87 billion in 1985—a calamitous 45 percent drop. Saudi oil export revenues had plummeted from a peak of $111 billion in 1981 to $25 billion in 1985. Few countries, if any, have experienced such a meteoric rise and fall in national income in so short a time span."[34] Vahe Zanoyan placed the combined revenues of the GCC states in 1986 at about $45 billion, dropping from a record high of $163 billion in 1981.[35] Huge investment in industrial projects has not generated real profit, as most factories continue to depend heavily on government subsidies. Left to their own means, which may be an eventual result of declining government revenues, most plants are likely to succumb to bankruptcy. Deficit spending for the GCC states exceeds 5 percent of the GDP, going up to 15 percent in Saudi Arabia.[36] Wary about curtailing huge food subsidies and levying income and sales taxes, for fear that they might exacerbate public discontent, the ruling elites drew on their countries' foreign assets until they virtually depleted them, and thus had to resort to borrowing.

The veneer of development erected by Arab conservative regimes in the Gulf, in which Saudi Arabia acted as the role model, camouflages an unfortunate experience of poor planning and lack of strategic foresight. Concentration on industrialization in sparsely populated states, where traditional mentality prevails, proved injudicious. Saudis generally shun manual work—which constitutes the backbone of industrial production—even when it involves high pay, viewing it as beneath them. Vocational schools in the kingdom attract the worst secondary students (between 1.5 to 3.6 percent), who would otherwise be out of school.[37] The extent of Saudis' contribution to the demands of industrialization, very low in terms of industrial recruits and quality of technical preparation, actually defeats the developmental objectives of the government. Saudi Arabia's sizable industrial edifice is inherently handicapped by the nonchalant attitude toward it by the national population, which raises important questions about the viability and soundness of such endeavor. Donald Wells, an American economist who specializes in the Saudi economy, voiced deep reservations about the kingdom's ability to Saudize the industrial sector: "In industry, Saudi Arabia will be dependent on foreign workers indefinitely for the same reasons this kingdom has been dependent in the past. First, Saudis will resist doing certain types of work, and will not accept the lower incomes associated with many types of employment within industry. Second, . . . the mixture of skills and experience required by heavy industry will not be available in the Saudi labor force for decades."[38]

It seems that modernization efforts in the Gulf have created complex problems whose management, let alone resolution, baffles the region's traditional ruling elites. The private sectors are booming thanks to heavy governmental subsidies, but there is no evidence in sight that they are ready to survive on their own according to conventional market transactions. Gulf states' budgets and economies are still as dependent on oil revenues as they were in the mid-1970s. Abundance of money, the ultimate dream of developing countries, has not eased off the GCC states' bid for modernity. The challenge of modernization remains as elusive as ever.

Far from the Gulf, the conservative monarchy of Morocco has had disabling difficulties in steering the economy toward modernization. The vast majority of Moroccans have not benefited from the economic policies of King Hasan. The country's industrial output has been severely depressed because of the paucity of spare parts and raw materials.[39] Shrinking purchase power domestically and stiff competition in the international market have dealt a heavy blow to Moroccan nascent industry. In order to maintain political control over his subjects, the king controls the economic resources and dispenses them selectively on the basis of patronage.[40] Naturally, this policy has strained the economy and, when coupled with the sharp fall of its hard currency earnings due to the decline of the price of phosphate in the world market, has had a drastic impact on its prospects in the foreseeable future.

The poor performance of Arab polities did not stop at the failure of economic development but deeply affected its political components. Nowhere in the Arab world have the ruling elites been successful in creating modern political institutions. They elected to rule autocratically and cherished their absolute powers to keep the population under tight control and to eliminate the opposition. They paid lip service to the idea of democratization, although they mightily feared abiding by the rules of the game which it entails.

Sticky Democracy

Army officers during the 1950s did away with parliamentarianism in core Arab countries and introduced populist regimes instead. The challenge presented by the ascendancy of doctrines advocating secular pan-Arabism and socialism in Egypt, Syria, and Iraq instilled fear in the conservative monarchies, as well as in the British-dominated shaykhdoms and emirates in the Gulf, thus arresting whatever potential they might have had for political evolution. Talk about democracy quickly retreated in the face of ambitious plans for bringing about material abundance. Nasser made it clear, when he proclaimed socialism as the instrument of Egypt's modernization, that ". . . the freedom of voting, without the freedom of earning a living and a guarantee to this freedom, lost its value and became a deceit, misleading the people."[41] Arab leaders viewing their forms of government as progressive endeavored to enlist the support of their populations for the regime and its stated policies toward modernization and confrontation with Israel. They strove to create mobilizational political systems (open hegemonies) along the Soviet model, but the predominance of traditional values among the masses, including the obstinacy of particularistic tendencies, stalled their efforts. Wars, religious and ethnic strife, and dwindling financial assets compelled the ruling elites to shift the focus of their attention to regime survival. This transition first took place in the progressive republics as early as the late 1960s but in the 1980s became characteristic of the conservative regimes, especially the oil-producing ones thanks to the crash in the price of hydrocarbons.

Economically beleaguered governments outside the Arabian peninsula found it useful to loosen restrictions on political participation. It seemed quite practical to involve the populations in the regimes' economic difficulties without enabling them to influence strategic decision making that might induce political elite rotation. Therefore, Egyptian President Anwar al-

Sadat, having just launched an open-door economic policy entailing painful social dislocation, abolished the ASU and held nominally competitive parliamentary elections that have continued to take place on a regular basis since 1976.[42] In 1990 Syrian voters elected deputies to the People's Assembly in which, according to Michael Hudson, only tame parties were allowed to participate besides the innocuous independent candidates.[43] Social unrest, often taking the form of bloody confrontations between demonstrators and security forces, persuaded the authorities (namely in Algeria, Tunisia, and Jordan) to call for elections in order to appease the large numbers of disaffected members of society.

Algeria ventured into the domain of genuine parliamentary elections, but when the ruling elite realized the undesirable implications of free choice on their own political survival they chose to rescind toying with democracy. A military coup on 11 January 1992 canceled the second round of parliamentary elections scheduled five days later, which the Islamic Salvation Front (FIS) seemed poised to win against the ruling National Liberation Front (FLN). The result of failing to abide by the rules of the game set by the government itself has engulfed Algeria in a raging civil war that has consumed the lives of tens of thousands of people, many of whom were massacred in a most gruesome manner. An equally unfortunate experience shocked the republic of Yemen four years after its southern and northern parts merged on 22 May 1990. Unsuccessful attempts to create real pluralism in the country that would have made the Yemeni Socialist Party (which ruled the former People's Democratic Republic of Yemen) an equal partner with the northern San'a'-based General People's Congress resulted in a devastating civil war in 1994 that terminated Yemen's prospects for democracy in the near future. Certainly tribal politics among Yemeni southern and northern politicians do not foster transition to democracy unless new values, promoted by shared economic interests, supplant segmentary modes of behavior. The discharge of Yemeni political transactions reveals the malaise of Arab politics in its pristine shape; Hudson found the former saddled by "violence, intrigue, assassinations, and often ruthless suppression of opposition."[44] Lebanon—the Arab world's most liberal and participatory political system—succumbed to a protracted civil war in 1975, basically because the modus operandi of its democracy failed to integrate newly mobilized social forces. The Algerian, Yemeni, and Lebanese examples show the susceptibility of democratization in the Arab world to sociopolitical upheaval.

Elsewhere in the Arab world, the rulers saw to it that legislative elections revitalize their aging authoritarian systems by pointing to a semblance of broad participation in making public policy, which did not expose their political tenure to any sort of threat. According to official figures, Mubarak's bid for a third presidential term in 1993 received endorsement by 439 of Egypt's 448-member People's Assembly. A nationwide referendum approved his nomination by more than 96 percent of the valid votes cast in an unusually high 84 percent turnout.[45] When the third term approached its end, Mubarak did not lack the audacity to amend the constitution to allow himself indefinite terms in office, a step that emboldened Tunisian President Salih Bin ʿAli to follow his example. In 1996 legislative elections, Mubarak routed the candidates of the opposition, including those of the popular Islamic groups, and secured a landslide victory for his political party which he called the People's Democratic Party. Much the same happened in Jordan as a result of the second full legislative elections in 1993, called for after King Husayn dissolved the House of Representatives.[46] The elections of 1989, which occurred after serious riots instigated by economic difficulties, brought twenty-two deputies from the Islamic groups into Jordan's new legislature. A change in the rules governing casting votes, according to which voters could vote for just one candidate rather than candidates equal to the number of parliamentary seats allocated for a single constituency, cost the Islamic groups six of their members. Vehemently opposed to peace with Israel, it looked as if the king wanted more flexible representatives to ratify the approaching peace treaty with the Hebrew state.

Lebanon's two controversial parliamentary elections, since the Taʾif Agreement (in 1992 and 1996 respectively) ended the civil war in the fall of 1989, reduced the country's prewar democratic standing and brought its political practices closer to the Arab hinterland. On both occasions the government announced the regulations governing electoral procedures only a few days before voters went to the polls. The government introduced electoral constituencies of different sizes in a way that favored its own candidates and weakened those of opposition groups. A major irregularity occurred during the summer elections in 1996 when the governorate of Mount Lebanon was exempted from a new ruling making each of the other four governorates a single electoral constituency. The manipulation of electoral laws which recognized six electoral constituencies in Mount Lebanon secured a position for the Druze chieftain Walid Junblat in the parliament and denied the Maronites, who represent the backbone of political opposition, the opportunity of forming a parliamentary bloc led by them. In an ominous precedent the parliament amended the constitution in order to extend the expiring term of President Elias al-Hrawi for three additional years. The 1990s will probably go on record as the decade of Lebanon's pacification and undemocratization.

The political situation in the GCC states best exemplifies the dilemma of Arab democracy. There, the traditional ruling elites' acquisition of significant material resources and their ability to dispense them without worrying about intervention by legal or legislative institutions put a tight lid on widespread domestic dissent, except probably in Bahrain. Robert Rothstein accepted the importance of oil money in attenuating political unrest in the Gulf where "rulers have substituted material benefits for political liberalization."[47] Kuwait's liberalism and al-Sabbah's modest democratic gestures, characteristic of the 1960s period, showed signs of fatigue a decade later and reverted to instability and intolerance the decade after. In 1990 the Iraqi army invaded a Kuwait riddled with political vacuum thanks to the dissolution of the parliament, the Gulf's oasis of liberalism. It is ironic that the exiled al-Sabbah family reacted with ambivalence to the Kuwaiti resistance movement, fearing (not unrightly) that it may lay claims to political participation after the reinstatement of Kuwait's statehood.

The political quandary of Saudi royals exceeds that of their brethren in the GCC. For years they took pains to avert the thought of political reform in the kingdom. They indulged the masses in easy living by heavy public expenditure even if it meant deficit spending. Concern about articulation of public demands for inclusion in the system and accountability of the ruling elite caused the Saudi government to refrain from raising badly needed revenues from taxation. Hypersensitivity to political enfranchisement induced King Fahd to pay token tribute to *majlis al-Shura* (consultative council), which he promised to decree as soon as he succeeded his deceased brother Khalid to the throne in 1982. The repercussions of the Gulf War in 1991 and the stationing of U.S. troops on Saudi soil finally persuaded him to make a symbolic democratic gesture to Saudis by declaring, on 1 March 1992, the establishment of majlis al-Shura. Its sixty appointed members convened for the first time some two years later in a closed session. Coming in the midst of a baffling succession problem—since all of the eligible children of the late king 'Abdul'Aziz, the founder of Saudi Arabia, are over seventy years of age—the idea of political reform presents itself as a dangerous step in the dark. The bleak future prospects for the Saudi economy and the emergence of religiously inspired and democratically coated political opposition in Bahrain and Saudi Arabia itself confound the kingdom's political spectrum. The most active Saudi opposition group is the Committee for the Defense of Legitimate Rights, whose leaders, as well as charismatic religious preachers, strongly condemn rampant corruption and deplore al-Sa'ud's ties with the United States.[48]

Saudi royals seem determined to preserve their political system's institutionalized traditional legitimacy, agreed upon nearly 250 years ago between Imam Muhammad Bin Sa'ud (the initiator of this family's drive for territorial control in the Arabian peninsula) and Shaykh Muhammad Bin 'Abdul Wahab (the founder of the Wahabi movement). They understandably refuse to undergo political changes that could quickly erode the very political foundations of the kingdom. Thus the defensive political discourse of King Fahd, which reveals aversion to political modernization and dwells on the kingdom's distinct position emanating from its revered place as the guardian of Islam's holiest shrines and its "unique customs, traditions, society, culture and civilization."[49] Ironically, Zanoyan determined that the greatest threat to U.S. vital interests in the Gulf region do not come from Iraq's adventurism or Iran's expansionism but rather from the ". . . slow but sure decay of the economic and political structures of [its] key regional allies."[50]

Arab regimes have invariably failed to transform their societies in the direction of genuine democracy, and they have not managed to place them on the right developmental track. Iliya Harik traced the origins of Arab undemocratic political systems to cultural authoritarianism that ". . . prevail in the family, the religious community, the workplace, and between social classes."[51] One of the most enduring obstacles to the transition toward democratic relationships in the Arab world, be they at the level of ruling elites or publics, relates to the strength of ". . . traditional solidarities [which] constitute the most common social bonds, whether tribal, ethnic, communal, religious, or kinship-based."[52] Civil society is weak to virtually nonexistent in the Arab world. Where interest groups and nongovernmental organizations exist, they tend to serve local or regional groupings, even when they purport to represent a national audience. In the less repressive Arab polities where the regime recognizes the right of assembly and formation of demand groups, numerous hurdles stand between the mobilized segments of the population and their ability to function without undue official harassment, unless they agree to glorify and deify the head of the state.

Insecure leaders have not done enough to encourage building the masses into citizens capable of playing a constructive role in society. This has resulted, according to Sa'dun Hamadi, in the emergence of a restless Arab character that is little prepared to deal with the complexities of the developmental process.[53] The idea of the state, as well as the privileges and obligations that ensue from identification with it, remains largely alien in the Arab world although decades have passed since the Western-type territorial state came into being. Hamadi arrived at the conclusion that tribalism and regionalism, among other narrow forms of identification, complicate the superficial and pale sense of citizenship of most Arab publics.[54] Lack of discipline and understanding of the law, not to mention adherence to its tenets, make it quite difficult for most Arabs to interact in a well-functioning civil society. Hence Arab politics suffers from the virtual absence of upward political communication, viewed as an indispensable component of participatory governments. This state of affairs, which is complicated by a general failure in the performance of the political system at almost all levels of policy outputs, has created an environment of siege exempting not a single Arab country.

Besieged States

During the nineteenth century Arabs sought to redefine their political identity and compensate for lagging far behind Western Europe, a regressive process that had lasted for several centuries. Western military occupation extinguished the glimmer of hope in the beginning of the twentieth century. Subsequent opportunities for starting modern polities were weakened by tribal factiousness, regionalism, and particularism. Lack of strategic vision, ideological vacillation, and political inexperience damaged the chances of building a collective Arab order. Interstate cooperation did not materialize, while domestic efforts to bring about economic abundance and political legitimacy met little success. Even in Algeria, which in the late 1970s seemed poised to achieve a developmental breakthrough, the legitimacy generated by the war of independence began to wane as the National Liberation Front, "which had stood at the interface between the Algerian state and its society, proved corrupt and unable to mobilize the population any further."[55] Instead of evolving the political system in a way that established rapport with the population, the ruling elite developed the military to protect the regime. Insurrection in Algeria, Sudan, northern Iraq, and upper Egypt demonstrates that regime heavy-handedness in dealing with the opposition offers no panacea for deep-seated conflict in society. Arab leaders, who until recent years considered the countries they ruled confrontationist states with Israel, fell short of transforming their armies into effective fighting forces. In fact, the qualitative military gap between Israel and Arabs, which gives the former overwhelming superiority, appears to have become unbridgeable.

Table 5.1 gives statistics about the size of the Arab countries' armed forces and the extent of military expenditure in relation to the economy and provides comparative data with the three non-Arab states in the Middle East. The table shows that Israel spends more money on defense than the combined expenditure of the three countries operating the strongest mili-

Table 5.1. The armed forces in relation to population and gross domestic product (GDP) in selected Middle Eastern countries, 1995

Arab countries	Armed forces	Population (million)	Defense expenditure	GDP ($bn)
Algeria	123,700	28,795,000	1.300	49.0
Egypt	440,000	58,731,600	2.400	56.0
Iraq	382,500	21,740,000	2.700	18.3
Jordan	98,650	4,560,200	.440	6.6
Kuwait	15,300	616,356	3.100	26.7
Lebanon	48,900	4,073,000	.407	7.7
Libya	65,000	5,608,200	1.400	25.0
Morocco	194,000	28,250,200	1.300	31.5
Saudi Arabia	105,500	13,307,478	13.200	125.0
Sudan	89,000	29,630,000	.389	9.1
Syria	421,000	14,814,000	2.000	30.1
Tunisia	35,000	9,226,000	.369	18.2
Yemen	42,000	14,792,800	.345	9.1
Non-Arab countries				
Iran	513,000	66,769,800	2.500	62.5
Israel	175,000	4,693,024	7.200	78.0
Turkey	639,000	62,253,200	6.000	153.0

Source: *The Military Balance 1996–97* (London: Oxford University Press for the International Institute for Strategic Studies, 1996).

tary forces in the Arab world (Egypt, Iraq, and Syria), whereas Turkey commits as many funds.

The figures in Table 5.1 imply that the strongest regional powers in the Middle East are non-Arab, even though more than two-thirds of the total population of the Middle East and North Africa is Arab. The magnitude of Arab military weakness is even greater than what numbers may suggest. Israel and Turkey, for example, coordinate military activity including joint maneuvers and cooperate in the domain of technology transfer. On the other hand, Arabs have not been able to conclude serious military cooperation plans and maintain them for any length of time.[56] Numerous inter-Arab military treaties proved counterproductive, or useless at best. The Arab Joint Military Command created by a 1964 Arab Summit (in order to defend Syria, Jordan, and Lebanon during their conversion of the tributaries of the Jordan River) did not deter Israeli retaliatory raids leading to the Six Day War. More recently, the GCC neither ensured the security of the member states during the Iran-Iraq War nor prevented Iraq's invasion of Kuwait in 1990 (this issue will be discussed at length in chapter 6).

Instead, Arab armies became instruments of domestic repression and participants in civil wars. The Syrian army succeeded in brutally destroying the Muslim Brethren's insurrection in the city of Hama in 1982, as well as in pacifying Lebanon without bringing real peace to it, but fell short of achieving strategic parity with Israel or in challenging its occupation of the Golan Heights. In May 1994 the Yemeni army split between north and south, and rival army units—organized along tribal lines—fought a vicious civil war that wasted the lives of thousands of troops before a weary north prevailed in the conflict. In Algeria, the army staged a coup in January 1992 to prevent the arrival of the Islamic activists to political power in the country, thus igniting a civil war that so far has cost the lives of more than 60,000 persons. As the bloody encounter between the army and Islamic militants escalated, sheer butchery of unsuspecting civilians by unidentified assailants became a matter of daily routine.

Arab armies, so essential for regime survival and bestowal of might and authority, haunt the ruling elites as prime suspects. The Moroccan army attempted to overthrow the monarchy in two botched coups in 1971 and 1972, and some army units participated in an ill-fated uprising in 1973. Egyptians prone to interpret accidents from a conspiracy-theory perspective have accused President Sadat of ordering in 1981 the assassination of Marshal Ahmad Badawi, the commander-in-chief of the army. They base their argument on grounds that Badawi grew to become more popular among the officers than Sadat himself.[57] Shortly afterward, an Islamist army officer put an end to Sadat's life during the 6 October military parade. Most Arab armies today, deprived of a sense of national mission, have devolved into instruments of suppression and potential elements of civil strife and scheming. The future role of Arab armies very much hinges on how the elites manage to contain social unrest, reverse the process of economic decline, and liberalize their political systems. The current ruling elites appear incapable of successfully managing complex or severe problems. The weakness of civil society in the Arab world and the officers' veto on the accession of Islamists to power mean that the army is the only feasible alternative to a decaying monarchy.

Reinforced by idle and unmotivated military, the state of siege confronting Arab political orders consists of thick walls of illiteracy, a sociopolitically unintegrated population, and declining rates of economic growth. Arab developmental plans have not been successful in eliminating illiteracy, a key to societal and economic transformation. Table 5.2 shows the persis-

Table 5.2. Levels of illiteracy in selected Arab countries

Country	Year	Male %	Female %	Year	Male %	Female %
Algeria	1987	36.6	64.2	1995	26.1	51.0
Egypt	1986	41.6	67.2	1995	36.4	61.2
Iraq	1985	9.8	12.5	1995	29.3	55.0
Jordan	1991	9.2	24.9	1995	6.6	20.6
Kuwait	1985	21.8	31.2	1995	17.8	25.1
Lebanon	—	—	—	1995	5.3	9.7
Libya	1984	23.1	57.7	1995	12.1	37.0
Morocco	1982	56.3	82.5	1995	43.4	69.0
Qatar	1986	23.2	27.5	1995	20.8	20.1
Saudi Arabia	1982	28.9	69.2	1995	28.5	49.8
Sudan	1983	55.5	79.0	1995	42.3	65.4
Syria	1981	26.4	63.0	1995	14.3	44.2
Tunisia	1989	30.8	54.8	1995	21.4	45.8

Source: *Statistical Yearbook* 41 (New York: United Nations Department for Economic and Social Information and Policy Analysis, 1996).

tence of this problem, especially among women. Although illiteracy rates for both men and women seem to decline with time, the quantitatively encouraging statistics raise disturbing questions. First, the literacy rate difference between males and females remains unacceptably high and points to serious societal imbalance. Illiterate mothers negatively affect the cognitive and evaluative dimensions of their children's personalities—even if the fathers are literate—and jeopardize their contribution to various aspects of life. Second, the percentages vary considerably from one Arab country to another, probably reflecting different positions along the traditional/modernity continuum, or varying degrees of accuracy in official publications. One might safely add that government-published vital statistics in Third World countries lack reliability.[58] Among oil-producing countries, Libya reports greater success in eliminating illiteracy, although one can always question the instrument of measuring literacy. Gulf states' reports sound conservative; they point to important progress with regard to eliminating illiteracy among females since the early 1980s, compared to very little change in the level of literacy among males. Despite the reduction in the rates of illiteracy, the currently existing levels of illiteracy are alarmingly unacceptable for societies desiring to modernize themselves. The inability of states in the Gulf to decrease literacy among males over a fifteen-year period suggests the limited utility of financial resources alone in transforming the population beyond the initial take-off stage.

Table 5.3. Daily newspaper circulation (per 1,000 inhabitants) in selected Arab countries

Country	1980	1992
Algeria	24	38
Bahrain	40	83
Egypt	39	41
Iraq	26	35
Jordan	23	53
Kuwait	222	248
Lebanon	109	185
Libya	18	15
Morocco	14	13
Qatar	131	135
Saudi Arabia	36	43
Sudan	6	24
Syria	13	22
Tunisia	43	49

Source: *Statistical Yearbook* 41 (New York: United Nations Department for Economic and Social Information and Policy Analysis, 1996).

Table 5.2 draws attention to an inauspicious trend in Arab plans to eradicate illiteracy. The literacy situation in Iraq has inexplicably deteriorated in the decade after 1985. Levels of illiteracy among males and females increased threefold and fourfold respectively. It would have been understandable if the cumulative effect of Iraq's two Gulf wars had arrested, or even modestly reduced, the country's literacy outlook. But for the rates to drop so sharply and very quickly reveals one or two things: notoriously unreliable statistics and/or shallow literacy definitions that drastically regress into illiteracy. The example of Iraq is a cause for concern since it hints that other Arab countries' achievements in the field of education may be nominal.

Nothing speaks of the Arab world's political and economic dilemma better than the low circulation of daily newspapers. Dailies keep the readers abreast of societal issues and aware of day-to-day developments of general public concern. It is difficult to imagine the existence of a well-functioning political system in which the population is shut out from information that affects their livelihood and well-being. Unfortunately Arab political systems do not avail their publics of politically relevant information through the print media, especially daily newspapers. Only Lebanon, Kuwait, and Qatar (whose combined population represents only 2 percent of the Arab

Table 5.4. Per capita gross domestic product (GDP) and growth rates (GR) in selected Arab countries

Country	1986		1994	
	GDP $ U.S.	GR %	GDP $ U.S.	GR %
Algeria	2,802	1.5	563	2.3
Bahrain	7,446	1.6	8,223	-0.5
Egypt	1,143	2.0	760	1.2
Iraq	3,056	8.1	2,855	-5.0
Jordan	1,534	7.7	1,095	4.7
Kuwait	9,678	-18.1	16,285	6.0
Lebanon	1,132	23.3	1,692	8.5
Libya	5,473	-8.7	4,220	1.3
Oman	4,978	3.3	5,698	-1.0
Qatar	13,091	3.7	13,020	-0.5
Sudan	365	3.9	62	0.0
Syria	2,375	-5.0	2,827	3.3

Source: *Statistical Yearbook* 41 (New York: United Nations Department for Economic and Social Information and Policy Analysis, 1996).

world's grand total) have modest levels of circulation. Table 5.3 demonstrates how little the situation has improved over a twelve-year period.

The damage to public involvement in the political system does not stop at low circulation, in itself detrimental to sound relationships between the ruling elites and the masses, but extends to the quality of available print media. Most mass media outlets, dailies included, are controlled by the government and disseminate information that commends official policies and glorifies autocratic leaders. The regimes, unable to induce economic modernization and afraid of the consequences of political liberalization, submit to the lure of oppression and brainwashing, in which media control and censorship play a major role. High illiteracy rates make it easier for the regimes to manipulate the masses through a process of misinformation and distortion of reality. Illiteracy and the dearth of independent media information encourage the circulation of clandestine literature and promote word-of-mouth communication, a situation which militant religious groups find most appropriate for propagating their political programs.

State-run or censored media act in a manner that stultifies the minds of the population by telling them, for example, about improving economic conditions when objective indicators suggest the opposite. Table 5.4 introduces information, available for some Arab countries, on the evolution of

GDP and GR over an eight-year period. The trend reveals general economic decline and portends gloom.

Declining oil revenues (GCC and Libya), internal strife (Sudan, Lebanon, Algeria, and Yemen), and destructive military adventurism (Iraq) have had debilitating economic consequences. The fact that economic conditions continue to depend very heavily on oil-generated hard currencies implies a basic weakness in the operations of the productive sectors. Lately, the exploitation of newly discovered oil fields in Syria has alleviated its economic difficulties which, in the 1980s, threatened to destabilize the regime. Continuance of dependence on oil, despite years of major investment in economic development projects, invokes bewilderment. For this to happen, Arab rulers must have, by implication, pursued faulty developmental strategies. Fiddling with socialism by inexperienced army officers and then returning to capitalism by disillusioned politicians without introducing workable bureaucratic reform measures have stalled successful economic transformation. This occurred in Egypt, which, in addition to everything else, did not proceed with fortitude in enacting legislation appropriate for economic *infitah* (open-door policy). Coupled with an inherent incapacity to expand political recruitment beyond the inner circles of the stagnating ruling elite, for fear that this might destroy the pillars of the existing order, most Arab political systems seem besieged by the cumulative consequences of their own deeds.

By the end of the 1970s, political decay, disheartening to many Arab leaders, underlined the need for political renewal, a suggestion inviting insomniac woes. In this atmosphere of uncertainty the Islamic revolution in Iran triumphed in 1979, immediately putting itself on a collision course with the GCC states' traditional elites and Iraq's secular but autocratic leadership. War against the militant Islamic threat coming from the east gave Iraq, with apparent Saudi blessing, the only hope they could think of to prevent domestic social disorder. Iran, struggling to come to peace with itself, while in the midst of post-revolution tumult, loomed as an easy prize. Thus a war broke out in September 1980 when the Iraqi army invaded Iran in a senseless war that lasted for eight years. Chapter 6 treats the subject of Iraq's road to that war and considers its subsequent implications on Iraq, the Gulf region, and the rest of the Arab world.

6

Trauma in the Gulf

The Persian Gulf first received international attention when in the sixteenth century Christian Europe realized its strategic importance to trade with the Orient. The Portuguese occupied Hormuz and Muscat in 1507 and Bahrain in 1521. Although other European maritime powers such as France and the Netherlands showed interest in the Gulf, the British established themselves forcefully as the dominant power in the region less than a century later, becoming the coastal sultans most favored ally. In the nineteenth century they developed interest in controlling the region politically, which they considered absolutely necessary to preserve intact their presence in India. Therefore they concluded as of 1880 a series of treaties with Arab shaykh-doms in the Gulf according to which Arab rulers ceded external legitimacy to the British empire.[1] Britain's control lasted without interruption until after oil was struck in the second quarter of the twentieth century (Bahrain in 1932; Saudi Arabia in 1938; Kuwait in 1946). The British maintained stability and security in the Persian Gulf until they decided to terminate their naval presence there in 1971. When the British took charge of key coastal outposts along the western shores of the Gulf, most of its people subsisted under conditions of abject poverty since they depended on meager returns from trade and fishing. By the time Pax Britannia ended more than 350 years later, the Gulf had become an affluent region containing at least 40 percent of the world's proven oil reserves.

The Issue of Gulf Security

British departure from the Gulf created an immediate power vacuum and threatened to destabilize the region. The shah of Iran seemed intent on giving his country the role of the Gulf's policeman. He dispatched Iranian paratroopers to assist Sultan Qabus of Oman in suppressing the revolt in Dhufar, supported by China, the Soviet Union, South Yemen, and Palestinian guerrilla organizations. Aggressive Iran expropriated three islands (Greater and Lesser Tunbs and Abu Musa) in the strait of Hormuz from the

United Arab Emirates (UAE) shortly after the British had withdrawn. In 1972 Iraqi troops entered Kuwaiti territory but pulled out immediately after coming under intense regional and international pressure. Weary Arab states in the Gulf did not succeed in their efforts to persuade the United States to replace Britain as the guardian of peace in this sensitive part of the world. Immensely disturbed by the war in Vietnam, Washington expressed disinclination to act as the policeman of the Gulf, preferring to pursue a policy of nonintervention in accordance with the Nixon Doctrine. Instead the United States, waging an unpopular and stalemated war in Vietnam, introduced a Twin Pillar Policy by which Iran plays a major role in defending the Gulf against foreign aggressors, with Saudi Arabia assuming a complementary role, and the smaller Arab states assuming responsibility for maintaining their own domestic peace.[2] Toward this end, the United States built up the Iranian armed forces to such a level that they became the uncontested military power in the Gulf. However, the breakout of the Iranian revolution and the establishment of an Islamic state in Teheran has undermined stability in the Gulf, which was further exacerbated by the eruption of the Iran-Iraq War in September 1980.

The pledge of Iran's new leader, Ayatollah Khomeini, to export his version of revolution to all Islamic countries caused trepidation among the Arab states' rulers in the Gulf. The fact that the populations on the Arab side of the Gulf include significant Shi'is (both of Arab and Persian ethnic origin), in a region where religious loyalty competes favorably with state identification, obsessed the ruling elites with tremendous apprehension and uncertainty about the future. The ensuing war between Iran and Iraq (the Gulf's two most populous and militarily powerful countries), two countries dreaded and loathed by the conservative Arab regimes for their universalistic ideologies and proneness to expansionism, revived the issue of security in the Gulf. The leaders of Saudi Arabia, Kuwait, the UAE, Bahrain, Oman, and Qatar took serious action to cope with the increasingly unstable political and military situation in the region. Just five months after the inception of war in the Gulf, the foreign ministers of these six littoral states convened in Riyadh and agreed on the establishment of the Gulf Cooperation Council (GCC).[3] On 25 May 1981, their heads of state held a summit in Abu Dhabi and signed the charter of the council. Article four of the charter focused on economic, educational, cultural, media, touristic, technological, and legislative and administrative aspects of cooperation. Wary about other Arabs' reaction to the formation of the GCC, the signatories made an indirect reference to military cooperation, the central objective of the new bloc. The opening statement in article four worded the first objective of the GCC as follows: "To effect coordination, integration and interconnection between member states in all fields in order to achieve unity between them."[4]

Aside from immediate U.S. approval of the formation of the GCC and belated Soviet endorsement of its defensive outlook, reactions in the Arab world and Iran were less than wholehearted. The Iranian leadership interpreted the move as an unfriendly gesture toward them, whereas Iraqi officials, now heavily dependent on Saudi and Kuwaiti largesse in their costly war with Iran, privately expressed discomfort at the GCC, at least because they were excluded from membership. Most Arabs viewed the GCC as a reactionary bloc whose aim was to isolate the rich and thinly populated littoral Gulf states from their poorer Arab brethren.

The GCC has managed to create a semblance of institutionalized presence, in spite of basic differences between some of its member states.[5] These states have formed a tribally based community of interests that manifests a low level of institutional capacity at the level of external threat, without being necessarily capable of coordinating sustained and consequential military cooperation in crisis situations. Apart from holding a number of limited-size military exercises, the GCC member states created a modest deterrence force composed of 7,000 men (the Peninsula Shield Force), hardly sufficient to participate in the defense of the region against foreign threats.[6] The inherent inadequacy of the GCC revealed itself during the Iran-Iraq War and also in reaction to the latter's invasion of Kuwait. The government of Kuwait, for example, found no way to protect its oil tankers navigating in the Persian Gulf from Iranian attacks other than reflagging them. Again, the GCC states succeeded neither in deterring Iraq from occupying Kuwait nor in taking the initiative to deal with the implications of this enormous event. In both instances, U.S. intervention proved decisive in remedying the situation.

The GCC states reacted passively to the threats building up around them, although they seemed to realize their intensity and urgency. They made sincere efforts, no doubt, to found a basis for broad cooperation particularly with regard to essential defense matters, but they were constrained by multiple interests of a local nature. Their tribal systems lacked the vibrant and dynamic political processes that are essential for making effective and timely decisions. In looking back on past events in the Gulf since the fall of the shah of Iran in 1979, one discerns a trail of fateful miscalculations by all regional actors in the Gulf including the GCC states, Iraq, and Iran. For many years to come, most Arabs will find themselves compelled to endure the implications of momentous events that went contrary to their expectations.

The Iran-Iraq Conflict: The War That Did Not Have to Happen

On 22 September 1980 the first Gulf War started when the Iraqi air force attacked Iranian airfields in a clumsy replication of Israel's air campaign during the opening hours of the Six Day War. Extensive media coverage in the Middle East and the West considered Iraq's decision to declare war on Iran as an impulsive action aimed at improving its strategic position vis-à-vis the new leadership in Teheran, mainly with regard to the dispute over the Shatt al-'Arab waterway. It goes without saying that Iraq was mightily disturbed by having to sign, under duress, the 6 March 1975 treaty with Iran that redrew the boundaries in the waterway to Iran's advantage. The treaty legalized Iran's 1969 unilateral abrogation of the 1937 treaty, according to which Iraq controlled the entire waterway except for a short strip between 'Abadan and Khorramshahr. The Iraqi leadership's nullification of the Algiers Agreement just five days before sending its military inside Iran gave the impression that it was waiting for an opportunity to reverse an unfavorable treaty. Stephen Pelletiere volunteered to analyze the behavior of Iraqi leaders on the basis of social class. Thus he unwarrantedly concluded that ". . . in keeping with the lower-class character of their movement, the Ba'thists were disposed to seek violent solutions to problems that beset them."[7] The truth differs greatly from this simplistic interpretation. Iraqi President Saddam Husayn initially reacted with openness toward the leaders of the Islamic Republic, offering them friendship and cooperation in good faith.

In the first few months after the revolution, Iraq tried hard to be on Iran's good side, but to no avail. Iran's Islamic leaders seemed determined to export their brand of revolution to neighboring Islamic countries; Iraq, with its politically underrepresented and economically disadvantaged Shi'i majority lured Iran's mullahs to taunt Iraq's leadership and exhort its people to topple the "infidel" Ba'thists. Iraq implicated Iran in sabotage activities on its territory that included an attempt on Tariq 'Aziz's life in April 1980. Khomeini declined a request by Ayatollah Muhammad Baqir al-Sadr, the spiritual leader of Iraq's Shi'i community, to defect to Iran and urged him to hold on until the fall of the regime, an imprudent piece of advice that resulted in the execution of al-Sadr and his sister. Nita Renfrew submitted that, although Iraq invaded Khuzestan in southwestern Iran, "the truth . . . is that . . . Iran started the war."[8] In addition to applying tremendous political pressure on Baghdad, taking the form of meddling in domestic Iraqi matters and inciting rebellion in a country divided by sectarianism (Sunnis vs. Shi'is) and ethnicity (Arab vs. Kurd), Iran initiated hostile military actions. Iranian gunboats intercepted Iraqi ships in Shatt al-'Arab, while its artillery shelled Iraqi oil installations and several towns across the border (such as Khanqin, Mandali, and Zurbatiyya).[9]

Iranian intransigence limited the Iraqi leadership's options in dealing with the militant Islamic threat coming from the east. There is no adequate evidence to infer that Iraq's war decision was short-sighted. Quite to the contrary, available evidence suggests a rational decision, if one evaluates the Iraqi action on the basis of Middle Eastern political dynamics and previous episodes of belligerency. It would probably be safe to propose that the developments leading to the unfortunate Iran-Iraq War, and its continuation for eight years, resulted more from the mullah's myopic worldview than the Iraqi leadership's irrational policies. Philip Robins gets to the core of the issue in unraveling the factors that prompted Iraq to go to war, which he attributes to "[t]he essentially negative prognosis formed by the Iraqi leadership about Iranian intentions . . . [which was] fed by Iranian actions. These included the renewed encouragement given to the Kurdish opposition groups in northern Iraq. . . . the new Iranian regime was not interested in observing the modus vivendi struck between the two states in 1975. Once convinced of the essential malice of the Iranian regime, the Iraqi authorities changed their strategy. Instead of attempting to conciliate Teheran they turned to an attempt materially to reduce its ability to subvert the Iraqi state."[10] Before he decided on war, President Husayn visited Riyadh on 5 August 1980 and obtained full Saudi endorsement for the military option and a strong commitment to provide monetary assistance to ensure the success of the operation.[11] Iranian opposition leaders Shahpur Bakhtiar and General Gholam Ali Oveiss planted in the mind of the Iraqi president the idea that Iran, beset by political turmoil and collapse and military disorganization, would quickly give in to a determined Iraqi offensive.

Iraqi leaders developed realistic war plans to put them in the service of theoretically achievable political objectives. Their military strategy was to advance rapidly into oil-rich Khuzestan and then negotiate its return to Iran from a strong bargaining position. They reasoned that wars in the Middle East and in most parts of the world do not last longer than a month after which the Security Council intervenes and issues a cease-fire resolution, after which the erstwhile belligerents negotiate a peaceful settlement. The Iraqis assumed that the strategic importance of the Gulf and the proximity of the battlefront to the oil fields would urge the United States to take quick measures to stop military action, but they were wrong. An adamant Iranian leadership rejected the suggestion of concluding a cease-fire with Iraq as long as Saddam Husayn remained in power. The U.N. Security Council, according to Mohamed Heikal who expressed surprise, exhibited an unusually slow reaction to the Gulf War and did very little to pressure the parties concerned to halt the war.[12] For eight years, Iraq found itself fully absorbed in a war that it nominally won at a staggering cost in terms of human life and material resources. Conservative figures place Iraq's losses at 420,000 casualties and at least $120 billion.[13] Iran's indeterminable toll is believed to be substantially greater.

The Iran-Iraq War debilitated society in the two countries and reversed the possibility of their economic development and political evolution. This self-destructive war did not have to happen at all, and it is largely attributable to changes in revolutionary Iran that combined religious dogma with the strength of Persian ethnic consciousness.[14] Iraq—a country plagued by ethnic and sectarian divisions and haunted by the specter of Iranian intervention in its domestic affair—responded with lethal defensiveness. Baghdad's reaction glaringly reveals the acuity of the crisis of legitimacy and identity in the Western-created Arab system of states. Concerning the Arab world, the Iran-Iraq War confirmed the salience of two very important variables on the conduct of inter-Arab affairs: the demise of the inherently defective Arab order and the paramount significance of the West in determining the outcome of regional conflicts.

The first Gulf War further split the Arab world on yet another issue, but this time it set a precedent whose repetition on a much larger scale proved disastrous to the Arab system following Iraq's invasion of Kuwait in 1990.[15] Immediately after the beginning of the war in 1980, Syria and Libya took the side of Iran, while Egypt, Jordan, and the oil-producing Gulf states rallied behind Iraq. The defection of Syria and Libya from the Arab camp and their unrestrained political support for Iran against a fellow Arab country demonstrated that personal grudges between Arab leaders (for instance, Hafiz al-Asad vs. Saddam Husayn) overshadow the matter of pan-Arab solidarity. Arab states that lined up on Iraq's side did not function in a concerted manner to satisfy strategic national interests. Instead, they assisted with Iraq from a narrow, almost self-serving, perspective. Along one track, Saudi Arabia and Kuwait gave Iraq billions of dollars to fight Iran and contain the threat of its Islamic revolution, and they prayed that the war would devastate it as well. Along another track, Egypt benefited from supporting Iraq in at least three ways. First, the increasing demand on Egyptian labor to replace Iraqis bearing arms against Iran multiplied their remittances back home. Second, its military factories provided the Iraqis with much of the ammunition needed to keep their guns roaring, for which the Egyptians received handsome compensation. Third, Egypt used the Iraqi connection to reenter the arena of Arab politics after the Camp David

Agreement ostracized it in the Arab world. On the other hand, the Syrian leadership thought that Iraq's entanglement in the Gulf War would improve the regional posture of Damascus thanks to its good relations with Iran and the GCC states. While the Iran-Iraq War raged unchecked, Syria used its good offices to allay the fears of the littoral Gulf states about possible Iranian escalation of the conflict beyond Iraq's borders. The great ideas that propelled Arab politics in the 1950s and 1960s (the Palestinian issue, Arab nationalism, and the struggle against Western colonialism) degraded to petty politics in the 1980s. The dusk of Arab nationalism and the reorientation of Arab affairs from pan-Arabism to territorialism trivialized political discourse in the Arab world. Hence the ruler cult appeared in most Arab countries, an untoward development pointing to a deep societal malaise that verified the demolition of the notion of citizen building. The Arabs sat tight until the utterly devastating blow finally arrived.

Iraqis boasted about their triumph in the war against Iran, which their state-run media proclaimed Saddam's Qadisiyya, an allusion to a battle in 636 in which Arab Muslim armies conquered Iraq from the Sasanid dynasty. Spectacular victories in the last four months of the war decisively tipped the balance of power in favor of Iraq and pervaded its leaders with an exaggerated sense of accomplishment. The Iraqi army lost its offensive momentum just two months after the beginning of the war as Iran readied itself for a long showdown. In September 1981 Iraq suffered its first major defeat at ʿAbadan in a confrontation that ended with the flight of the Popular Army Units.[16] The Iraqis pulled out of Iran and settled on fighting a defensive war until a face-saving settlement could be reached with Iran. When field conditions deteriorated for President Husayn's military commanders as a result of Iranian territorial advances across the borders, he ordered (beginning in 1984) the extensive use of chemical weapons to help stabilize the front. The inflow of financial aid from the Gulf states and the steady supply of Western military supplies and technological know-how—in addition to other sources of armament—eventually enabled the Iraqis to force Ayatollah Khomeini to accept a cease-fire in the summer of 1987. U.S. overt hostility to Iran's Islamic rulers and its determination to contain their regional influence encouraged many nations to participate, rather unflinchingly, in building up Iraq's military capability beyond the requirements of its war with Iran (specifically Iraq's nuclear programs). U.S. satellite information about the deployment of Iranian units in the southern front proved its worth in helping the Iraqis achieve a military breakthrough in the final phase of the war.

Saddam Husayn's tragic experience with Iran and the West brings to mind the example of Egypt's Muhammad 'Ali who, in the nineteenth century, challenged the Ottoman sultan and built up an impressive military machine with French assistance. Lord Palmerston, then British foreign secretary, rallied European powers (Prussia, Austria, and Russia in addition to Britain) to defeat Muhammad 'Ali's forces in Syria and confine his suzerainty to Egypt. Even since Napoleon's troops landed on Egyptian shores in 1798, the West has not blinked at important developments in the Middle East. For more than one hundred and fifty years Britain and France set the rules of the political game in the region, but America's turn has arrived at last. Arabs nowadays bear the full weight of American might as it presides on the top of the world in a unipolar international system. The paramount role played by the United States in mobilizing and leading the world to defeat Iraq, following the latter's invasion of Kuwait, deserves close attention.

Precursors to the Conflict over Kuwait: The War That Had to Happen

Iraq emerged totally exhausted from the war with Iran. With an economy at a standstill, a huge foreign debt, a social tragedy of phenomenal proportions, and an overrated military capability, Iraq pondered its future without reason for celebration. Its financial burdens belied the government's capacity to cope with them. A staggering foreign debt totaling $86.2 billion and an estimated $63 billion bill to cover the cost of the damage caused by the war with Iran and complete a few development projects, against less than $13 billion of annual oil revenues, snagged all of Iraq's economic revitalization plans.[17] Unable to raise sufficient revenues to simultaneously purchase essential imports and service its foreign debt, not to mention the principal, put the country on the verge of bankruptcy. In view of its evidently deadlocked financial situation, Jeffrey Record made a sobering assessment about Iraq's future, in which he said: "Once-prosperous Iraq seemed headed for the status of a permanently and hopelessly indebted Third World state, despite its vast oil revenues and usable military powers."[18] Patrick Clawson contested this type of interpretation and claimed that the Iraqi economy fared better in 1989 than in 1986, due to a 70 percent increase in its oil earnings.[19] He put the blame for Iraq's economic woes solely on the person of Saddam Husayn, who spent beyond his means on grandiose projects and noncritical food purchases.[20] Clawson's analysis ignored the fact that, with the end of war with Iran, Iraq was no longer receiving Arab financial assistance which helped offset its declining oil earnings. One should keep in mind that Clawson belonged to the pro-Israel academic school that did not sympathize with Iraq, even before the beginning of the crisis over Kuwait, and ridiculed its megaprojects. No matter how we look at it, the fact remains that Iraq confronted difficult financial problems on the eve of invading Kuwait. Saudi Arabian discreet antipathy, Kuwaiti condescension, Israeli watchfulness, and U.S. dryness in dealing with the Iraqi leadership interacted to constitute the elements of an imagined conspiracy that dominated the thinking of President Husayn.

Iraq, ever striving to attain a position of preeminence in Arab politics, has never been popular in official Middle Eastern circles. War with Iran, which the Ba'thist rulers tried to market as a struggle for the existence of the Arab nation against Persian expansionism, only increased the apprehensions of Iraq's neighbors about its potential for regional subversion. Self-congratulatory Iraqi officials sought Arab appreciation for defeating Iran and recognition for Baghdad's playing of an enhanced role in Arab affairs. Instead they received mixed reactions ranging from aversion to trepidation. Calculating and inoffensive Saudi Arabian leaders chose to appease Iraq and wrote off its substantial debts to the kingdom. However, Kuwait adopted an unaccommodating policy toward Iraq, and in doing so it grossly miscalculated. The issue of Kuwaiti provocation and Iraqi retaliation resulted from the behaviors of political actors operating at differing levels of analysis, a situation that has encouraged conspiracy theory interpretations. The present study shuns the conspiracy approach and considers the political developments leading to the second Gulf War as elements of a dynamic, not necessarily preconceived, set of interactions. The assembling of the events that occurred between the end of the Iran-Iraq War and its successor that pitted Iraq against the U.S.-led coalition over Kuwait reveals, almost deterministically, that the conflict could not possibly have been averted.

Decreasing oil prices stifled Iraq's desperate need to raise larger sums of money to cope with its implacable economic crisis.[21] Overproduction by some GCC states, mainly Kuwait, beyond their OPEC quotas brought oil prices down and mightily angered hungry-for-cash Iraq. During the Baghdad Arab summit on 28 May 1990, President Husayn alerted Arab leaders to the gravity of the situation, describing it as a virtual war against Iraq. Tariq 'Aziz, Iraqi minister of foreign affairs in the 1980s, reiterated to U.S. Secretary of State James Baker, when they met in Geneva on the eve of the war, the devastating consequences of Kuwait's excessive oil production. He said: "In December 1989 and January 1990 we used to sell oil for $26 per barrel, but in February the rulers of Kuwait began to flood the market with oil bringing the price down to $11 or less."[22] The political establishment in Baghdad expressed thorough conviction that the Kuwaitis, who steadily ignored its repeated complaints, were part of a grand conspiracy to cripple Iraq. Heikal researched the viewpoint of Iraqi leaders concerning their conflict with Kuwait on the issue of the latter's oil overproduction, and he made the following assessment about their decision to use force: "Iraq determined that Kuwait had decided to overlook its complaints regarding oil. The general impression in Baghdad was that Kuwait would not dare do this unless it had security guarantees from the United States. Iraqi suspicions reached a degree of conviction about Kuwait being used to pressure Iraq to inhibit its potential and curtail the development of its military might."[23] Kuwait never denied charges of overproduction. Nearly a year before the Iraqis finally spoke out in condemnation of their tiny neighbor's oil policy, the Kuwaiti minister of petroleum announced that his country did not intend to abide by its OPEC quota of 1,037,000 barrels per day, and that it wanted to increase it by one-third. In fact, Kuwait's actual production exceeded its quota by 70 percent.[24]

Kuwaiti oil policy disclosed the strategy of its rulers' financial planning; it was not at all the outcome of an anti-Iraqi plot. The al-Sabbah family simply pursued what they thought was in the best interests of their country, although in a manner displaying a great deal of arrogance and little sensibility. Kuwait (much like Saudi Arabia and the UAE) preferred to export as much oil as it could at reasonably low prices rather than the other way around. Unlike Iraq who merely exported crude petroleum, Kuwait—as an investor in international oil companies—did not seem to worry about low oil prices. Kuwaiti officials who defended their country's oil policy presented their case disdainfully and behaved wantonly. Amid reports about a massive Iraqi military buildup along its borders with Kuwait, Egyptian President Husni Mubarak flew to Baghdad on 24 July 1990 to defuse the mounting tension between the two countries. He succeeded in persuading the leaders of Iraq and Kuwait to attend a summit meeting in Jiddah on 31 July, but the emir of Kuwait chose to boycott the meeting, thus adding personal insult to the Iraqi leader's entrenched notion of collective injury for his people. This Kuwaiti indiscretion uncapped the Iraqi president's restraint and swayed him to unleash his army. In the early morning hours of 2 August 1990 Kuwait succumbed to Iraq's formidable military juggernaut. Jeffrey Record wrote a critical note in evaluating Kuwait's behavior toward Iraq, which he found reckless because a ". . . small state lacking defenses, allies, and a willingness to appease is an open invitation to aggression, especially if it is either rich in natural resources or strategically critical territory—and certainly if it pursues a foreign policy based on the illusion of its own inviolability."[25]

Instead of taking the time to realize the gravity of Iraq's financial situation, the leaders of Kuwait adopted a nonchalant approach, mainly blaming the rulers in Baghdad for undertaking ungainly policies. The actions of Kuwait coincided with the beginning of an anti-Iraqi campaign in Washington, supported by Israel and its friends in Congress and the U.S. media. The timing of pressures coming from different directions convinced Iraq's rigid and closed political leadership that Kuwait was conniving with the United States and Israel to bring down the regime in Baghdad.

From the beginning of 1990 Western media, especially in the United States, took aim at Iraq and its thin-skinned president. Press releases about Iraq's efforts to manufacture a supergun with nuclear delivery capability, as well as its nonconventional weapons production programs, suddenly aroused the journalistic instinct of many American reporters. Thus *U.S. News and World Report* announced that Saddam Husayn had become the most dangerous man in the world, while *Newsweek* decided that he was the number-one enemy of the American people.[26] A disbelieving Tariq 'Aziz asked James Baker: "How have we become the number-one enemy of the American people without killing a single U.S. citizen, or threatening any of your interests?"[27] The Iraqi leadership failed to understand that the media in the United States is independent and does not necessarily reflect official views or planned policies. Unknowing Iraqi leaders, prisoners of a political system in which the media acts as a mouthpiece for the regime, ascribed to the media in the United States the same role played by its counterpart in Iraq. There is no basis for claiming that the U.S. administration worked in concert with the critics of Iraq in Congress and the media. To be sure the two countries had a fairly good, although obviously not cordial, working relationship. A successful visit by 'Aziz to Washington in October 1989 convinced President George Bush to open up to Saddam Husayn. Bush issued a memorandum to concerned members of his administration requesting the development of normal relations with Iraq, because this would, in his view, help stabilize the Middle East.[28] He followed this up, in January 1990, by authorizing an increase in the volume of U.S. trade with Iraq. In return, the Iraqis adopted favorable policies toward Washington such as the termination of their involvement in the Lebanese civil war in support of the anti-Syrian faction, attended two disarmament conferences in Geneva, and fostered a flexible attitude on the issue of Arab-Israeli peace.[29]

Rapprochement between the United States and Iraq bred discontent in Israel. A relatively strong Iraqi military with active weapons development programs threatened to upset Israel's military superiority, which the Hebrew state has pledged to preserve at any cost, including launching preemptive strikes, ever since its creation. Although Iraq is not a confrontationist state, in the sense that it shares borders with Israel, it has participated in major Arab-Israeli wars (those of 1948, 1967, and 1973). The emergence of Iraq as a regional power in the early 1970s, its decision to acquire nuclear capability, and daring to invade Iran caused worry in Israel. Taking advantage of its war with Iran, Israeli jets destroyed on 7 June 1981 Iraq's Osirak nuclear reactor near Baghdad. In fact, determination to stall the rise of a strong Arab military power did not deter Israel from selling arms to Islamic Iran to defeat secular Iraq. In the beginning of 1990 Israel, in collaboration with its strong pressure groups in the United States, started a massive political and media campaign against Iraq's military buildup and threatened to repeat the Osirak operation. The trick achieved the objective of angering the Iraqi president, who swore, on 2 April 1990, to destroy half of Israel if it made good on its threat. The synchronization of Kuwaiti oil policy and Israeli media war suggested a conspiracy in the making to the Iraqi leadership. President Saddam Husayn, a captive of personal fears and a narrow worldview, decided to act. He miscalculated, because he failed to realize that the bipolar world order that he knew was in the throes of a complete transition toward unipolarity. Husayn also seemed yet unaware that the fragile concept of Arab solidarity had crumbled under the march of territorial nationalism. The United States, a superpower in search of new enemies to replace the dying Soviet Union, found in the Iraqi invasion of Kuwait an ideal starting game for the new world order it was contemplating. Iraq presented itself as a toothless foe to the American military might; the leaders of Egypt and Saudi Arabia took it upon themselves to trap Iraq in the inferno of American might, while Israel's U.S. allies made sure that it stays there.

From Desert Shield to Desert Storm

As soon as Iraqi troops occupied Kuwait, the Bush administration made it obvious that it preferred the use of military might to evict them. The speed and resoluteness of U.S. diplomatic action to isolate Iraq and stigmatize its leadership leave little doubt that it ruled out a peaceful solution to the crisis. It seemed as if the Americans were waiting for the Iraqis to make the foolish mistake of violating Kuwaiti sovereignty to implement previously prepared contingency plans for military intervention in the Persian Gulf.[30] Shocked by the Arab oil embargo during the 1973 October War, the U.S. government pledged to prevent any future disruptions in the supply of hydrocarbons, perceived as vitally strategic to its national interests. The establishment of the Rapid Deployment Force (RDF) for intervention in the Gulf should another oil crisis develop, the initiation of the Bright Star military maneuvers with Egypt, and U.S. policy in the Horn of Africa in the 1970s were all elements of a comprehensive policy that aimed at ensuring the uninterrupted flow of oil to Western markets. Given the central importance of Gulf oil to America—and the inviolability of the area's constituent states as a corollary—the Bush administration decided, once Iraqi tanks crossed into Kuwait, to accept the demand of the strong pro-Israel lobby to dismantle Iraq as a regional power. It is necessary to point out that U.S. officials had no reason to feel jolted by the Iraqi invasion of Kuwait. The Iraqis did not rule out the possibility of military action and made a point to alert Washington to this possibility. Alex Hybel studied the unfolding of the Iraq-Kuwait crisis and the former's method of mobilizing its troops in preparation for action. He determined that the Bush administration ". . . cannot plead for forgiveness for being deceived by Saddam Hussein . . . [who] did not attempt to achieve surprise, and U.S. officials had more than sufficient evidence to conclude that an invasion of Kuwait was probable."[31] To make sure that Washington fully understood what he wanted to do next, on 25 July 1990 he met with U.S. Ambassador April Glaspie in Baghdad. She assured him of the neutrality of her government's standing policy on interstate Arab conflicts. The Iraqi leadership understood the importance of Gulf oil to the United States and professed no intention to tamper with it; they took it for granted that Washington knew this as a constant in Iraqi foreign policy. The Bush administration reacted to the invasion as if it did not know Iraq's commitment to U.S. interests or, notwithstanding, considered it completely unforgivable.

Bush quickly outlined for his country a belligerent and uncompromising course of action vis-à-vis Iraq, one that shunned diplomacy and avoided serious rationalization. The awkward plan comprised the following major elements:

1. Iraq's invasion of Kuwait is totally unacceptable and provides no basis for negotiations;

2. American and world public opinion must be mobilized to support the forthcoming U.S. response;

3. The liberation of Kuwait is the sole responsibility of the United States, hence its operational plans must prevail;

4. Saudi Arabia must be contacted because its territory will provide the launching pad for envisaged military activity against Iraq.[32]

Margaret Thatcher, then the prime minister of Britain, heavily influenced the thinking of Bush on how to punish Iraq. An adamant Thatcher advised the American president that withdrawal from Kuwait was insufficient, and she persuaded him to exact a crippling blow to Iraq. She succeeded in focusing the attention of Bush on the need to destroy Saddam Husayn's military machine, his country's industrial infrastructure, as well as the need to keep it under severe economic sanctions even if it complied with U.N. resolutions.[33]

Having decided to destroy Iraq, President Bush immediately dispatched Secretary of Defense Dick Cheney to Saudi Arabia to enlist the support of reluctant King Fahd. Armed with U.N. Security Council Resolution 660 of 2 August 1990, which condemned Iraq's invasion of Kuwait, an insistent Cheney demanded and obtained the king's approval of his war agenda that included sending about 240,000 U.S. troops to Saudi Arabia. The success of U.S. strategy against Iraq hinged on the failure of a peaceful Arab solution to the crisis. To ensure the derailment of Arab diplomacy, Bush phoned the president of Egypt, literally ordering him to comply with Washington's vision. Bush scoffed at Mubarak's preference to convene an Arab summit to look into the matter, saying that Iraq had crossed the point of no return.[34] Thus Iraq's decision, hours after the invasion, that it intended to announce the withdrawal of its army from Kuwait in the Jiddah summit in which it would participate, did not prevent Egypt from sending a condemnatory note to Baghdad. By canceling the Jiddah summit, King Fahd gave valuable assistance to President Mubarak, who knew that his escalatory rhetoric would anger an image-conscious Iraqi leadership. Coordinated efforts to condemn the Iraqi president and radicalize his political moves culminated in the theatrical Cairo summit, held on 10 August, 1990.

The speeches of the Egyptian, Saudi Arabian, and Syrian heads of state revealed that they came to the summit without a will or intention to resolve the issue among themselves, but only to endorse and legitimize U.S. intervention. After censuring Iraq, Mubarak demanded immediate withdrawal from Kuwait, without offering to help resolve the outstanding problems between the two countries. He warned against the alternative of American intervention, "which we can neither stop nor control, and whose objectives aim at fulfilling the interests of the forces behind it."[35] King Fahd told Arab leaders that he had already requested military assistance from many countries—Arab and non-Arab—to assist in training the Saudi army. He stressed that the only task of "these foreign troops [American] is to assist in repelling aggression against Saudi territory, not to attack Iraq."[36] Obviously, King Fahd lacked the courage to admit that these troops came to the kingdom to eliminate Iraq's military strength, as part of their goal to put Kuwait back on the map. Following consultation with the Saudi king less than three months later, President Bush ordered the deployment of 200,000 U.S. troops (in addition to the 240,000 troops already there) to the kingdom to give him "an adequate offensive option."[37]

Speaking defensively at the summit, Syrian President Hafiz al-Asad blamed Iraq for forcing Arabs to entrust the United States with the task of reinstating Kuwait. In a move that served Bush's preference to involve token Arab and Muslim military units in his war plans (to placate Saudi Arabia's outraged religious establishment by giving them the impression that U.S. troops were part of an international coalition against the person of Saddam Husayn, not the Iraqi people), Asad declared his willingness to commit Syrian troops to liberate Kuwait "so that history will not damn us for inaction as foreigners come to defend our brothers in distress."[38] Before the end of the day, Mubarak, who was obliging to Bush's wish to rule out an Arab solution, succeeded in mustering enough support among the conferees to pass a resolution condemning Iraq and demanding its unconditional withdrawal from Kuwait. The head of the PLO, Yasser 'Arafat, cried out after Mubarak announced the resolution: "All of you are [American] agents." Predictably, Iraq denounced the resolution and was forced to dig in, while Bush achieved his objective of dragging it into an unwinnable showdown with the United States.

By refusing to talk to Saddam Husayn, the United States completely shut in the Iraqis, simply demanding that they pull out of Kuwait without assurances that compliance with U.N. Security Council resolutions would end the crisis. To the contrary, U.S. officials emphasized that withdrawal from Kuwait was not necessarily going to avert military retaliation or end economic sanctions. Muhammad Hallaj excellently summarized the predicament of Iraq, arguing that

> . . . American demands on Iraq reached a level whereby Iraq was expected to consent to its own military emasculation, economic strangulation, and political abdication. The Bush administration made it clear that Saddam Hussein was not even to be offered an opportunity for a face-saving way out of the confrontation. It was as if the Bush administration feared Iraqi acquiescence to its demands and sought to prevent it by demanding . . . humiliating capitulation . . . indemnities, the disarming of Iraq, war crime trials, and the removal of the Iraqi leadership. The Bush administration was in effect serving notice that it would be in the interest of the Iraqi leadership to take its chances on war.[39]

The United States, now a world power without a clear foreign policy direction, searched for enemies in the Third World.[40] Its leaders saw in Iraq an ideal enemy who erred, but they did not want to give it the opportunity for redemption. Therefore it opposed the proposal of Moroccan King Hasan II in November to convene an Arab summit to search for a peaceful solution; instead the United States pressured the Security Council to issue Resolution 678 authorizing the use of military force against Iraq if it did not evacuate Kuwait by 15 January 1991. Similarly, it rejected a last-minute initiative by France to call for an international conference on the Palestinian question, which would have satisfied the Iraqi leadership as a precondition for leaving Kuwait. War broke out on 16 January 1991 and, as expected, resulted in the destruction of Iraq and ended its leading regional role, as well as putting it on the verge of territorial disintegration. Antun Maqdisi viewed the second Gulf War as evidence that the United States would not tolerate dissension in the Third World against its will. He considered the consequences of the war as the greatest Arab loss since the loss of Spain in the fifteenth century.[41] Indeed, it created a multifaceted Arab trauma of the severest magnitude.

The Conflict from a Western Perspective

Most Western writings on the Gulf conflict endorse the official interpretation of the events leading the war, as well as the evaluation of its staggering consequences. Steve Yetiv saw in the invasion of Kuwait an attack against the security of all Persian Gulf states and countries interested in securing their oil needs at moderate prices.[42] He insisted that Saddam Husayn, obsessed with self-aggrandizement, wanted to resurrect Babylonia and that he "fancied himself a modern-day Nebuchadnezzar."[43] Yetiv isolated three reasons for Washington's decision to defeat the objectives of the Iraqi president. First, if Iraq prevailed in Kuwait, it would most certainly intimidate other Gulf states and elevate the status of Saddam Husayn into a regional power. Second, the U.S. administration seemed quite confident (on the basis of Iraqi military deployment near the Saudi borders) that Iraq intended to invade Saudi Arabia, a move that would allow Baghdad to control more than half of the world's known oil reserves. Third, the loss of Saudi Arabia carried the possibility of a sharp increase in oil prices and threatened the occurrence of a world recession.[44] In turn, Elaine Sciolino identified three factors behind Saddam Husayn's decision to invade Kuwait: finding a quick solution to Iraq's deep financial crisis, transforming the country into a naval power, and punishing his Arab neighbors who, allegedly, tried to prevent Iraq from achieving a position of preeminence in the Gulf, the latter presuming it to be their country's legitimate role.[45] In verification of her assessment of Saddam Husayn's belligerent designs, Sciolino pointed to Iraq's heavy military investment in missile, chemical, biological, and nuclear programs.[46] Michael Mazarr summed up the negative evaluation of the Iraqi regime by the mainstream Western discourse. He labeled what he perceived as an ambitious, aggressive, and subversive leadership in Baghdad as a major threat to U.S. vital interests in the Middle East, primarily access to oil and the security of Israel.[47]

Alan Munro concentrated on what he categorized as the suspicious, brutal, and impulsive character of Saddam Husayn. By showing how these negative character qualities shaped the aggressive foreign policy conduct of the Iraqi president, Munro appeared intent on justifying U.S. military, economic, and diplomatic containment of Iraq.[48] To be sure, President Bush had a difficult time articulating a recipe for winning public support for the extravagant buildup of U.S. troops in Saudi Arabia in the wake of Iraq's invasion of Kuwait. In a brilliant essay, Edward Luttwak traced the confusion of the American president who dispatched an awesome military machine to defeat Iraq, before working out a convincing motive. In the words of Luttwak, George Bush

> . . . would have avoided the wild hyperbole of the Hitler comparison—Iraq has not the capacity of the meanest province of Germany—and he would have kept matters in proportion by delegating diplomacy to the diplomats instead of doing it all himself on the telephone. . . . George Bush threw himself into crisis management on a full-time basis with boyish enthusiasm, barely turning aside to explain, most unconvincingly, the reason for it all. . . . Had Bush resorted to deterrence he would have nothing to explain. Had he then quickly proceeded to issue a withdrawal ultimatum, beginning to bomb Iraq as soon as it expired, that too would have been accepted by most Americans. Instead of deterrence and bombing, he chose defence by an expeditionary force, followed by . . . the assembly of an army of reconquest. . . . Bush was insistently pressed to explain why American "boys"—and women, and reservist fathers and reservist mothers, had to be sent to Arabia of all places. After trying and failing to evoke support for the imperative of restoring the Al Sabah family over its enterprise of Kuwait, and keeping the Al Saud family in ownership of its own larger enterprise . . . the Bush Administration tried the "oil needs of the industrialized world" argument.[49]

When this argument very quickly collapsed, the Bush administration ". . . did finally come up with a new, fully original justification for taking on

Saddam Hussein ever so slowly, with troops on the ground, under the mantle of the UN: the (Post–Cold War) 'New World Order': when public opinion reacted very negatively, foolish television pundits explained that the idea was much too abstract for the untaught masses, which could not be expected to understand."[50]

The Americans were very slow to admit that their strategic objectives in the Gulf entailed the destruction of the Iraqi military machine and the strangulation of its regionally ambitious leadership, who violated the tenets of the Western-created Middle Eastern state system. Early in the conflict, a commentary in a British daily advised the U.S. administration to define its war aims, which included ". . . the destruction of Iraq's ability to develop and deploy chemical and nuclear weapons."[51] It also called for the removal of Saddam Husayn, not just because of the tyrannical nature of his rule, but because of his "expansionist ambitions."[52]

Once the lopsided war started, the United States waged it against the lame Iraqi armed forces with maximum force that far exceeded the requirements for reclaiming Kuwait. The massacring of thousands of retreating Iraqi troops at Mutla Ridge opened a window on the magnitude of unscrupulous use of overwhelming firepower to achieve stated war aims. The maximum use of force confused many American Arabists who found it convenient to focus on the erratic aspects of the Iraqi president's personality. Writing defensively, Bill Quandt thus put all the blame for the losses in human life and the material destruction on Saddam Husayn, whom he regarded as the worst world leader.[53] But Zbigniew Brzezinski, former U.S. National Security Adviser, spoke critically about the war, regarding it a moral disgrace to his country. He condemned the ". . . intensity of the air assault, the demolition of the life-support environment and the callous massacre of retreating troops."[54]

The Kuwaiti and Saudi Perspective

Kuwaiti and Saudi officials viewed the course of events leading to crisis in the Gulf mainly in terms of Iraq's demands to annex parts of Kuwait and its urgent need for huge sums of money to stimulate its depressed economy and to reconstruct its infrastructure after the devastating war with Iran. They sharply disagreed with President Saddam Husayn's interpretation that the countries of the GCC owed it to Iraq to stop the spread of the Iranian revolution, which safeguarded the eastern flank of the Arab world against Persian penetration. Arab writers from the Gulf region often repeated the charge that Iraq invaded Kuwait and threatened the territorial integrity of Saudi territory in order to fully control the oil policy of the Gulf states and break Saudi hegemony on oil markets.[55]

'Uwayd al-Mish'an, a Kuwaiti author, rejected Saddam Husayn's claims that his country took advantage of Baghdad's preoccupation with war against Iran by taking possession of Iraqi territory and siphoning oil from al-Rumayla oil field.[56] Instead, he accused the cash-poor Iraqis of trying to use intimidation to coerce Saudi Arabia, Kuwait, and the UAE into allocating billions of dollars for an Arab version of the Marshall Plan for Iraqi reconstruction.[57] Al-Mish'an felt that Iraq's Arab neighbors did not cause Iraq's travails—therefore, they were not responsible for their consequences—which he attributed to Saddam Husayn's injudicious policies, reckless adventurism, and psychopathic personality.[58]

Khaled Bin Sultan, the joint forces commander of the anti-Iraq coalition, best expressed the Saudi view on the events that led to Desert Storm. He stated that Iraq's invasion of Kuwait mightily upset King Fahd, who felt the move had destroyed the existing order in the Arabian peninsula which, for years, he sought to maintain. The Saudi king came to realize that Saddam Husayn turned out to be a false friend who broke all the rules of Arab politics and personally stabbed him in the back.[59] Bin Sultan believed the Iraqi president intended to become the Arab world's uncontested leader, and to outdo at that the charismatic leadership of Egypt's former president Gamal 'Abdul Nasser.[60] But by the spring of 1990 the Iraqi president finally realized that his country was broke, an appalling situation for a leader whose image, not to mention political survival, depended on large-scale public spending and investment in extravagant projects. The dire need for cash impelled Saddam Husayn to send his prime minister to Kuwait ". . . with a peremptory demand for $10 billion . . . [of which] the Kuwaitis offered him a mere $500 million which he took as an insult."[61] According to Bin Sultan, this incident played a crucial role in convincing Saddam Husayn that invading Kuwait—a rash decision for whose results he is fully responsible—seemed to provide an immediate opportunity to redress Iraq's financial standing.[62]

An Arab Trauma

Numerous years will pass before the trauma befalling the Arabs as a consequence of the second Gulf War dissipates. The war waged by the United States and its make-believe coalition against Iraq, ostensibly to liberate Kuwait, has destroyed the last vestiges of Arab solidarity, rendering Arab states totally ineffectual in Middle Eastern politics. This war, in which many Arab states chose to side with the United States against one of their own, came as a logical conclusion of many years of failure at different levels of performance, be they in relation to political and economic development, confrontation with Israel, or attaining a workable Arab order. American aggressiveness, heightened and emboldened by the stunning eclipse of Soviet power, infringed upon the Arabs in their despair and indirection. The United States, a great power in perpetual search for convenient enemies, took advantage of its new status as the sole superpower to cow Arab leaders to commit their countries' material and human resources in a war against Iraq, a major center of Arab-Islamic culture and civilization.

A milestone in inter-Arab relations in that it jeopardized mutual cooperation and undermined interelite trust even among erstwhile friends, the war for Kuwait also served to reintroduce direct Western intervention in Arab affairs. Thus, the United States established a permanent military presence in the Gulf and a preeminent role in setting the pattern of appropriate political behavior and determining defense priorities. In the meantime, U.S. policy of containing Iraq meant that Iraq would languish indefinitely under severe U.N. sanctions, which have caused the deaths of hundreds of thousands of civilians and devastated its potentially promising economy, previously described as a Middle Eastern tiger in the making. It also meant that any attempt by Iraq to protest the conduct of certain U.N. weapons inspectors or challenge the two no-fly-zones would invite heavy American and British reprisals such as the Desert Fox Operation in December 1998 and the daily bombardment during the winter of 1999.[63] A collective disaster of the highest magnitude, the war for Kuwait that pitted Arabs against one another came after a century of repeated injuries to Arab pride and aspirations. It attested to the futility of Arab political elites and the bankruptcy of their developmental designs.

The second Gulf War gave a tremendous boost to militant Islam, already on the rise for twenty years. Demonized by erratic policies and paranoia, many ruling Arab elites found themselves compelled to cope with an uncontainable extremist version of political Islam bent on destroying the regime and installing an Islamic system of government on the basis of pristine orthodoxy. Wherever political groups took on Arab (and other Middle Eastern) governments, they were invariably militant Islamic groups. True, their activities antedated the Gulf crisis, but its outcome contributed to further militarize them. Indeed, the pace of militant Islamic terror dramatically increased in the 1990s, as strongly suggested by gruesome evidence from Algeria, Egypt, the Palestinian Territories, and even Saudi Arabia, previously considered an oasis of peace in the Arab region. Chapter 7 focuses on Islamic revivalism in its bid to fill the vacuum generated during years of stagnation and malpractice by miscalculating political elites.

The Case for Islamic Revival

The Islamic faith commands a pervasive influence on Muslims, whether they are devout or irreligious. Nearly all of them adhere to shariʿa to the letter on matters pertaining to civil status such as marriage and inheritance. The rituals of praying and fasting are so frequent that they are not generally regarded as strong indicators of religiosity. As Muslims grow in age many of them tend to dedicate more time to religious matters, eventually performing Hajj (pilgrimage to Mecca), the fifth pillar of Islam, which seals their destiny as true believers. The exceptionally strong bond between Muslims and Islam has baffled not a few Western observers, some of whom have oversimplified this seemingly irresistible relationship as a tense one. Manfred Halpern interprets the influence of religion on Muslims in terms of Islam being a common fate rather than a common faith.[1] In saying this, he probably refers to the Prophet's endorsement of the tribe, in the 622 A.D. Constitution of Medina, as the major organizational unit in Islamic society. This arrangement did not erase intergroup contradictions but made them subservient, even if sometimes nominally, to Islam, the overarching source of unity. For a millennium, this unique arrangement provided relative societal stability and legitimate political continuity, but eventually it eroded because of inner contradictions, lack of renovation, and encroachments from mighty Europe.

The Rise of Political Islam

Political Islam first made its mark in the second half of the nineteenth century when it seemed so obvious that the Ottoman empire, the carrier of the banner of Islam, was on its way to rapid extinction unless something drastic could be done to salvage the situation. The works of Muhammad ʿAbdu and Jamal al-Din al-Afghani, as well as several others, dwelt on the matter of reconciling Islam to modernity, including the compatibility of the former with the latter. Religious reformers and movements strived to delete from faith foreign practices that, in the course of many years of stagnation and damaging Sufi influences, penetrated Islam and traditionalized it. But the momentum of political Islam was short-lived; it quickly retreated in the face of Arab nationalism (especially after the coup d'état of the Young Turks which overthrew Sultan 'Abdul Hamid in 1908) and the onslaught of Western colonialism. The Sanusiyya movement fell as Italian troops occupied Cyrenaica and Tripoli, and the Mahdiyya movement succumbed to the British conquest of the Sudan. Only the Wahabiyya movement survived in Najd without being able to reach out elsewhere, even to the peripheries of Arabia. The termination of the caliphate added spiritual insult to the political injury caused by subjugation to the West's might. Arab protests mounted, but they lacked in persistence, clear purpose, and continuous mobilization. The Muslim Brethren appeared in Egypt in 1928, under the leadership Hasan al-Banna, during the zenith of Western control of the Arabic-speaking world. Within a decade of its formation it transformed itself into a politicized group seeking to expel the British, topple the monarchy, and introduce an Islamic state in the Nile Valley. Its political potential, great during Egypt's turbulent years in the 1940s, was ravaged by Nasser's secular regime in the 1950s. In 1954 Taqiy al-Din al-Nabahani, a Palestinian shaykh, formed the militant Hizb al-Tahrir al-Islami (the Islamic liberation party), which demanded the restoration of khilafa and the initiation of jihad to realize this objective as well as to liberate Palestine. Severe repression by Arab regimes kept the party underground and its membership minimal.

During the 1950s and most of the 1960s, Arab publics did not view militant Islam favorably. Although Islam maintained its sway as a belief system, its political relevance did not. Influenced by Soviet revolutionary slogans and the collapse of Anglo-French colonialism, the political mood in the Arab world was supportive of strong ties with the countries of the socialist bloc. Arab nationalism flourished again in the early 1950s, as Arab masses saw redemption and national salvation in its now pronounced secular tenets. Military defeats at the hands of Israel and the failure of development discredited Arab ruling elites and did away with the concept of pan-Arabism. Islamic sentiment accelerated immediately, readily transforming itself into radical political movements. The political seeds planted by the Muslim Brethren in various Arab lands (such as Syria, Lebanon, Jordan, Sudan, and North Africa) formed the Islamist nucleus from which originated the plethora of contemporary Islamic groupings. The militants saw in the military, political, and developmental setbacks suffered by the secular leaders an affirmation of the untenability of their programs and a sure revelation of the wrath of God. They felt the time had finally arrived for them to introduce the reign of Allah on the ruins of the nationalist political orders, through the implementation of their religious creed.

The Islamists' Creed

The reciprocally dependent concepts of jihad and caliphate feature prominently in the creed of the Islamists, forming their raison d'être. The resurrection of the Islamic state, according to the Islamist thesis, cannot possibly occur without jihad which, in turn, relies heavily on support from the Islamic state. The notion of jihad is central to Islamic teachings; it calls for constant confrontation with perceived infidels, oppressors, and evil doers. The Qur'an instructs the community of believers to prepare for jihad, as the following statement clearly indicates: "Against them make ready your strength to the utmost of your power, including steeds of war, to strike terror into [the hearts of] the enemies, of Allah and your enemies, and others besides, whom ye may not know, but whom Allah doth know. Whatever ye shall spend in the Cause of Allah, shall be repaid unto you, and ye shall not be treated unjustly."[2] This and similar Qur'anic statements convinced many authors that the Muslims are a community of fighters, ordered by God to maintain vigilance and readiness for war, for which they receive earthly and heavenly rewards.[3] Prophet Muhammad exhorted all able-bodied Muslims. In a saying attributed to him, he said: "He who fights for the word of God, fights in the name of God."[4] Muslims from different walks of life, irrespective of their political persuasions, tend to accept these themes, although the politically organized and militarily mobilized Islamists are obviously better prepared to act on them.

It is erroneous to claim that, among Muslims, only the militants believe in jihad and commit themselves to it. It is safer to state, however, that the militants are better equipped to invoke it in their practice. The simple fact remains that the Islamic faith instills in the minds of believers the notion of constant exposure to and suffering from the forces of injustice and evil. It also assures Muslims that God stands by them, provided that they fight back. Consider the following Qur'anic verses: "To those against whom war is made, permission is given [to fight], because they are wronged;—and verily, Allah is Most powerful for their aid;—[They are] those who have been expelled from their homes in defiance of right,—[for no cause] except that they say, 'Our Lord is Allah.' . . . Allah will certainly aid those who aid His [cause];—for verily Allah is Full of Strength, Exalted in Might, [Able to enforce His Will]."[5] In return for Muslims' steadfastness and promptness to fight in the name of God, the Almighty will successfully intervene on their behalf. The serious implication of the Qur'anic exhortation to fight is that the faithful may choose to go to war without due preparation or sufficient thoughtfulness. Sureness about God's forthcoming help can lure Muslims into unwinnable situations or cause them to sacrifice their lives to win God's praise and secure a place in heaven.

The ultimate aim of jihad is the installation of an Islamic order, for short of that Muslims will always be subject to violation by the infidel. The Islamists can easily enlist the support of a litany of examples to verify their point. The clamor of the Islamists' drive to reconstruct the Islamic state does not cover up for their theoretical weakness. After everything is said about the centrality of the Islamic state in the Islamists' creed, the fact remains that, in their view, the most important function of the state is *al-Da'wa,* that is, to spread the word of Allah to every corner of the world.[6] Very little is mentioned about how such a state can operate viably in a secular international order modeled by the West! Instead of elaborating a workable model for the idea of the Islamic state, the Islamists focus on the limitations of the Western model of the state and condemn democracy, its political instrument of governance. Arabs and Muslims' uneven interaction with the West during the last two or three centuries, a period that witnessed the ascendancy of Western values and ways of doing things, probably lies at the heart of radical Muslims' abhorrence of Western cultural and political values.[7]

The Islamists condemn Western-inspired notions of nationalism, seeing them as largely responsible for decimating the Muslim community and weakening the faith of believers. Islamist reasoning articulates the view that the Arabic language never formed a societal bond. Unity in spoken language did not cause the Arabian tribes in the pre-Islamic period of paganism to forge mutual bonds of cooperation. To the contrary, they immersed themselves in endless conflicts, often collaborating with foreigners (Byzantines and Persians) against fellow Arabs, only to be saved by the rise and spread of Islam in the Arabian peninsula.[8] Over and over again, the Islamists lean on the Qur'an for support as attested by the following verse: "And hold fast, all together, by the Rope, which Allah [stretches out for you], and be not divided among yourselves; and remember with gratitude Allah's favour on you; for ye were enemies and He joined your hearts in love, so that by His grace, ye became brethren; and ye were on the brink of the Pit of Fire, and He saved you from it. Thus doth Allah make His Signs clear to you: that ye may be guided."[9]

The Islamists see more than just a faith in Islam, conceiving it as a system of life upon which a universal society can be founded. Accordingly, it supersedes the tribe and abolishes ethnicity as a differentiating factor among distinct groups of individuals. Thus the Islamic state consists of a community of believers in God, Prophet Muhammad, and shari'a, rendering other sources of belief not just superfluous but worthy of forcible elimination. Of all radical Islamic movements, Hizb al-Tahrir al-Islami provides the most comprehensive program for the functions of the imagined Islamic state. Even theirs seems severely inadequate in terms of modern political dynamics. Suha al-Faruqi reviews the Islamic state model as proposed by Taqiy al-Din al-Nabahani, the founder and theoretician of Hizb al-Tahrir, and identifies four basic criteria: application of shari'a, institution of khilafa, denouncement of territorial nationalism, and rejection of democracy.[10]

Al-Nabahani's model, an undertaking fraught with conspiracy thinking, is essentially defensive, aiming at undoing the legacy of more than two centuries of Western penetration of Arab-Islamic territories. This is how the Islamist argument goes: the West, wary about the great potential of Islam, has always desired to destroy the Muslim identity. Hence, it decided, beginning in the nineteenth century, to pollute the minds of Muslims by planting the idea of ethnonationalism in their societies.[11] Al-Nabahani and other Islamists at once spurn democracy—proclaiming it a system of disbelief—suggesting to the faithful, as always, a Qur'anic alternative:

> O ye who believe! obey Allah, and obey the Messenger, and those charged with authority among you. If ye differ in anything among yourselves, refer it to Allah and His Messenger, if ye do believe in Allah and the Last Day: That is best, and most suitable for final determination. Hast thou not turned thy thought to those who declare that they believe in the revelations that have come to thee and to those before thee? Their [real] wish is to resort together for judgment [in their disputes] to the evil [Tagut] though they were ordered to reject him. But Satan's wish is to lead them astray far away [from the right]. When it is said to them: "Come to what Allah hath revealed. And to the Messenger": Thou seest the Hypocrites avert their faces from thee in disgust.[12]

These verses confirm the salience of shari'a and the office of the caliph in Islamist thinking and provide ample ammunition to their loathing of Western-type democratic principles. They stress obedience to God and the Prophet (shari'a) and those charged with authority (caliphs), not persuasion or compromise. Insofar as perfunctory efforts by certain Western students of Arab affairs to reconcile Islam to democracy simply failed to do the trick, their putting the blame on narrow American definitions of the concept did not induce any theoretical revisiting of it.[13]

The Islamists vehemently denounce the two pillars of democracy, which vest sovereignty and the power of legislation in people as opposed to God, and appeal to all Muslims to do the same. The starting argument for them is that democracy, which the "infidel West" is trying to market in Muslim lands, is a system of incredulity totally incompatible with Islam.[14] Westerners sought democracy as a means to get rid of despotic monarchs who abused them in the name of religion. Hence, their philosophers envisaged a new form of governance in which man controlled himself, not oppressive rulers hiding behind religious dogma. The Islamists' response to the proponents of democracy is straightforward. They argue that there are limits to the prerogatives of the caliph in Islam, who is merely an executive implementing shari'a. The argument proceeds to assert that inability to legislate places great curbs on the caliph to deviate from the path of righteousness.[15] Radical Islamic thinking voices strong objection to freedom and individualism, since the span of freedom is curtailed by religious norms and values, whereas individualism is deemphasized in favor of conformity with a community structured along egalitarian criteria. In defending aversion to the infusion of democratic values in Muslim societies, the Islamists think of a grand Western conspiracy to deprive Muslims of their faith, the source of past glory and the promise of future rejuvenation. They evince serious doubts about Western hostility toward Muslims that are often supported by readily convincing examples. The Qur'an always provides verses that seem to seal the argument of the Islamists on whatever issue they tackle, as the following does on the matter of relations with the West: ". . . Rank hatred has already appeared from their mouths [Muslims generally interpret this as Christian and Jewish hostility]: What their hearts conceal is far worse. . . ."[16]

Militant Muslims believe there is collusion between the West and local proxies, be they individuals spoiled by secular education or elites either benefiting from economic interaction with Westerners or dependent on their politico-military support. They also claim that the majority of Muslims have lost touch with the essence of true Islam and fallen victim to superficial religious interpretation and redundancy. In their view, the West and their proxies deserve confrontation, while the masses require religious reeducation. Even though militant Muslims accept the merits of diplomacy and persuasion, they do not rule out resorting to violence when pacifist measures fail to produce results.

Militant Transformation

In a damning book that received little attention at the time of publication following the Six Day War, Sa'd Jum'ah, a former Jordanian prime minister, announced the bankruptcy of all Arab regimes and urged Arabs to return to Islam in order to come to terms with themselves and cope with a rapidly changing world around them. He spoke of deceived Arab masses led by tyrannical and lame rulers.[17] Jum'ah used disparaging terms to condemn the state of Arab society, which he deemed was sinking because of disintegration, corruption, baseness, atheism, sectarianism, servitude, and agentry to the West.[18] He noted in a clamorous tone that ". . . we [Arabs] have raised every slogan known to humanity . . . except the slogan of jihad to liberate the stolen homeland [Palestine] and usurped holy sites. We imported every ideology from every corner of the earth, forcing them on our people so that they would abandon their religion, civilization and belief in God. . . . Our peoples are lethargic, drugged, exhausted, pulverized, and our leaders are fake and immoral. . . . We lost incentive, pride, hope, even the ability to feel disgrace!"[19] Jum'ah concluded his argument by appealing to Arabs to equip themselves with pristine Islamic faith and lay the grounds for a new Islamic revival, as the surest way to stand up to the enemies of the Arabs, namely Israel and the West. Muslims must find a way, Jum'ah insisted, to get rid of Sufi practices which emphasizes withdrawal from the challenges of life, mysticism, isolationism, and abandonment of the notion of jihad.[20]

Despite the emergence of voices such as Jum'ah's, calling upon Muslims to take matters into their own hands in the name of God, the first waves of militancy in the Arab world were stirred by leftist organizations, mainly Palestinian organizations. The first incident on record goes back to 23 July 1968 when members of the leftist Popular Front for the Liberation of Palestine hijacked an Israeli airliner and forced it to land at Algiers airport. From that date until June 1982, when Israel invaded Lebanon with the declared aim of ousting PLO fighters from the country, nationalist and leftist groups—mainly associated with the Arab-Israeli conflict—took responsibility for almost all belligerent activities. In the wake of the Israeli invasion, Hizbullah appeared in Lebanon. With this development, the center of militant activity shifted from the discredited leftists to the rising Islamists. It would be erroneous to explain the use of violence in terms of protest; the radicals, be they leftists or Islamists, have a political program that they seek to accomplish. The Islamists began where the leftists stopped. Radical Islamic groups believe they launch terror missions for a holy cause. They claim that their aim is to reinstate the Islamic state which Kamal Ataturk, the founder of secular Turkey, formally abrogated in 1924. According to the Islamists, it is completely unacceptable for Muslims to be ruled by any system of government unless it is based on shari'a. Western-inspired secular laws, now applied in most Islamic states, contradict Islamic tenets, and most Islamists wholeheartedly reject the application of these laws. The fact that radical Islamic groups constitute mainly domestic movements against state authority within the boundaries drawn by Western colonial powers does not mean that they necessarily accept the existing Middle Eastern state order. The Islamists realize that they remain some way from the ultimate construction of a universal Islamic state. Even the nonviolent Muslim Brethren movement expresses commitment to the accomplishment of the Islamic state, although it advocates a moderate approach. The primary goal of the movement is to contribute to Muslim awakening by revitalizing religious values and eliminating Western cultural influences, which they regard as a major threat to the Arab-Islamic culture. The Muslim Brethren's eschewal of militant activities emanates from their empirical conviction that they cannot possibly win against the state which commands a formidable machinery of coercion. The operating motto of the Muslim Brethren focuses on forming exemplary brothers for other Muslims.

Other Islamist groups do not commit themselves to peaceful tactics. They employ violence as a recipe for change toward the "right path." Moreover, in their view, fighting the state represents a duty that binds all able Muslims; without it, the concretization of the Muslim state remains wishful thinking. Radical Muslims view militancy as a means to topple their countries' corrupt and illegitimate regimes, which they also conceive of as Western lackeys. They argue that jihad is sanctioned by God, and they consider it as the only means to resurrect the Islamic state.[21] R. Hrair Dekmejian contended that ". . . confrontation is an important part of the world view of Islamic militants and many conventional Muslims."[22] Muhammad ʿAbdul Salam Faraj, an Egyptian Islamist ideologue, carried the idea of jihad to the point of regarding it an absent obligation, or a forgotten pillar of Islam.[23]

The Islamists capitalize on the crisis of identity which plagues all Arab political systems, and they benefit from the ruling elites' invariable failure to convince the populations that they symbolize their cherished goals and aspirations. To be sure, Arabs do not accept the consequences of the collapse of the Ottoman empire which resulted in the formation of arbitrary political units. Iraq, Jordan, Syria, and Lebanon provide living examples of the fragility of Middle Eastern states. It is worth noting that the Arab-Islamic mind remains essentially unionist, a reality not missed by the radicals who capitalize on it to find young and frustrated recruits.

Islam conferred upon the Muslims a sense of attachment to the *umma* of believers (the Islamic community). The fall of the Ottoman empire finally shifted the focus of affinity from Islam to Arabism.[24] Similarly, community orientation—not comparable to Western definitions in terms of rigor and strength of attachment—drifted some way from religion in the direction of nationalism. Arab nationalism reached its peak in the mid-1950s but received a severe blow as a consequence of the 1967 Six Day War. The demise of the idea of Arab nationalism led to an instant rise of militant Islam. A three-dimensional perspective governs, at this stage, the ensuing political environment in the countries gripped by the surge of Islamist influence: overthrowing the existing ruling elite, eliminating Western cultural and political influences, and reintroducing shari'a-based, Islamic rule. Many radicals have prescribed unmitigated violence to achieve these stated objectives.[25]

Despite the vociferousness of Islamic militants and their unwavering pledge to combat the West, one must bear in mind that most acts of international terrorism take place outside the Middle East, and by movements other than Islamic militants. In 1995, 441 acts occurred in 51 different countries.[26] There are at least three reasons for the current Western fixation on Islamic-inspired terrorism: geographic proximity to Europe, Islamist rhetoric, and Western hostility. First, the southern shores of the Mediterranean are exclusively Muslim and include some of the most active Islamist groups. In addition, there are millions of North African Muslims living in Europe many of whom support, or at least empathize with, the mission of their Islamist coreligionists. Second, Islamist spokesmen never miss an opportunity to remind the world that "Islam and the West are locked in an ongoing battle, dating back to the early days of Islam . . . and which today is the product of a Judaeo-Christian conspiracy."[27] Third, Daniel Pipes admitted that there has been considerable historical hostility by Christians toward Muslims. He explained it in terms of the rapid Muslim conquests in the early days of Islam which threatened European culture and its Christian faith.[28] This sentiment has been graphically articulated by Samuel Huntington who, in addition to charging that Islam has bloody borders, added that they—as well as other Easterners—do not quite understand "Western ideas of individualism, liberalism, constitutionalism, human rights, equality, liberty, the rule of the law, democracy [etc.]."[29]

The Islamists and the Islamic Revival Movement

The Islamic revival movement is a universal occurrence that goes far beyond the phenomenon of Islamic militancy. For the most part, Islamic revivalism is a benign societal movement that provides a proper linkage between increasingly religious Arab-Islamic publics and the government in countries where political mobilization is insignificant. In this capacity, religious groups perform the functions of political parties on the basis of co-optation rather than participation. This unfolding mechanism has been fairly successful in serving as an avenue for the expression of public needs and acting upon them, in societies where religion provides a workable frame of reference for collective identity. Religious groups have noticeably proliferated in the Arab world in recent years. This is not to say that the appearance of Islamic groups is in itself a negative development, even though they are emerging at the expense of other essential components of civil society. Three factors readily account for the fast growth of religious groups: regime suppression of political organization (especially opposition groups), public resistance to group association outside the domain of religion, and general distaste for Western cultural values, which remaine peripheral to Arabs' core value system.

Islamic militancy denotes frustration, acute proneness to conspiracy thinking, absence of effective two-way communication with the governing elite, and state manipulation. Conversely, pacifist Islamic groups demonstrate a desire to cooperate with the state, often taking upon themselves the task of performing functions that are normally administered by the public sector or agencies of the civil society. The radicals constitute only a fraction of the Islamic revival movement, a fact largely missed because of the militants' uproar. The Islamists are associated with sectarian conflict (in Egypt, for example), opposition to corrupt state socialism and single political party hegemony (in Algeria), anti-Americanism (in Saudi Arabia), political disenfranchisement (in Bahrain), and resistance to Israeli occupation (in southern Lebanon). The inherent weakness of post-caliphate Arab political orders seems irremediable to certain religiously motivated elements in Arab societies, unless the Islamic state is resurrected sooner than later. By the mid-1960s, the limitations of existing regimes became obvious not only to politically mobilized groups in the Arab world but to the informed sectors of the populations as well. Since then, the religiously militant elements of politically mobilized Arabs have chosen to implement their own version of how society ought to be patterned and governed.

Egyptian Islamists, then benefiting from Sadat's support, unleashed their wrath against Coptic fellow citizens.[30] Clashes erupted as early as 1974 over the issue of church building, to which the Islamists vehemently objected, and also to the preconceived notion of a Coptic conspiracy to Christianize Egypt.[31] In Algeria where Islam played a crucial role in confronting French colonialism, the FIS appeared in 1989 as a direct reaction to severe economic crisis which, according to Yahia Zoubir, led to a ". . . flagrant marginalization of large segments of society especially among the youth, coupled with the impoverishment of the middle class and the pauperization of the popular masses. . . ."[32] The FIS, applying the name of Islam, quickly took command of the widespread but leaderless protest movement that had destabilized the FLN government since the early 1980s. The weakness of civil society and the absence of a democratic tradition in Algeria transformed the Islamist movement there into another hegemonic establishment.[33] Adam Abdel Moula concurred with Zoubir's point of view, asserting that the FIS ". . . parallels itself with society and considers opposition to it opposition to the whole society necessitating retaliation and liquidation."[34] Then he shifted his attention to the National Islamic Front (NIF), which has been in control of the Sudan since the military coup of 30 June 1989, to conclude that its human rights record is probably among the world's worst.[35] Abdel Moula accused the government in Khartoum of intimidating the population, monopoly of wealth and economic activity, denial of freedom of religion, and ethnic cleansing.[36]

The political experience of Islamist groups, whether in government or within the opposition, does not bode well for the future of political Islam. The militants' contestation of political power has been the norm in Islamic countries, but their hold on it has been the exception (Sudan, Iran, Afghanistan). In all cases, the advent of political Islam has not resolved outstanding political, economic, and social issues; it has aggravated them in most cases. Fortunately, the majority of Islamic groups are not militant. Although radical groups operate in most Arab countries, pacifist groups are spreading at a more rapid pace. Muslims have absorbed the thrust of Western cultural advances and appear determined to reassert Islamic values. This does not mean undoing the changes of the past two hundred years of direct Western influence but restoring some sort of cultural balance by revamping archaic traditions such as veiling, gender segregation, and Islamic business transactions. Besides, pacifist Islamic groups partially compensate for inadequate public services by engaging in philanthropic and welfare activities. Among the many successes of such groups has been their contribution to better medical services in their communities. Preliminary research by Janine Clark on the Islamic clinics in Egypt shows that they are extremely useful in making up for grossly inadequate government-provided health facilities. Her significant assumptions attribute the work of local charitable organizations to a "strong Islamic tradition . . . and religious devotion,"[37] not to militant zeal. In a pathbreaking book more than forty years earlier, Halpern had already attested to the prominence of community webs that predominated in Middle Eastern societies long before the advent of Islam.[38] In view of this, it would be pretentious to concentrate on the militants' attention to urgent public needs, without due attention to the greater role of the pacifists in this respect. A final word may be said on the matter of providing public services. Whereas the motive of Islamist groups (primarily concerned with ousting non-Islamic regimes) is essentially political, hence bearing on their relations with the constituencies they try to win, the philanthropic activities of the pacifist Islamic groups tend to be terminal in objective.

Components of the Islamist Challenge

An intensive debate raged in the West during the 1990s concerning whether Islam posed a real threat to Middle Eastern societies and Western regional interests, as well to their domestic security. Martin Kramer represents the group of scholars who believe that militant Islam constitutes a potent threat (at the state, regional, and international levels) that must be contained before it becomes uncontrollable. He dwells on the assertion that Islam must have power in this world since, in accordance with the Islamists' reasoning, it is befitting to God's true religion.[39] In addition to being worried about the prospects for an escalation of Islamist terror in the Middle East, Kramer seems thoroughly disturbed by their ability to spread their operations in the West. He voices deep concerns about the presence of large Muslim immigrant communities in Western Europe and North America. Although most of them are innocuous, ". . . there are those who simply await a word of encouragement or inspiration offered by a visiting cleric or a foreign diplomat."[40] His effort to register an objective note falters when he summarily condemns Lebanese Islamists for the 1984 assassination of Malcolm Kerr, the president of the American University of Beirut, without giving evidence or documentation of any sort.[41] Kramer's wide-of-the-mark analysis is probably understandable since he was part of a scholarly drive that deliberately tried to put Islam on a collision course with the West.

John Esposito wrote extensively to dispel the notion that Islam and the West were diametrically opposed, more specifically to allay Western fears about the perceived threat of radical Islamic groups.[42] In a sharp contrast to Kramer's thesis, Esposito quickly denies that the Islamists represent a global threat on grounds that: "For a Western world long accustomed to global vision and foreign policy predicated upon superpower rivalry for global influence if not dominance . . . it is all too tempting to identify another global ideological menace to fill the 'threat vacuum' created by the demise of communism. . . . As Western leaders attempt to forge the New World Order, transnational Islam may increasingly come to be regarded as the new global monolithic enemy of the West."[43] Even though he recognizes the problems associated with militant Islamic groups on the national political systems in which they operate, Esposito calls for patience and understanding as he points to similar domestic challenges that beset Europe when its monarchs contemplated ways to cope with the consequences of the withering away of the continent's feudal orders.[44] His conciliatory approach, though commendable, necessarily tones down—consciously or otherwise—crucial components of the Islamist challenge. It is essential to examine what the Islamists say about their own mission in order to best determine the nature of their challenge.

The Islamists indefatigably defend the position that Islam provides an ideal model for the righteous state that is intrinsically superior to the West's liberal democratic paradigm, which they brand as hegemonic, conspiratorial, and materialistic.[45] Militant Islamic groups, subject to unrelenting state suppression, took advantage of the general failure of Arab regimes and succeeded in integrating considerable numbers of the opposition, mobilized by frustration and despair, into their ranks.[46] All such groups believe that Muslims must rise from their current state of torpidity to resurrect the Islamic state and apply religious tenets in all aspects of society. Their ultimate aim is to reinstate the type of pristine Islam that prevailed during the early Islamic period. Islamist thinkers who allege that nationalism, socialism, communism, and capitalism have not been able to solve the problems of the world insist that the time has arrived for implementing the Islamic model of governance in all societies.[47] Islamic society, they add, is superior to all others, simply because its faithful members behave in a most perfect way.[48] The reason lies in the perfection of the Islamic religion and its presentation in clear and readily understandable terms. According to Islamist thinking (a perception accepted by traditional Muslims as well), disbelievers in the world of Allah have nobody to blame but themselves, because ". . . they have hearts wherewith they understand not, eyes wherewith they see not, and ears wherewith they hear not. They are like cattle,—nay, more misguided: for they are heedless [of warning]."[49] They declare that shari'a contains a package of laws that covers all aspects of man's life on earth and guarantees believers a smooth transition to the afterlife. The mechanism for belief in the tenets of Islam is largely subjective since it emphasizes the role of the heart, ears, and eyes, whose interactive processes are ignited by a spark of intuitive faith, not intellect.

The Islamists aim to convince Arab-Islamic publics that shari'a is superior to all other forms of spiritual belief (including Christianity and Judaism) and earthly systems of governance (notably secularism). They do not content themselves with mere conviction but demand Muslims to join them in a bid to destroy existing political orders in order to institute the caliphate instead. Their program of action involves organization, preaching, and jihad. Jihad, as indicated earlier, is mandatory in Islamist terminology, since the fate of the Islamic state is contingent upon the outcome of confrontation between the faithful and the infidel. The Islamists' agenda is reminiscent of the defunct communist mission in its determinism, plea for unquestioning obedience of higher authority, and the duty of proselytism. It differs from communism in its emphasis on state omnipresence as a final arrangement, not a transitional stage. The Islamists promise glory for Islam and material abundance for the faithful in a solidary political system where individualism gives way to collectivism.[50]

The vehemence of the Islamists' propositions make them assaultable on at least two grounds: defensiveness and nostalgia. They are unhappily aware of the steady influence of Christendom on Muslim societies for the last seven centuries and distressed by the suggestion that Islam today is "a semi-inert mass receiving the destructive blows of the formative influences from the West."[51] Militant Muslims are equally dismayed with the ruling elites in their societies, whom they label as Western lackeys, and would like to see them removed from power at any price. Engrossment in the past, fixation on religious dogma, and unattentiveness to the tremendous ideological and conceptual changes that occurred in the Arab-Islamic world obviously make the Islamist project nostalgic, hence uncreditable. The clean slate upon which early Muslims created a religious social system has, since then, developed in complexity of knowledge and diversity of informational sources so that the resurrection of the once thriving Islamic system seems quite remote if not virtually impossible. Nostalgia acquires such nourishment from endemic stagnation at the economic, social, political, and societal levels that medieval Islam currently presents itself for the militants as the only solution.

The Islamists no doubt present a compound problem of variable degree at the domestic, regional, and international levels, even if there is a tendency to unduly magnify their strengths. Their influence in recent years confirms more the inherent weaknesses of the territorial state in the Arab world and chaos in international relations than brilliant Islamist strategies or superior organization. Terror operations by certain Islamists, often bizarre and morally repugnant, have instantly resulted in strong opposition to the idea of Islamic government. The Islamists are however less of a security problem than a side effect emanating from the injudicious policies of incompetent national elites, as well as a reaction to Western arrogance toward Arabs and slighting of Islam. Even though Islamist groups may gain more influence in the years ahead, the fact remains that they are a spent force fighting an unwinnable battle mainly because they appear out of touch with the reality of contemporary politics. Militant Islamic groups that have been present on the political scene in the Gaza Strip and the West Bank since 1980 illustrate the point. Their militancy disrupted transition to peace in the Holy Land and boosted the political imperatives of Jewish religious radicalism, thus strengthening the anti-peace segment in Israeli society. Suicide bombings against Israeli civilians did not escalate into an Islamic popular war for the liberation of Palestine, with the explicit objective of establishing a shari'a-based state there.[52] Islamic radicalism actually emboldened Israel's Likud government to proceed with its controversial project of Judaizing the West Bank. Palestinian Islamists regard Israel as an embodiment of Western modern challenge to Arabs and Muslims, and they deal with it from the perspective of an Islamic solution that seeks to restore psychological balance to the world of Islam.[53] Judged by the results of the militants' tactics in confronting Israel, the Jewish state is becoming increasingly stronger, and the West that it embodies is reasserting its hegemony.

Future Outlook

Recent years have witnessed a dramatic surge in the influence of Islamist groups in many Arab countries. Political Islam has been transformed into a vehicle of organized protest against inept, secularly structured but functionally ill-adjusted political systems, although there is meager evidence to link the surge of militant Islam to enhanced faith. Current militant trends are largely a translation of the frustration felt by the masses in connection with the regimes' failure to achieve political development, solve the riddle of political identity, and bring about balanced economic prosperity.[54] Muslim scholars hint that the Islamist agenda may not, after all, be a tenable alternative. The West has already won after a millennium of confrontation with Islam. In this regard, George Joffe determines that ". . . within the temporal, collective arena of modern society and politics, the Islamic cultural paradigm seems apparently unable to cope with the implications of modernism . . . "[55] Khurshid Ahmad accepts that Western-type institutions have invaded Muslim societies ". . . to such an extent that even the army now is being restructured and 'modernized' along Western models."[56] In spite of the developmental legitimation constraints besetting Arab ruling elites, Arab publics are probably inclined to recognize their authority, provided they perform efficiently and impartially. Two eminent problems continue to arrest the launching of national politics in the Arab world: personal politics and unruly populations. There is no doubt that the elites have subdued the masses—aside from the Islamists' outbursts of random violence—but they never managed to sway them to identify with broader public issues. Until a genuine societal transformation occurs, the militants will probably continue to do their share in stalling Arab political evolution. In the meantime failure to successfully deal with the requirements of modernity and the resolution of the identity crisis have created an Arab impasse, which will be the central topic in chapter 8.

The Arab Impasse

The Arabs have experienced two centuries of attempts to stem the tide of retreat vis-à-vis the West and create the conditions for their own *nahda* (renaissance). On balance, Arab societies underwent significant changes in recent generations although they failed to modernize, let alone catch up with the West. Three-quarters of a millennium of steady decline made the realization of nahda quite difficult. The task was further exacerbated by the introduction of certain Western concepts without successfully integrating them into the system of Arab cultural and politically relevant values. Thus Western concepts such as secularism, nationalism, and liberalism began to compete, rather inconclusively, with hitherto impregnable notions of shari'a, religious solidarity, and political dogma. As the forces of modernism gained ground, the concomitant erosion of traditional societal values was neither sweeping nor irreversible. Tradition, best represented by religiosity and rural style of living—has made a forceful comeback in most Arab countries since the late 1960s. In addition to the revival of religious zeal and ruralization of major urban centers due to heavy internal migration, retraditionalization struck the political arena as well. The conservative states in the Gulf held back the initiation of token political reforms; similarly the ruling elites in the former progressive states abandoned claim to populism and contented themselves with narrowly based political systems. The idea of the state as a private enterprise, a characteristic of Arab conservative states, spread to other countries as well (notably to Egypt, Lebanon, Tunisia, Iraq, Syria, and Algeria). It seems that the last two centuries of reforms and setbacks have completed a full cycle as Arabs find themselves at the starting point once again, facing the same basic issues that tormented them before. The accumulation of unresolved societal problems and the bleak political picture have created a situation of systemic impasse.

This chapter argues that unfavorable historical developments decimated the first Arab-Islamic nahda and prevented post-eighteenth-century reformers from inducing its resurgence. Twentieth-century Arab statesmen longing to modernize their societies failed in their objective because they overlooked the importance of political transformation. They also fought shy of defining the role of religion in public life. The result was an impasse that involved a severe political identity crisis and a society at war with itself. Among the main characteristics of the state of Arab affairs nowadays are intellectual stagnation and the elites' inability to determine sustainable and achievable objectives, mainly because of the absence of a charted plan of action. The unpleasantness of the current situation has obviously encouraged vast elements of the populace to seek peace of mind in the sanctuary of past glory. In terms of procedure, the analysis first examines the setting in which the impasse takes place, then it dwells on some of its major symptoms according to the following order: (1) political identity in coma, (2) society in crisis, (3) intellectual stagnation, (4) blurry vision, and (5) sanctuary in past glory.

The Setting

Except for the office of the caliph that survived for more than twelve centuries, mostly as a symbol of religious identification and nominal authority, Arab historical evolution did not lead to the rise of political institutions or the dissolution of feudalism into a class society. The roots of contemporary Arab decay date back to the middle of the ninth century when the caliphs in Baghdad gradually began to lose their authority to provincial governors and Seljuk mercenaries. Although some Arab caliphs took genuine interest in promoting culture and knowledge, their patronage generally reflected personal taste, not societal commitment. Unlike in the Renaissance that spread throughout Europe by the seventeenth century, only members of the upper strata of Arab-Islamic society were introduced to the cultural richness of the period of Arab ascendancy. The European Renaissance thrived and survived until the present because it established grass roots in European societies, whereas the Arabs Golden Age of Harun al-Rashid declined too soon because of its failure to become a mass phenomenon. Hudaytha Murad noted that administrative corruption, military chaos, intellectual backwardness, ethnoreligious discrimination, political despotism, and moral degeneration[1] persisted in the Arab-Islamic state even during the zenith of its influence.

The survival of feudalism in Arab lands and its alliance with the non-Arab ruling elite prevented the modernization of production and delayed incorporation in the world economy, thus precluding the possibility of comprehensive societal reforms. Excessive taxation impoverished the peasants, causing most of them to eventually lose their land; it also overburdened the traders and artisans, ruined the crafts, and preempted the rise of the middle class. Ottoman political, social, and economic reforms in the nineteenth century, which applied to the Arab provinces, did not induce worthwhile changes in society. Murad located two reasons for this failure: first, reform did not result from a felt societal need aggregated by organized individuals; instead it emanated from intense Western European pressure on the Ottoman sultan. Second, reform remained an internal affair involving the ruling and feudal elites. As a consequence, the process failed to spark a breakthrough in domestic interactions that would have paved the way toward enfranchisement and integration in the modern economy.[2] This barred the appearance of crosscutting cleavages, an essential element in the formation of inclusive societies. Subsequent mobilization meant that societally active groups would line up on the basis of sect and region. Arab nation-states in the twentieth century created conditions whereby divergent groups became visible to one another, thus inviting unmitigated recourse to the forces of religion and tribe in society.

The Arabs, circumscribed by the wall between them and the currents that shaped the West of today, currently languish as a result of ideological deprivation, intergroup conflict, and oversimplification of modern reality. They have paid a terrible human and material price by refusing to take bold steps to disengage themselves from those elements of their past that are incompatible with the requirements of the modern age. Some regimes squandered tremendous resources on military adventurism, useless arms purchases, and controversial nonconventional programs. A few others created facade democracies, but all of them exhibited unusual intolerance of the opposition. Development came to a near halt, social problems raged unchecked, and the future seemed more bleak than ever.

Political Identity in Coma

The crisis of political identity, inherent in the process of transition to modernity, afflicted many Arabs in the second half of the nineteenth century. Egypt, obviously responding to British occupation, quickly—but uneasily—developed a semblance of European ethnonationalism, even though under the watchful guidance of Islam. In North Africa, a surge in atavistic Islam prompted local resistance to French, Spanish, and Italian incursions. The historical leaders of resistance, 'Abdul Qadir (in Algeria), 'Umar al-Mukhtar (in Libya), and Abd el-Krim (in Morocco's Rif), all were religious men. The most acute form of identity crisis occurred in Iraq and the Levant, mainly because of sharp ethnic and sectarian differences. There, Islam retreated in the face of a host of Western ideological and cultural cross-currents. Although Western penetration was not decisive, it succeeded in ending Islam's hold on identity in the countries of the Fertile Crescent.

The question of political identity among Arabs represented an inevitable outcome of the decline of traditional political legitimacy, which was based on a symbiosis between Islam as a belief system and tribe as a basic unit of social organization. This loose political arrangement accommodated the segmentary nature of population formations, while the modern blueprints for change adopted by many Arabs did not. Erosion of the Islamic community was not compensated for by the appearance of a new community having distinct characteristics and a clear sense of mission. Equally missing has been the lack of development of a civil society without which normal transactions in a modern polity, namely the construction of a democratic edifice, cannot possibly take place. Exposure of traditional individuals to the pressures of a modern way of life, as opposed to immersion into it, generates interpersonal friction and animosity. Unhealthy patterns of interaction prevail in the Arab world and stall progress. ʿAbdul Hadi al-Bakkar maintained that mutual hatred is the modern Arab plague.[3] Indiscreet hatred and suspicion, two characteristics of particularistic people, assumed a major role in wrecking Arab politics at the domestic and interstate levels. They have had a paramount impact on derailing economic development, inhibiting social change, and precluding the fulfillment of nationalistic aspirations, be they pan-Arab, pan-Islamic, or territorial.

Misgovernance made a mockery of independence and drove the masses to alienation. The inability, possibly unwillingness, of the ruling elites to invoke a minimum of solidarity dissuaded politically active Arabs from pursuing the goals of pan-Arabism. In due course, repressive leaders eradicated dissident groups, sending their remnants either underground or abroad. Elite preoccupation with cultivating territorial nationalism failed for the same reasons that caused the decline of Arab nationalism. Both types of identification require the presence of an anonymous sense of community, severely wanting in Arab social organization. The lengthy civil war in Lebanon and massive Arab intervention in it through pumping money and arms to its many combatants demonstrated inherent problems in the Arab order. Indisputably, the greatest sign of disorder came from the deceivingly tranquil shores of the Gulf when the Iraqi army overran defenseless Kuwait. The colossal consequences of the ensuing international crisis laid to rest all claims about the existence of an Arab regional order, arguably one that was only deficient in terms of having an institutional mechanism.

The ascendancy of Islamic revivalism during the last quarter of the twentieth century, sometimes assigned hyperbolic dimensions, is more a symptom of an identity coma than revival. It would certainly be impossible for a level-headed individual to find even a trace of evidence about revivalism in the frequent slaughtering of innocent civilians in Algeria, or the cold-blooded massacring of unsuspecting tourists in Egypt. Islamist movements, aside from being out of step with the times, are symptoms of societies that have lost hope in progress via conventional processes and sought redemption in obscurantism. Their gains attest to the incompetence of Arab ruling elites in dealing with the problems of society, namely in the arenas of politics and economy. An Indian writer sympathetic with the version of Arab nationalism of the 1950s noticed the presence of widespread poverty amidst plenty, which prompted him to conclude that ". . . the institutional structure of Arab society was unsuited for rapid economic development."[4] R. K. Karanjia was baffled by the frequency of cabinet turnover in Egypt and the countries of the Fertile Crescent during the 1940s and 1950s, a phenomenon that reached alarming levels in Syria with a cabinet's average life expectancy of four months.[5] Revolutionary Arab leaders dashed Karanjia's baseless hopes that they would succeed in putting their countries on solid developmental grounds.

Salahuddin Hafiz thought that he had solved the riddle of the Arab elites debacle. He isolated it into two types of pressure: domestic (poverty, repression, frustration) and foreign (subjugation to U.S. hegemony).[6] Partial genuineness of these pressures must not absolve the Arab elites from their great responsibility for the unimpressive performance of their political systems. They certainly had rational policy options to choose from, but they did not. Arab elites, mostly bereft of liberal ideas, either lacked the experience of governing a mosaic society or were solely concerned about personal aggrandizement. In both instances they missed the purpose of modern polity, driving large segments of their populations into oblivion. A combination of frustrated nationalistic hopes, degradation of military defeats, and insensitivity of despotic leaders unyielding to the needs for change have resulted in what Sa'd al-Din Ibrahim called nationalistic dim-sightedness.[7] Unable to deal with the sources of frustration, whatever they might be, Arabs have displaced their aggression from its imagined origins to self-destruction. Thus they tend to belittle the negative peace implications of Israeli Prime Minister Benjamin Netanyahu's intransigence, wink at the impact of the severe U.N. sanctions on the Iraqi people, exhibit no emotion at the horrors of random throat slitting in Algeria, and fail to react to the heartbreaking consequences of Somalia's drought or flooding.

Sudden involvement with a rapidly changing world, without the shield of a solidary identity, caught most Arabs by surprise. They did not generally develop a multidimensional process of cognitive evaluation to help them make politically relevant decisions in complex settings. This resulted in systemic confusion and an overwhelming sense of individual inefficacy, paving the way to a deep crisis in the fabric of society.

Society in Crisis

The kind of contractual arrangements that govern relations between Western governments and publics has no equivalent in the Arab world. There, the expanse of government functions pervades the social order, leaving very little work for private initiative. The modus operandi of elite-mass interaction in Arab politics involves positioning the state as a provider of welfare in exchange for unquestioning public obedience. According to unwritten covenants, the ruling elites serve as patrons, whereupon the masses waive the requirement of government accountability for its actions. This pattern of elite-mass relationship has occurred in most Arab countries, especially in those having substantial hydrocarbon resources. Although the formula has not produced impressive results anywhere, its most dramatic failure derives from the Algerian example, whose unhappy story was told by John P. Entelis: "By the middle 1980s, however, as world oil and natural gas prices declined and massive industrial projects faltered or collapsed altogether, it had become obvious that something had gone seriously wrong with this particular model of development. In other words, the ruling bargain had become unstuck as the economic conditions which financed this arrangement began to disintegrate. . . . Autonomous social forces, long regarded as either impotent or subservient to state control, emerged with incredible vigor, if not vengeance, to challenge hegemony of state power. Workers, farmers, students, street people, Islamic militants, feminists, and Berberists all rose in violent protest to their continued condition of marginality and subordination."[8] Events in Algeria took on a negative turn that demonstrates the magnitude of contradictions in society, the potential for conflict that exists in most Arab societies, and the fragility of existing political arrangements. The wounds of civil war in Lebanon, which ended inconclusively after raging for fifteen years, are still open. They remind Arabs that their social orders are not particularly any better than Lebanon's.

The nation-state is indeed retreating in the Arab world, not in favor of globalization or regional bloc formation, but in the face of strong visceral pressures. ʿAbdul Razzaq ʿId warned that sectarianism, parochialism, and the universalization of corruption might eventually liquidate the idea of state in Arab societies.[9] One dimension of the dilemma of Arab societies relates to the failure of national movements to free themselves from the past, including nonrational religious belief and denial of secularism.[10] Arab societies have consistently resisted dealing with pressing matters on the emancipation of women, liberal culture, or vesting sovereignty in the people. As a corollary, Arabs accepted the fruits of Western technology, not the system of knowledge that produced it (namely rationality and complex analysis).[11]

The past still survives in Arab societies because they did not produce the equivalent of a Martin Luther to break religious monopoly, a Niccolò Machiavelli to free politics from metaphysics, a Nicolaus Copernicus to emancipate the natural sciences from theology, or an English gentleman to provide a link between the aristocracy and the masses. To the contrary, Arab societies have been plagued by unenlightened, self-aggrandizing despots, religious mysticism, and a preponderance of segmentary identifications. Thus Arab societies seem ill-equipped to devise a workable formula capable of ensuring smooth transition into modernity. The problem also entails elite resistance to change, political incompetence on the part of the masses, and an unsuitable system for disseminating impartial information and sound knowledge. In this situation, the gap between elites and masses widens, tension among the classes increases, and subnational antagonisms heighten. Growing demands on the government from the public for better standards of living, which the elites cannot provide, clash with the elites' use of coercion to extract more resources from an already impoverished population. Escalation of tension causes unresolved grievances to mount, placing the system on the brink of civil strife.

Intellectual Stagnation

A country's intellectual life is a thermometer measuring the overall health of society. Advanced societies have vibrant intellectual atmospheres, whereas those of underdeveloped countries are casualties of stagnation. Political authoritarianism, subservience, economic underdevelopment, and overdependence on the outside world make Arab intellectual life unavoidably stagnant. Arab societies seem to suffer, almost invariably, from the same attributes of intellectual torpidity. In this context, al-Bakkar claimed that very few Arabs deal with reality in an objective and rational manner.[12] Sa'id Hija, the most prominent Moroccan intellectual in the late 1930s, noted that "Moroccan thinking has not tangibly developed, as it still maintains the form of the ancient past. The pillars of Moroccan culture [rest on] fragile foundations. . . . Our contact with the new Western way of life did not aid in effecting a *coup de main* in our mental concepts and methods of comprehension. We continue to suffer from mostly sagging intellectual life whose roots are stagnant and obsolete."[13]

Munir al-Hamash saw a connection between the intellectual crisis in the Arab world and the weakness of inquisitiveness among the masses, which he ascribed to illiteracy and low standards of living.[14] There are conceptual problems in this line of thinking. Do literacy and prosperity necessarily enhance a process of intellectual debate in the absence of independent thinking and active political will? There are grounds to assume otherwise. Placing emphasis on the denial of basic human rights, including self-expression, brought Husayn Jamil closer to grasping the dilemma of human resource development in the Arab world.[15] The speedy amelioration of the situation is difficult, partly because the ruling elite, besieged by the political legitimacy question, seems afraid of the consequences of promoting independent thinking. A study by the International Committee for Human Rights in the Gulf and the Arabian peninsula complained that Arab regimes in the Gulf region have revoked the promises they made to their populations about political liberalization, as soon as the U.S.-led coalition expelled the Iraqi army from Kuwait.[16] Salahuddin Hafiz blamed the intellectual stagnation that plagues Arab societies on historic crises and misfortunes that eventually debilitated the Arab mind. Missing the age of science and technology meant to Hafiz that Arabs would miss the age of reasoning, freedom, and progress as well.[17] He summarized his strong argument saying: "The essence of the current crisis of the Arab mind lies in its inability at innovation and creativity. . . . The continuation of this trend causes extinction in the end!"[18] The Arab intellectual class has abandoned its role in society since many of its members chose to abstain from taking a stand on burning societal issues (be they political, cultural, economic), contenting themselves instead with acting as apologists for the regime. Intellectual vacuum made it easy, to use the words of Hafiz, for ". . . the beasts of darkness, the enemies of the intellect and freedom to destroy independent thinking and creativity."[19]

The weakness of civil society in some Arab countries (such as in Lebanon, Egypt, and Morocco) or its virtual nonexistence in others (the Persian Gulf states, Yemen, and Libya are pertinent cases) make it extremely difficult for the emergence of public opinion, whose absence, or ineffectiveness, denies the intellectual life of a society from a major tributary. The infelicitous conditions of civil society and public opinion are reinforced by the crisis of public awareness. Defensive regimes worried about sheer survival deliberately confuse the populace by providing them with incorrect bits of information. The state-controlled print media and so-called intellectual lackeys preach democracy and human dignity but behave autocratically and violate basic human rights. There is a chasm in the Arab world between what the elites tell their peoples and how they actually treat them. The unworthiness of official rhetoric, lack of faith in government statements or actions, loss of self-confidence, deliberate marginalization of sincere individuals, hiding of truth from the public, and forging of vital statistics all result in a society plagued with hypocrisy. It is hardly possible for such societies to have dynamic intellectual milieus. Yasin al-Hafiz attempted to determine the underlying causes of his assumption about Arab political irrationality. He ruled out progress and political predictability as long as the Arab intelligentsia, deemed unfit to engage in politics, remains reactionary.[20] Condemning the injudicious policies of Arab military juntas, al-Hafiz concluded that their ruralization of major Arab cities has contributed greatly to irrationality.[21] To sum up the debilitating effects of existing systemic conditions in the Arab world on its intellectual life, it would suffice to state that gold strands are not spun from straw.

Blurry Vision

Arabs seem unable to deal with the post–Cold War era. The rulers are busy quelling the opposition in order to stabilize increasingly vulnerable regimes. They refuse to admit fault in their regimes, finding it expedient to blame unnamed foreign powers for their domestic travails. Arab leaders only pay lip service to the issue of political legitimacy by introducing sham participatory policies. Many of them appear more concerned with international recognition than with recognition from their own peoples. Some leaders shun a Middle Eastern economic and military order; nevertheless, their efforts to create an alternative Arab order have not achieved any tangible results. The countries of the Gulf Cooperation Council want to create a unified military force to ensure viable defense against foreign aggression but are held back by narrow interests and interpersonal distrust. Leaders seek peace with Israel but worry about its technological and democratic challenge.

The masses desire change; nevertheless, they exhibit little interest in political mobilization unless it puts on a religious cloak. They dream about democracy without struggling to make it come true, and they yearn for modernization but evince unwillingness to work hard to realize it. In other words, they aspire to enjoy the amenities of Western societies without the responsibility attached to them.

Arab leaders, unable to marshal adequate popular support for their policies, have difficulty planning the future of their countries. Having relied on co-optation and repression to pacify the populace, without sincerely trying to transform them from subjects into citizens, Arab leaders seem ill at ease with an emerging international order inclined toward globalization. An impasse has finally arrived whereby the rulers operate in a foggy environment, and the masses, long isolated from the currents of enlightenment blowing in every direction, lack the operational requisites for immersing themselves in constructive domestic politics, let alone a rapidly emerging international system. As a defense mechanism, many Arabs turn to the past, seeking refuge from the unfamiliar complexities of contemporary challenges.

Sanctuary in Past Glory

Deprived of modern achievements of import to their societies or humanity at large, Arabs turned to the past, searching for purpose in life and pride in accomplishments. Early Arab nationalists such as Butrus al-Bustani (1819–83) and Jurji Zaydan (1861–1914), attempting to found a legitimate basis for separation from the Ottoman empire, revived Arab culture and extolled the heroism of Arab warriors. Nonfulfillment of the doctrine of Arab nationalism, partly due to the absence of a political program, transformed a carefully rewritten legendary past into a nostalgic exercise. Muhammad 'Abdul Salam Kafafi asserted that Arabic culture, bolstered by the advent of Islam (reaching its peak during the medieval period), which unified Arabs' hearts as well as aspirations and high principles, still possesses a strong influence on the determination of their future.[22] Like many Arab authors, Kafafi derived great satisfaction from the tenets of Islam and from Arab poetry, way of life, and system of governance. He proudly recollected the contributions of Arab-Islamic men of learning to philosophy (al-Farabi), mathematics (Abu Kamil), geography (al-Mas'udi), and history (al-Tabari).

Engrossment in glorifying past achievements manifests itself in school curricula, political discourse, and the shaping of today's way of life. The legacy of the past seems to impose itself heavily on the lives of Arabs in the present. Visitors to book fairs in Arab countries invariably notice that most books on display deal with *turath* (cultural and religious legacy). Focus on the past reaches—probably because of defensiveness about the present—the point of attributing the great ancient civilizations of the Nile Valley and Mesopotamia to the Arabs. Anwar al-Rifa'i thus discovered Arab origins for the ancient peoples of the Middle East including the Egyptians, Sumerians, Acadians, Babylonians, and Arameans.[23] He determined that Hannibal, the Carthaginian general who challenged the Roman empire, was an Arab hero, and he insists on attributing the Code of Hammurabi to Arab legislative genius.[24]

The underdevelopment of a society sometimes brings stigma to its members, especially if they had a brilliant past. Occasionally it encourages denial of the need to learn new technological skills and behavioral traits, since their acquisition tends to be exceptionally difficult, or even unwarranted by the strength of traditional values. People may choose to seek shelter in past glory instead of mustering courage to cope with foreign cultural prerequisites of development. Certain Arab authors succumbed to the temptation of resisting change, finding solace in medieval days. Ahmad ʿAbdul Rahim al-Sayih, for example, reminded his readers about the bright aspects of Arab-Islamic civilization but came up short of using it as a launching pad for a new nahda. He implored Arabs to return to pristine Islam and establish a direct association with God. Al-Sayih contaminated his argument by leaning on Qurʾanic verses, such as the following: "Call on Me; I will answer your (prayer)."[25] The author led us to the conclusion that all Arabs and Muslims need to do in order to break the vicious cycle of backwardness is to rediscover Islamic turath.[26] By establishing a causal relationship between religion and the medieval successes of Islamic society, without obtaining canonical correlation, al-Sayih demanded the institution of an Islamic scale for discharging all functions in society.[27] He used a generalization from the Qurʾan to disarm potential critics of his undefined proposal for modernization: "This is the Book / In it is guidance sure, without doubt / To those who fear Allah."[28]

The jolt of Western imperialism and Arab coolness to the cultural sources nourishing the advancement of their former colonizers, or their unintelligibility to them, create a buffer between Arabs and the ability to grasp the nuts and bolts of modernity. The failure of major drives for modernization in the Arab world during the nineteenth and twentieth centuries (first by Muhammad ʿAli, and more recently by secular leaders in Egypt, Syria, Iraq, and Algeria) appears to have convinced many people in the region to flee the complexity of the modern age.

Aversion to cultural renovation and resistance to the incorporation of fresh precepts into the analytical processes of Arab societies led to intellectual paralysis and perpetuated the loss of political will. The mismatch between the cultural frame of reference and superficially modern government structures watered down the content of public-oriented decisions, usually compromising the effectiveness of legislated policy outputs. Arab ruling elites, who oppressed the masses and stifled their hopes for meaningful living, bear false witness to the quagmire of their societies. They have continuously bombarded their populations with pep talks about an imminent developmental breakthrough that never came to pass. Deprivation from independent sources of information about domestic affairs, international developments, and the influx of ideas on free thinking facilitated the return of many Arabs to the imagined peace of past glory.

Arabs must find a way to break out from the yoke of cultural encapsulation and analytical frigidity. This requires an expansion of their worldview to encompass broader awareness of what goes on in this vast village called the globe. Arabs need to attend to their tremendous societal problems by entering the world, a step that requires self-confidence, attention to abstraction, and commitment to hard work. Elites and masses would do well to revisit their understanding of political and cultural identity and integrate the concept of plurality in deeds rather than words.

9

Negotiating the Future

The Arabs, having wallowed in a continuous ideological mire for more than two hundred years, find themselves surrounded by gloom as they trudge into a new century unprepared to deal with its challenges. A long journey to determine a valid identity linking them to the modern age has finally completed a full cycle of vain search. The contemporary surge of militant Islam, after other modes of governance have been unsuccessfully attempted, demonstrates the predicament plaguing the Arab World's ruling elites. A legacy of defeat, a sense of helplessness, endless divisions on every aspect of social and political subjects, unruly publics, and overwhelming state repression and violation of basic human rights do not invite much hope in an unfolding era of economic globalization and steady political openness. The Arabs must make their exit from the past without divorcing themselves from it. They need not relinquish the roots of the much-valued Arab-Islamic culture; however, they need to invigorate it with new values and modes of behavior to make possible their transition toward modernity and beyond. The list of important steps that they must take in the years ahead include (1) understanding the West, (2) believing in the myth of Arab nationalism, (3) defining and pursuing collective objectives, (4) nurturing respect for authority, and (5) realizing the inevitability of political representation. To relieve themselves of the self-perceived sense of siege, the Arabs must graciously accept the fact that the West has convincingly won after a millennium of confrontation against Arab Muslims.[1] This is certainly not an invitation to divest themselves of their religio-cultural traditions but to integrate in their thinking certain functional requisites that made the West reach its pinnacle of societal and economic achievements. This makes understanding the West a matter of utmost urgency for Arabs puzzled by the requirements of modernity.

The Need for Understanding the West

Ever since the appearance of Islam in the seventh century, the history of Arab interaction with the West has been marred by misconception, stereotyping, and prejudice. The aim here is not to assign blame on either party but rather to make a case for the Arabs' need to come to terms with the fact that a better future for them requires a greater understanding of the West. The West—ecstatic with its cultural contributions, political achievements, and technological superiority—now sets the pace of universal progress and judges what is admissible and what is not. The disbanding of the Soviet Union and the adoption of market economy principles by Eastern European countries hastened the arrival of globalization, the giant offspring of capitalism. During the 1998 commencement at the American University in Dubai, James Baker, former U.S. secretary of state, advised the young graduates to prepare themselves for the professional challenges presented by the advent of globalization, which he said has come to stay.[2] Rapid global changes in the economic and political domains require the Arabs to rethink their present situation in earnest. The deterioration of the position of Arab countries vis-à-vis their non-Arab neighbors reveals advanced political decay and utter failure to influence their own destinies.[3] The Arabs must get rid of the Crusaders' syndrome which lurks deep in their collective consciousness and affects their perceptions about the outside world. In other words, they have to abandon the time-honored belief that they are locked in a perpetual struggle with the West. Similarly, the Arabs must resolve the lingering Hulagu memory and the consequences of the Spanish reconquest, which destroyed the two greatest centers of Arab-Islamic civilization in Baghdad and Andalusia.

Today, the Arabs face the arduous task of having to reconcile themselves to the loss of the Islamic state, accept and learn the new rules of interstate interaction as set forth by the West, and reform their societies accordingly. In medieval times, Arabs and Muslims played a major role in the Old World's politics and excelled in culture and civilization; a grudging Europe, duly recognizing its inferiority, found no harm in altering its value system and broadening its cultural and civilizational horizons. European determination resulted in an outstanding breakthrough that caused the West to become the political, civilizational, and economic hub of the world. The Arabs cannot escape dealing with the West. To do this properly, they must understand what made the West powerful, without forgetting that previous experiences, especially in different cultural settings, cannot be replicated elsewhere. The modernization of the West is indeed the result of complex societal processes anchored in progressive rationality and legitimacy. Arabs do not need to—probably they cannot—replicate every aspect of Western ascendancy to eminence. It is obvious, however, that the successes of the West would not have been accomplished without the resolution of the identity question; hence, this brings to the fore the issue of Arab identity, long mired in ambiguity and indecision.

The Arabs first came into contact with Western notions of nationalism as early as the middle of the nineteenth century. Impressed by the West, they sought to follow their example and develop their own version of ethno-national identity as a necessary step toward modernity. They failed partly because they did not integrate in their system of behavior values such as hard work, punctuality, individualism, anonymous citizenship, respect for state authority, informational inquisitiveness, commitment to basic human rights, and acceptance of the idea of broadly shared political responsibility. The Arabs are left with no choice but to tackle the consequences of the communication revolution, namely the advent of the era of a global information system. It is becoming increasingly difficult for Arab leaders to masquerade as successful rulers, when in reality their tenuous political edifices seem on the verge of falling apart. The rise of Israel as the Middle East's superpower, the strangulation of Iraq, domestic quandary, Islamic revival, and awe of the West all combined put the Arabs in a tight situation indeed. Arab troubles have come home; they no longer lend themselves to patched up solutions. Arabs implicate the West for their travails. Although there is a certain truth to this charge, the Arabs must realize that denial of the West will not get them very far on the road toward modernity. Contact with the West may have been venomous to the Arabs, but many Western modernizational values provide the necessary antidote for their regeneration. Before anything else can be done, Arabs must resolve their lingering identity crisis.

Believing in the Myth of Arab Nationalism

Even though Arab nationalism clearly has serious limitations, it has presently become a compelling need for the Arabs nevertheless. Chronic inter-Arab divisions eventually made their influence in the Middle East secondary to Israel's, Turkey's, or even Iran's, despite the fact that Arabs constitute more than half the population of the region. In North Africa, the Arab states are either wholly dependent on the West (Morocco, Algeria, Tunisia), or quarantined by it (Libya). The role of the Arab League—once regarded as epitomizing Arab hopes for political solidarity and economic cooperation—as a harmonizer of Arab views and coordinator of collective policies has been shattered by suspicion and feud, much of which results from personal rivalries among Arab rulers. The establishment of the Arab League in 1945 was intended to provide a viable mechanism to shore up Arab interests as a new world order set in the aftermath of World War II. Flawed since its inception by bickering and lack of commitment, it duly lost its significance as a forum for rallying Arab aggregate objectives. Further weakened by the second Gulf War, which ushered in a unipolar world order, the league currently finds itself even unable to perform ceremonial functions beyond perfunctory protesting of Israel's apparent disengagement from the peace process. Arabs' search for a unifying identity capable of allowing them to collectively confront the challenges of modernity and geopolitics has been dealt a disabling blow. As the situation stands today, the Arabs are at a crossroads pondering their future. This is happening in an increasingly complex world characterized by nations' scramble to gain strategic allies and economic partners. Global trends toward political and economic associations (the Americas, Europe, and the Pacific region) have been reciprocated by an escalation in the level of Arab factiousness and disarray.

Undeniably, Arab nationalism lacks many of the functional prerequisites that allowed the successful launching of its European antecedents.[4] Peter Mansfield went a step further to say that the geographic stretch of the Arab world from Morocco on the Atlantic Ocean to the western shores of the Persian Gulf is deceptive. He highlighted the point that this vast territorial area ". . . is really an archipelago of inhabited islands on a desert sea."[5] Mansfield's "archipelago" notion is no longer admissible in our age of revolutionary transportation and communications technologies. The vast desert is no longer a barrier to Arab interaction; the real barrier now is the restless rulers preoccupied with the security of their illegitimate regimes. The truth is that the Arabs share important qualities that provide a basis for the commensuration of Arab nationalism: history, culture, and a sentimental, nearly inexplicable, attachment toward the native speakers of Arabic that has no equivalent among the corresponding speakers of English or Spanish. Using Ernest Renan's remark that "language invites unity, but does not compel it,"[6] Mansfield hit the nail on the head when he said that it ". . . has been shrewdly observed that the Arabs are linked by a huge invisible nervous system. If you apply pressure at one point, the reaction may take place at some wholly different branch of the complex. But, to carry the metaphor further, the Arab world lacks a skeleton."[7] Politically speaking, Mansfield's "skeleton" implies founding a pan-Arab institutional mechanism capable of defining and pursuing collective objectives. The Arab countries confront common domestic and external challenges which they attempt to deal with separately, and in the process they shoot accusations at one another. The argument that nations are historical accidents does not deflect the need for nationalism, all the more in the current emphasis on globalization.

The unfolding new world order leaves little room for individual states, especially the smaller ones, to make it on their own. Globalization with its emphasis on the formation of blocs of nations, essentially for economic purposes, underscores the triumph of capitalism over all sorts of socialism. It also signifies the retreat of political despotism in favor of transparency. Arabs must accept the new rules of the game as set by the West and integrate them in their behavior. Weak as they are in strategic terms, rebellion will most likely result in catastrophic consequences for the Arabs, as the living example of the devastation of Iraq clearly demonstrates. The Arab states have paid dearly for their divisions and now must realize that the formation of a viable bloc of Arab states has become a must for their survival and existence on the strategic map of world politics. To do this, they have no other choice but to believe in the myth of Arab nationalism, no matter how tenuous its theoretical grounds are. The ruling elites can certainly play a decisive role in this regard. Arab nationalism has been consistently constrained by lack of political elite commitment to its symbols and slogans. The time has arrived for the formulation of an Arab national ideology and winning over consensus for its tenets. A new Arab national consciousness must be founded on the principles of liberating reason, solidarity, cooperation, freedom, initiative, and inculcation of positive values.[8] The Arabs must come to terms with these principles and values which the West understands and appreciates. Unless they transform their political systems and learning to work collectively, the Arabs probably will face their doomsday much sooner than other peoples.

Defining and Pursuing Collective Objectives

Arab states have not been inattentive to the importance of pan-Arab policies, especially since the intensification of the Palestine crisis in the mid-1940s. The Arab League attempted, from its founding, to establish harmonious and mutually beneficial relations among the member states, but it achieved few tangible results. Personal rivalries, suspicion, and insecurity doomed Arab endeavors at forging close inter-Arab cooperation. The league's charter included a number of clauses on economic and military cooperation which were never put into action. Arab states signed numerous bilateral trade agreements that were either immediately discarded or were rather insignificant. The obvious merits of economic interaction did not result in improving inter-Arab political relations. To the contrary, political divisions preempted all aspects of meaningful cooperation and created an atmosphere of uncertainty among Arabs.[9]

Arabs' unwillingness to cooperate militarily proved even more disastrous than their failure to come together on economic matters. Often motivated by narrow political objectives, plans for military cooperation became an arena for settling personal scores, or a demonstration of subservience to international powers. In 1949 King Faruq proposed the formation of an Arab Collective Security Pact in order to avert the likelihood of a merger between Iraq and Syria. President Nasser advocated a similar plan in the mid-1950s, hoping to neutralize the Baghdad Pact project (whose aim was to complete the encirclement of the former Soviet Union), which monarchical Iraq thought would give it a claim to leadership in the Arab world. In 1964 Egypt, Syria, Iraq, Jordan, and Lebanon agreed to establish a Joint Arab Command to strengthen the military preparedness of Arab armies bordering Israel. The ultimate objective was to divert the tributaries of the Jordan River to prevent Israel from accommodating more immigrants in the Jewish state. The consequences of the 1967 Arab-Israeli war attested to the failure of genuine Arab military planning and cooperation. Needless to say, participation of key Arab states (such as Egypt, Syria, and Saudi Arabia) in the U.S.-led military coalition against Iraq signaled the demise of the tenuous Arab order. The trauma of the disastrous and unimaginable war touched the hearts and minds of Arabs, leaving deep scars in their collective consciousness. Nevertheless, it ignited an intense, albeit belated, debate on the need to found a new Arab order resting on defining and pursuing collective objectives.

Overbearing challenges, both domestic and external, necessitate the formation a community of Arab states capable of performing the functions of economic integration, military cooperation, and political coordination. For many years Arab economists and businessmen have pleaded for the establishment of an Arab market. Writing in 1982, Yusif Sayigh lamented the failure of efforts to achieve economic integration including the 1964 Arab Common Market. He blamed Arab states for inadequate conceptualization of development, weak commitment to development effort, and excessive dependence on the advanced industrial economies.[10] Apart from blaming the West and Arab political disarray for the regretful conditions of Arab economies, Sayigh did not offer a mechanism for bringing about Arab economic cooperation and complementarity.[11] A quarter of a century later, Arab economists began to see the issue of cooperation as a question of life or death for all Arab countries. Egyptian businessmen such as Muhammad al-Jundi, president of the board of directors of the International Company for Commerce and Investment, and Wa'il Lahhita, president of the board of directors of Egytrans, suggested that Arab economic cooperation had become an inevitable necessity. Short of it, Arabs would have to brace themselves for most undesirable consequences.[12] Ma'n Bashshur, an Arab nationalist, concurred with the views of economists and businessmen. He saw the formation of an Arab economic bloc as the only realistic possibility for Arabs to cope with the rigorous criteria of the U.S.-inspired new global order.[13]

The Arab states must produce a binding and lasting covenant to regulate inter-Arab relations. They must renounce the idea of the center state (a term coined by President Nasser to refer to the pioneering role of Egypt in achieving Arab unity) and relinquish the notion of an Arab heroic leader who would eventually unite the Arabs.[14] The Arabs must organize their reciprocal relations on the basis of conciliation, respect, understanding, and compromise for the purpose of integrating the Arab countries economically, politically, and militarily. Arab cooperation must be governed by the following considerations:

(1) Achieving unity of vision and solidarity in action.

(2) Quick and peaceful resolution of inter-Arab conflicts without impacting any aspect of cooperation or impinging on prior commitments or agreements.

(3) Provision of prompt aid, by all Arab states acting as a collective entity, to any Arab country threatened by whichever foreign power.

(4) Commitment to a genuine Arab economic market that ensures the free movement of trade, labor, and capital.

(5) Formation of an all-Arab military command capable of deterring possible foreign encroachments, although politics and economics will play a greater role in shaping events in the Middle East, at least during the first quarter of the twenty-first century.

(6) Dealing with foreign powers as a solid front on consequential economic and political matters.

In order for the Arab states to establish harmonious relations among themselves and to engage in fruitful transactions with the outside world, they must implement daring changes in their internal political environments. Domestic stability that emanates from good political performance is indispensable for projecting fruitful interactions with neighboring countries. Inter-Arab cooperation in the past was mightily hindered by the ruling elites' debilitating sense of political illegitimacy, as well as by their preoccupation with keeping the forces of local opposition at bay. Rulers' meddling in the domestic affairs of other Arab countries poisoned the Arab political climate and precluded the prospects for smooth relations. The frequency of intervention in the affairs of other Arab countries has sharply declined in recent years, but the rate of domestic change has been largely less than satisfactory for the purposes of better governance. The required changes entail instituting the rule of the law and enfranchising the population in decision making. The first change hinges on respect for authority, and the second on political representation.

Nurturing Respect for Authority

Rule of law demands public awareness of government intentions and endorsement of its policies. Respect for authority is essential for the successful implementation of public policies and the maintenance of law and order. Respect for authority requires its acceptance as legitimate; in turn, the latter presupposes approval by the majority of the population. Even when the minority dissents, it is obliged to respect authority in accordance with established rules of the game in a legitimate polity. The modern state, after which Arab governments are structurally modeled, is rooted in nationalistic identification and legitimate representation. Functionally, Arab states deviate from the model and succumb to a variety of particularistic tendencies. A few efforts in some Arab countries to create a sense of belonging (Egypt, Syria, Iraq, Tunisia, Algeria) were attempted ineffectually during the second half of the twentieth century, solely by depending on the single political party approach. Corrupt party machinery hardly provided an example to be imitated by populations grouped along visceral lines. Ideological vagueness, corruption, nepotism, and weak or nonexistent civil societies created societal mess. It normally reduced the authority of the state to brutish use of coercion, at best to buying off the mobilized segments of the population.

Territorial nationalisms (such as Saudism, Iraqism, Syrianism, Lebanonism) have utterly failed with the exception of Egyptianism and Tunisianism. Strong Arab tendencies prevail everywhere in the Arab world, even in Egypt, where significantly large segments of the population are increasingly accepting identification with the Arab world.

Respect for the authority of the state in the Arab world can be enhanced by resolving the nationalistic question, which the notion of Arabism seems quite capable of fulfilling. Equally important to nationalism is the issue of civil society, one that is grossly wanting in the Arab world. Three factors appear to have directly inhibited the development of civil societies in the Arab world: authoritarian regimes, particularistic identifications, and underdevelopment. First, most Arab rulers suppress professional associations and other types of demand groups, or simply manipulate them; the few others ban all forms of special-interest groups. Second, weak anonymous identifications make the concept of a community nebulous to many Arabs. For the most part, Arab societal identifications have not transcended the family sphere, localism, or regionalism. Interest-driven and duty-bound associations that cut across society are little known in the Arab world. Third, the small Arab economies and their lack of versatility do not promote the proliferation of viable interest groups.

Respect for authority is a learned behavior. It results from abiding by the rules of mass organizations, well-defined patterns of family interactions, and interpersonal relationships. Coercion is, unfortunately, the dominant instrument that regulates most Arab individuals' contacts with their environment. This results in resentment of authority and in the identification of its wielders as despots. Weak civil societies lack the ability to provide the public with the necessary preparation for working with authority figures on the basis of membership in an organic society, a notable predicament of all Arab countries.

Arabs tend to loathe authority and, if possible, evade it; they see it as arbitrary, oppressive, and unjust. Its monopolization by rulers who usurped power creates a wedge between the Arab populations and their ruling elites. The rectification of this anomalous situation requires empowering the people, a most desired development that would transform the publics from mere spectators into actual participants in the affairs of their countries. Participants find it relatively easy to respect authority, since it designates their desire to go through with the choices they make. It becomes clear now that authority cannot be separated from representation.

Realization of the Inevitability of Political Representation

The dilemma of development rendered political representation an immediate issue for action by harried Arab ruling elites. Certain Arab heads of state have tried, since the mid-1980s, to halt their loosening grip on society by faking representation. The trick did not work as the problem of political enfranchisement has now become graver than ever. The matter of political representation has been discussed at numerous regional and international conferences in recent years. In a notable scholarly event, Arab intellectuals convened in Abu Dhabi (UAE) in November 1997, in a seminar on the future of the Arab world and the role of the Arab League in coordinating inter-Arab relations. The participants expressed belief that the solution to Arab political travails lay in democratization and official respect for the law.[15] They condemned the Arab ruling elites for having twisted the political domain to furthering narrow interests, despite sweeping public enthusiasm for close ties with other Arab countries. The intellectuals came to the conclusion that representation will resolve the legitimacy crisis and ensure an institutional basis for genuine Arab cooperation.[16]

In an exceptional piece of scholarship, Charles William Maynes advised Arab rulers that the twenty-first century will not bode well for their obsession with political centralization. Demographic growth and successive technological strides are bound, according to Maynes, to transform the political contours of the Middle East. He articulated his viewpoint as follows: "States in the Middle East will have an ever harder time managing their internal pressures as technology begins to transform the relationship between governments and people in the region as elsewhere. . . . Today, technology seems to be siding with the decentralizers. The rise of the service economy, the development of the Internet, the explosion in the number of cable television channels, and growing mass literacy, all are strengthening the periphery at the expense of the center. All are empowering at the local level while undermining authority at the center."[17]

The Arab world's transition toward real representation has two sides: elite acceptance of broad public participation as an irreversible fact and the universalization of rationality and legality. Elite decision to expand the base of politics and introduce the practice of broad political recruitment are more conducive to regime stability than mere dependence on crude instruments such as repression or co-optation. Arab ruling elites are called upon to display a high degree of altruism; bent on achievement, nation builders are phenomenal individuals driven by sincerity and open-mindedness in their pursuit of universal objectives. There are no examples of competent polities in which the ruling elites resorted to petty behavior in order to lengthen their staying powers. Part of the problem with Arab elites is attributable to moribund Arab masses. The absence of lay activists with clear messages to transmit to the ruling elites on behalf of the masses has compounded the issue of representation, desensitizing the former to the aspirations of the latter.

To the extent that Islamic militancy represents one form of extremism, the advocacy of secularism is tantamount to another.[18] Rationality, with its emphasis on critical evaluation and scientific inquiry, provides a viable alternative to secularism. The intertwinement of Islam and culture makes secularism, an outcome of Europe's sociopolitical evolution, a useless concept in the Arab world. Tolerance, perseverance, commitment to public goals, and recognition of inalienable human rights all can occur without secularism per se.

Rationality is indispensable for legality, an enabling attribute of representation. Legality is a sine qua non for stability, a guarantor of peace, and a promoter of vibrant economic activity. To come about, there has to be a matching between state ideology and people's aspirations sanctioned by broad public participation in domestic politics. The Arab publics have an obligation toward themselves as collective entities to make their voices heard through peaceful means; otherwise the full scope of their demands will not ring out.

The twentieth century is entering the Arab collective consciousness as an era of great frustrations, astonishing defeats, and stunted aspirations. The twenty-first century presents paramount challenges but also great possibilities. The Arabs must fully comprehend the themes of past failures and integrate them in a recipe of success for the future, which is quickly becoming our present. The Arabs of today are a casualty of historical interactions. It does not matter at all if they put the blame on themselves or others. The fact is that they must do something about the situation. The malfunctioning Arab train has come to a halt, but the damage, extensive as it might be, is repairable. Unrepaired trains end up in junkyards.

Notes

1. The Search for Identity

1. Hamadi, *Tajdid al-Hadith ʿAn al-Qawmiyya al-ʿArabiyya*, 24.

2. In Lebanon, for example, the Association of Islamic Charitable Projects advocates a liberal version of traditional Islam. This approach has gained the association wide popularity within the country's Sunni Muslim community.

3. Arab scholars tend to accept Ibrahim Pasha's pan-Arab statements. See, for example, ʿImad ʿAbdul Salam Raʾuf, "Al-Jamʿiyyat al-ʿArabiyya wa Fikruha al-Qawmi ʿind al-ʿArab Munzu Matlaʿ al-Qarn al-Tasiʿ ʿAshar Hatta Qiyam al-Harb al-ʿAlamiyya al-ʾUla" (Arab societies and their nationalistic thought among Arabs since the beginning of the nineteenth century until the eruption of the First World War), in *Tatawur al-Fikr al-Qawmi al-ʿArabi*, 106.

4. Halpern, *The Politics of Social Change*, 22–23.

5. For more details, see Cleveland, *A History of the Modern Middle East*, 57–78.

6. Conversely, Sultan ʿAbdul Hamid accelerated other aspects of reform, especially those in the fields of education, administration, transportation, and telecommunications.

7. Cleveland, *A History of the Modern Middle East*, 115.

8. For a good analysis of al-Afghani's thoughts on political reform, see Abdelnasser, *The Islamic Movement in Egypt*, 27–30.

9. Some argue that the West aimed from these activities to create a wedge between Arabs and Turks to facilitate the destruction of the Ottoman empire. For a thorough representation of this view, see Al-Nabahani, *Al-Dawla al-Islamiyya*.

10. Carmichael, *The Shaping of the Arabs*, 282.

11. See Raʾuf, "Al-Jamʿiyyat al-ʿArabiyya wa Fikruha al-Qawmi," in *Tatawur al-Fikr al-Qawmi al-ʿArabi*, 131–32.

12. Al-Qabbani, *Mawqif Shawqi wal Shuʿaraʾ al-Misriyyin*, 12.

13. Ibid., 59.

14. *Al-Aʿaml al-Qawmiyya li Sati ʿal-Husry*, 991.

15. Khadduri, *Political Trends in the Arab World*, 19.

16. Ibid., 21.

17. Ibid., 185.

18. The implications of the Balfour Declaration were clear to Arabs in general, especially to Palestinians, who, from the early 1930s, watched as Jewish immigration to Palestine accelerated and the immigrants' political and military weight posed a threat to the local Arab population.

19. Transjordan was created in order to accommodate prince Abdullah, in partial British fulfillment to an earlier promise to his father, Sharif Husayn, about creating an Arab kingdom in exchange for his revolt against the Ottomans.

20. Mansfield, *A History of the Middle East,* 183.

21. Ibid., 180.

22. For additional details, see Entelis, "The Maghrib: An Overview," in Long and Reich, eds., *The Government and Politics of the Middle East and North Africa,* 381–90.

23. Nasser's initial successes included evicting the British from the Suez Canal area, concluding the breakthrough Czechoslovak arms deal, opposing the British-inspired Baghdad Pact, nationalizing the Suez Canal, surviving the consequences of the Anglo-French and Israeli military campaign against Egypt, and merging politically with Syria.

24. In fact, the main reason for Nasser's insistence on creating the Palestine Liberation Organization, during the second Arab summit held in Alexandria in September 1964, emanated from his fears that the Fat'h movement might soon launch raids against Israel that would destabilize the armistice lines with Israel. He obviously aspired to contain the rising Palestinian militancy by creating an organization that he could directly control. For further information, see Kimmerling and Migdal, *Palestinians: The Making of a People,* 215–20.

25. Michael Hudson, "State, Society, and Legitimacy: An Essay on Arab Political Prospects in the 1990s," Sharabi, ed., *The Next Arab Decade,* 24.

26. Ibid., 25.

27. For an informative point of view on the impact of tribalism on Yemeni politics, see Al-Bakr, *Harb al-Yaman,* 13–17.

28. Hallaj, "U.S. Gulf Policy."

2. Identity and Political Entity

1. Zdzislaw, *Symbols, Conflict, and Identity,* 3.

2. For a thorough study on the development of the modern state, see Morton, *The Evolution of Political Society.*

3. Kohn, *The Idea of Nationalism,* 188.

4. Ibid., 6.

5. Ibid., 13.

6. Kamenka, "Political Nationalism—The Evolution of the Idea," in Kamenka, ed., *Nationalism,* 12.

7. Kedourie, *Nationalism,* 38.

8. Deutsch, *Nationalism and Social Communication,* 87.

9. Gellner, *Nations and Nationalism,* 39.

10. Ibid., 39–40.

11. Smith, *Nationalism in the Twentieth Century,* 1.

12. Joseph R. Strayer, "The Historical Experience of Nation-Building in Europe," in Deutsch and Foltz, eds., *Nation-Building,* 17.

13. Ibid., 19.

14. Shibutani and Kwan, *Ethnic Stratification,* 444.

15. Talcott Parsons, "Some Theoretical Considerations on the Nature and Trends of Change of Ethnicity," in Glazer and Moynihan, eds., *Ethnicity: Theory and Experience,* 59.

16. Kamenka, "Political Nationalism," 7.

17. Smith, *Nationalism in the Twentieth Century,* 1.

18. Kohn, *A History of Nationalism in the East,* 5.

19. See Louis-Jean Duclos, "The Berbers and the Rise of Moroccan National-ism," in Gellner and Micaud, eds., *Arabs and Berbers,* 217–29.

20. Emerson, *From Empire to Nation,* 90.

21. Migdal, *Strong Societies and Weak States,* 4.

22. For a relevant discussion on the consequences of introducing state national-ism in the Third World, see Von Der Mehden, *Politics of the Developing Nations.*

23. Alford Carleton, "The Interaction of Education and Public Responsibility," in Hall, ed., *The Evolution of Public Responsibility in the Middle East,* 91.

24. Ibid., 92.

25. See Halpern, *The Politics of Social Change,* 7–22.

26. Emerson, *From Empire to Nation,* 95.

27. Presthus, *The Organizational Society,* 192.

28. Hugh Seton-Watson, "State, Nation, and Religion: Some General Reflec-tions," in Alpher, ed., *Nationalism and Modernity,* 25.

29. For more on this, see Castelli, *A Plea for Common Sense.*

30. Ibid., 16.

31. See Carter, *The Culture of Disbelief.*

32. Lowell S. Gustafson and Matthew C. Moen, "Challenge and Accommoda-tion in Religion and Politics," in Moen and Gustafson, eds., *The Religious Chal-lenge to the State,* 5.

33. Ibid., 10.

34. The strength of fundamentalist groups in the West is more than matched by the secular institutions of the state and the strong support they get from the public. Likewise, fundamentalist groups in Buddhist countries do not seem to present a serious challenge to state authority. This is probably due to Buddhist clergymen's dependence on state patronage, hence their unwillingness to confront the state. For an interesting analysis on the reasons for the weakness of militant tendencies among Buddhists, see Martin Southwold, "Purity and Power in Buddhist Sri Lanka," in Bax and Koster, eds., *Power and Prayer,* 201–14.

35. Van Der Veer, *Religious Nationalism,* 12.

36. Boullata, *Trends and Issues in Contemporary Arab Thought,* 57.

3. The Case for Arab Nationalism

1. Hitti, *History of the Arabs,* 197.

2. Ibid., 217.

3. See Lewis, *The Arabs in History,* 74.

4. Ibid.

5. Bishai, *Islamic History of the Middle East*, 362.

6. Al-Marayati, *The Middle East*, 62.

7. Halpern, *The Politics of Social Change*, 10.

8. Lewis, *The Arabs in History*, 93.

9. Shortly after the French had occupied Algeria, some Algerians, including prince 'Abdul Qadir, began to articulate the country's Arab national character, probably as a reaction to coming into a subordinate contact with France's robust, culturally rich and secular nationalism. This matter is discussed by Ra'uf, "Al-Jam'iyyat al-'Arabiyya wa Fikruha al-Qawmi," 103–34.

10. Issawi, *The Arab World's Legacy*, 50.

11. Antonius, *The Arab Awakening*, 33.

12. The situation in Egypt, where nationalism made certain advances, differed significantly. Isolation from West Asia by the occurrence of British occupation, as well as direct educational and cultural interaction with the West, produced a non-European version of nationalism in which religion continued to exercise paramount influence on politics and societal organization.

13. Ra'uf, "Al-Jam'iyyat al-'Arabiyya wa Fikruha al-Qawmi," 113–16.

14. Al-Nabahani, *Al-Dawla al-Islamiyya*, 184.

15. Ibid., 190.

16. Ibid.

17. James Jankowski, "Egypt and Early Arab Nationalism, 1908–1922," in Khalidi et al., eds., *The Origins of Arab Nationalism*, 246.

18. Zallum, *Kaifa Hudimat al-Khilafa*, 24.

19. The Eastern Question rose as a result of Ottoman conquests in Europe during the sixteenth century and gained acuity following the decisive Russian victories against Muslim armies in the second half of the eighteenth century. Intense conflict between the Turks and the plethora of ethnic groups whom they ruled, as well as the aggravation caused by direct intervention of the great European powers, underlay the Eastern Question.

20. Cited in *Thawrat al-'Arab Did al-Atrak*, 143.

21. Zallum, *Kaifa Hudimat al-Khilafa*, 29.

22. *Tatawur al-Fikr al-Qawmi al-'Arabi*, 131–33.

23. Al-Jabiri, *Mas'alat al-Hawiyya*, 40.

24. At later stages of its development, Arab nationalism took on further negative courses pertaining to anti-Europeanism, anti-Zionism, anti-Arab conservatism, and finally anti-Americanism.

25. Ra'uf, "Al-Jam'iyyat al-'Arabiyya wa Fikruha al-Qawmi," 131–33.

26. Mustafa 'Abdul Qadir al-Najjar, "Fikr al-Thawra al-'Arabiyya li 'Am 1916" (The discourse of the Arab rebellion of 1916), in *Tatawur al-Fikr al-Qawmi al-'Arabi*, 148.

27. Ibid., 143.

28. Ibid.

29. European consulates presumably played a role, among other things, in establishing Arab associations and parties. The list includes establishing Hizb alla

Markazia (the decentralization party) in Cairo and Jamʿiyyat al-Islah (the reform association) in Beirut. The fact that the Syrian Arab Congress convened in Paris is often reported as a clear indication of Europe's attempt to agitate Arabs in order to speed up the destruction of the Ottoman empire. These remarks are found in Munassa, *Harakat al-Yaqaza al-ʿArabiyya fi al-Sharq al-Asiawi,* 30.

30. Despite the controversy shrouding the issue, most Arabs evince strong conviction, tinged with bitterness and a sense of betrayal, that the British had actually promised to help them create a kingdom of their own in exchange for rising against the Ottoman empire.

31. Pipes, *The Hidden Hand,* 328.

32. Al-Jabiri, *Mas'alat al-Hawiyya,* 13.

33. Kramer, "Arab Nationalism," 179.

34. The proposition of an Iraqi-controlled Arab state seemed appealing to the pro-British Iraqi prime minister, who saw in it a way to stabilize Iraq—beset by ethnic and sectarian differences—for it would allow him to preside over a political entity with a decisive Sunni Arab majority.

35. *Al-Aʿaml al-Qawmiyya li Sati ʿal-Husry,* 991.

36. Arab nationalists accept al-Husry's analysis. See, for example, Walid Jamal ʿUmar Nazmi, "Fikr Satiʿ al-Husry al-Qawmi" (The nationalistic thought of Satiʿ al-Husry), in *Tatawur al-Fikr al-Qawmi al-ʿArabi,* 201–24.

37. ʿAbdallah Sallum al-Samirra'i, "Harakat al-Qawmiyyin al-ʿArab wa Dawruha fi al-Waʿy al-Qawmi" (The Arab nationalist movement and its role in nationalistic awareness), in *Tatawur al-Fikr al-Qawmi al-ʿArabi,* 168.

38. Ibid., 170.

39. Ibid., 171.

40. For a good study on how the Baʿth Party approached the idea of Arab nationalism, see NizarʿAbdul Latif al-Hudaithi, "Al-Qawmiyya al-ʿArabiyya wal Nazariyya al-Qawmiyya fi Fikr Hizb al-Baʿth al-ʿArabi al-Ishtiraki" (Arab nationalism and the nationalistic theory in the discourse of the Arab socialist Baʿth Party), in *Tatawur al-Fikr al-Qawmi al-ʿArabi,* 235–64.

41. For more on this, see Nutting, *Nasser,* 74–90.

42. Dekmejian, *Egypt under Nasir,* 91.

43. Cited in Beattie, *Egypt during the Nasser Years,* 117.

44. Abu Izzeddin, *Nasser of the Arabs,* 342.

45. Hopwood, *Egypt: Politics and Society,* 101.

46. Mohi El Din, *Memories of a Revolution,* 131.

47. Speech on 3 July 1960. Cited in Abu Izzeddin, *Nasser of the Arabs,* 343.

48. Speech on 29 September 1961.

49. Safadi, "Muhawala fi al-Bahth ʿan Muʿadil Siyasi li Harakat al-Qawmiyya al-ʿArabiyya," 24.

50. Nasser did not want to fight Israel, but he hoped to use the crisis as an instrument to reassert his power and prestige among the Arabs. Prior to the beginning of hostilities, he made it very clear that he wanted to restrain Israel from invading Syria, not to wage war against it.

51. Al-Samirra'i, "Harakat al-Qawmiyyin al-'Arab wa Dawruha fi al-Wa'y al-Qawmi," 175.

52. Al-Jabiri, *Mas'alat al-Hawiyya*, 16.

53. Hamadi, *Tajdid al-Hadith 'n al-Qawmiyya al-'Arabiyya wal Wihda*, 24.

54. Ibid., 26.

4. War and Peace with Israel

1. Haqqi, "Introduction," in Haqqi, ed., *West Asia since Camp David*, 5.

2. Heikal, *Secret Channels*, 18.

3. Haqqi, "Introduction," 3–4.

4. For more on this from a Zionist point of view, see Sinai and Sinai, *Israel and the Arabs*, 3–5.

5. Reich, ed., *Arab-Israeli Conflict and Conciliation*, 53.

6. Sinai and Sinai, *Israel and the Arabs*, 41.

7. Sura *Al-Hujurat*, verse 13.

8. Haj Hamad, "Al-Mafhum al-Qur'ani lil 'Uruba wal Dar fi Muqabil al-Qawmiyya wal Watan," 13–15.

9. Ibid., 15.

10. See Riad, *The Struggle for Peace in the Middle East*, 3.

11. Cited in Cleveland, *A History of the Modern Middle East*, 311.

12. Ibid., 200.

13. Cited in Khashan, *Palestinian Resettlement in Lebanon*, 1.

14. Ben-Gurion, *Israel*, 235–36.

15. Riad, *The Struggle for Peace in the Middle East*, 7.

16. The new Ba'thi regime advocated applying the Vietcong approach against the United States in the Vietnam War to the Arab-Israeli conflict.

17. Successive military coups, army purges, factionalism, and poor training rendered the Syrian army an ineffective fighting force.

18. The five-year-long Yemeni war revealed the inherent divisions in inter-Arab relations and resurrected an old tribal tradition of one Arab faction siding with a common enemy against a fellow Arab. The interests of Saudi Arabia, Jordan, and royalist Yemenis converged with those of Israel on the matter of defeating the Egyptian army in Yemen. For more on Israeli involvement in the Yemen war, see Heikal, *Secret Channels*, 124.

19. Nasser, although he accepted the political option to recover the Arab land lost in 1967, stressed that the Arabs must prepare for the likelihood of war if peaceful measures failed to bring about Israel's withdrawal.

20. It is worth noting that while the United States toughened on the PLO, allegedly in response to Palestinian raids that killed Israeli civilians, on 10 November 1975 the U.N. General Assembly passed Resolution 3379 which labeled Zionism as a form of racism.

21. In the second half of September 1970, the Jordanian army launched a murderous campaign against the PLO, driving them out of the country. Hostilities,

which highlighted uneasy coexistence between the two sides since the Six Day War, began when the Popular Front for the Liberation of Palestine hijacked three Western airliners to an airstrip in northern Jordan and blew them up after releasing the passengers.

22. In the late 1960s a dismissive Israeli prime minister, Levi Eshkol, asked "Who are Palestinians?" Unfortunately, only a wave of Palestinian radicalism (hijackings and killing of civilian hostages) eventually made the world community and the Israeli government concede the presence of a Palestinian people possessing a full-fledged national identity. See Gilmour, *The Ordeal of the Palestinians*, 34.

23. Cited in Reich, ed., *Arab-Israeli Conflict and Conciliation*, 107.

24. Ibid., 132.

25. Sadat triggered the October War in order to persuade the United States to assume a vigorous role in resolving the Arab-Israeli conflict. From the time he took office at the end of 1970, his speeches emphasized that the cards to end the conflict were on the American table. Hoping to erase Washington's apprehensions about Egyptian foreign policy formed during the Nasser period, he unexpectedly announced, in July 1972, the expulsion of Soviet military advisors from Egypt.

26. For an insider's observations on Sadat's handling of the talks, see Riad, *The Struggle for Peace in the Middle East*, 320–21.

27. Prince Fahd, who later became king of Saudi Arabia, proposed an eight-point plan which included an item "confirming the right of the countries of the region to live in peace." Cited in B. Raha Mothulla, "Camp David Accords and Prince Fahd Plan: An Analysis," in Haqqi, ed., *West Asia since Camp David*, 224.

28. Reich, ed., *Arab-Israeli Conflict and Conciliation*, 196.

29. The American president wanted to invalidate Iraq's stipulation that it would honor a U.N. resolution concerning withdrawal from Kuwait if Israel implemented similar resolutions on the Palestine issue.

30. Said, *Peace and Its Discontents*, 4.

31. Syria made two important concessions to Israel: it dropped its demand that Israel commit itself to a full withdrawal from the Golan Heights. It also waived its previous requirement that talks take place under the umbrella of an international conference.

32. Zisser, "Negotiations across the Golan Heights," 41.

33. Sura *Muhammad*, verse 34.

34. Ibid., verse 4.

35. In Khashan, *Partner or Pariah?* 18.

36. Ibid., 8.

37. Ibid., 27.

38. Ibid.

39. Ibid.

40. For more on these findings, see Khashan, "Are the Arabs Ready for Peace with Israel?" 19–28; and Khashan, "The Levant: Yes to Treaties, No to Normalization," 3–13.

41. Heikal, *Secret Channels*, 471–82.

42. Ibid., 508–30.

43. Cohen, "Negotiations across the Golan Heights," 46–49.

5. The Failure of Development

1. Al-Shahir, *Al-Ittijahat al-Fikriyya wal Siyasiyya fi al-Watan al-'Arabi*, 31.

2. Issawi, *The Arab World's Legacy*, 91.

3. Ibid., 85.

4. Interestingly, Morocco's maintenance of a semblance of liberalism and participatory politics has not by any means improved the quality of governance, nor has it created a higher standard of living than those of Arab countries in the East that parted from liberal politics in the 1950s. In Morocco, literacy rates, per capita income, and mass media exposure are below the levels in Egypt, Iraq, and Syria.

5. Badeau, "The Clashing Paths to Modernization," 3.

6. Ibid.

7. Ibid.

8. Britain, fearing that the Iraqi coup would give Nazi Germany access to the Middle East, reacted immediately. The British army quelled the rebellion and reoccupied Iraq until 1945, when it reinstalled 'Abdul Ilah and Nuri al-Sa'id.

9. Yapp, *The Near East since the First World War*, 53.

10. Ibid., 56.

11. Al-Jabiri, "Al-Haraka al-Salafiyya wal Jama'at al-Diniyya al-Mu'asira fi al-Maghrib" (The Salafi movement and contemporary religious associations in Morocco), in *Al-Harakat al-Islamiyya al-Mu'asira fi al-Watan al-'Arabi*, 190.

12. Ibid., 212.

13. Mark A. Tessler et al., "Kingdom of Morocco," in Long and Reich, eds., *The Government and Politics of the Middle East and North Africa*, 384.

14. Ibid.

15. For useful insights on this matter, see Torrey and Devlin, "Arab Socialism," 47.

16. Sayyid, *Al-Ruh Al-Thawriyya fi al-Mithaq*, 13.

17. For more on the effects of Western penetration of Arab lands, especially North Africa, see Findlay, *The Arab World*, 26–33.

18. Torrey and Devlin, "Arab Socialism," 47.

19. Dam, *The Struggle for Power in Syria*, 34–47.

20. Findlay, *The Arab World*, 91.

21. Allan, *Libya*, 237.

22. There is strong evidence implicating the United States, Britain, and Iran in instigating Kurdish belligerency in northern Iraq. See, for example, Khashan and Nehme, "The Making of Stalled National Movements," 126–36.

23. Naturally, the Iraqi leader's developmental policies were aided by his formal assumption of his country's key political position a year earlier, and by the simultaneous boom in oil prices.

24. In Allan, *Libya,* 254.

25. Findlay, *The Arab World,* 92.

26. Ibid., 94.

27. Ibid.

28. *Third Development Plan* (Saudi Arabia), 47.

29. Al-Farsy, *Modernity and Tradition,* 211.

30. Ibid.

31. Ibid., 177.

32. There are millions of expatriate workers and dependents living in Saudi Arabia. In fact, foreigners are clearly more visible in major Saudi urban centers than natives.

33. Al-Farsy, *Modernity and Tradition,* 211.

34. Kanovsky, *The Economy of Saudi Arabia,* 23.

35. Zanoyan, "After the Oil Boom," 2.

36. Ibid.

37. Kanovsky, *The Economy of Saudi Arabia,* 39.

38. Cited in Kanovsky, *The Economy of Saudi Arabia,* 38.

39. Tuomo Melasuo, "Maghreb Conflicts, Socioeconomic Crisis and Unity," in Raffer and Salih, eds., *The Least Developed and the Oil-Rich Arab Countries,* 50.

40. Tessler et al., "Kingdom of Morocco," 384.

41. Draft of the Charter, 35.

42. Sadat had motives other than economic for introducing a facade of democracy. He needed a cloak of legitimacy to sanction his preparations for signing a peace accord with Israel, and he desired to weaken the leftist and Nasserite forces of opposition to his regime.

43. Hudson, "After the Gulf War," 409.

44. Ibid., 420.

45. *The Middle East and North Africa 1997,* 387.

46. Satirical Jordanians like to call the kingdom's House of Representatives al-Majlis al-'Asha'iri (Clannish House), because many voters—namely the bedouins—tend to vote for someone with whom they identify through tribe or clan.

47. Robert L. Rothstein, "Democracy in the Third World: Definitional Dilemmas," in Garnham and Tessler, eds., *Democracy, War, and Peace in the Middle East,* 77.

48. For more on this, see Khashan, "The New Arab Cold War," 162–64.

49. Al-Rasheed, "God, the King and the Nation," 370.

50. Zanoyan, "After the Oil Boom," 2.

51. Harik, "Rethinking Civil Society," 45.

52. Ibid., 47.

53. Hamadi, *Tajdid al-Hadiih 'an al-Qawmiyya al-'Arabiyya wal Wihda,* 24.

54. Ibid., 26.

55. Elbaki Hermassi and Dirk Vandewalle, "The Second Stage of State Building," in Zartman and Habeeb, eds., *Polity and Society in Contemporary North Africa,* 22.

56. Egypt and Syria's success in coordinating a simultaneous attack against Israeli positions along the Suez Canal and the Golan Heights during the 1973 October War, which is often heralded as a unique feat of Arab cooperation, faltered two or three days after the beginning of military operations. The Syrian command complained that they took the brunt of Israel's counterattack, while the scope of operations in Sinai degraded to skirmishes.

57. See Fawzi, *Asrar Sukut Ta'irat al-Mushir.*

58. Poor data collection mechanisms, weak public cooperation with surveying agencies, and governments wishing to impress observers with their domestic accomplishments coalesce to produce unrealistic figures.

6. Trauma in the Gulf

1. Britain signed treaties with Bahrain, Trucial Tribalities, Kuwait, Najd, and Qatar between 1880 and 1916.

2. Al-Jaber al-Sabbah, "The Gulf Cooperation Council and the Security of the Gulf," 18.

3. Unlike other Gulf states, Saudi Arabia was lukewarm to the idea of foreign involvement in the Gulf, namely U.S. and Soviet competition, following the latter's invasion of Afghanistan. Saudi Arabia convinced the other five states to sign the charter in anticipation of President Ronald Reagan's decision to establish the Rapid Deployment Force to preserve peace in the Gulf and the Horn of Africa.

4. Al-Jaber al-Sabbah, "The Gulf Cooperation Council and the Security of the Gulf," 18.

5. The list of differences includes border disputes (Qatar vs. Saudi Arabia and Bahrain respectively), domestic political style (Saudi Arabia's reserved antipathy to Kuwait's political liberalism), and foreign policy conduct (the kingdom's displeasure with Qatari and Omani efforts to speed up the normalization of their relations with Israel).

6. Instead of concerted military effort to provide for their collective defense, the GCC states concentrated, at the initiative of Saudi Arabia, on matters of internal security especially after the discovery of a plot supported by Iran against the Bahraini government in December 1981. For more on this and other matters of internal security cooperation, see Ursula Braun, "The Gulf Cooperation Council," in Maull and Pick, eds., *The Gulf War,* 90–102.

7. Pelletiere, *The Iran-Iraq War,* 24.

8. Renfrew, "Who Started the War," 98.

9. Ibid., 103.

10. Philip Robins, "Iraq in the Gulf War: Objectives, Strategies and Problems," in Maull and Pick, eds., *The Gulf War,* 46–7.

11. Hiro, *The Longest War,* 75.

12. Heikal, *Harb al-Khalij,* 233.

13. Cordesman, *The Iran-Iraq War and Western Security,* 9.

14. The strength of the religious orientation of the Iranian revolution should not

detract us from the essentially nationalistic perspectives of Iran's domestic and foreign policy. The Islamic order in Iran continues to uphold the shah's approach in dealing with Iran's numerous ethnic minorities, that is, denying them the right of self-determination. In regional affairs, Iran is as persistent as ever in carving out for itself a prominent political role in the Middle East.

15. Issues with regard to the Palestine question, peace with Israel, accusations of intervention in intrastate affairs, and numerous border disputes had already poisoned the entire Arab political environment.

16. Pelletiere, *The Iran-Iraq War,* 41.

17. Al-Khafaji, "Al-Iqtisad al-'Iraqi ba'd al-Harb ma' Iran," 189–92.

18. Record, *Hollow Victory,* 20.

19. Patrick Clawson, "Iraq's Economy and International Sanctions," in Baram and Rubin, eds., *Iraq's Road to War,* 71.

20. Ibid., 71–73.

21. Several oil price reductions in 1990 shocked the leaders of Iraq, prompting them to speak out about a conspiracy to strangulate their country's emaciated economy. For details, see Shuqayr, "Azmat al-Khalij."

22. *Nusus al-Harb,* 19.

23. Heikal, *Harb al-Khalij,* 47–48.

24. Ibid., 255.

25. Record, *Hollow Victory,* 21.

26. In *Nusus al-Harb,* 17.

27. Ibid.

28. Heikal, *Harb al-Khalij,* 235.

29. Ibid., 236.

30. Rishani, "Al-Siyasa al-Kharijiyya al-Amirikiyya," 99.

31. Hybel, *Power over Rationality,* 33.

32. See Heikal, *Harb al-Khalij,* 377.

33. Primakov, *Muhimmat fi Baghdad,* 85.

34. Ibid., 381.

35. 'Assasa, *Watha'iq Harb al-Khalij,* 21.

36. Ibid., 57.

37. Eilts, "The Persian Gulf Crisis," 9.

38. 'Assasa, *Watha'iq Harb al-Khalij,* 76.

39. Hallaj, "U.S. Gulf Policy," 2.

40. For a good analysis of U.S. foreign policy toward the end of the 1980s, see Maynes, "America's Third World Hang-Ups," 117–40.

41. Maqdisi, *Harb al-Khalij,* 27.

42. Yetiv, *The Persian Gulf Crisis,* 3.

43. Ibid.

44. Ibid., 12.

45. Sciolino, *The Outlaw State,* 185.

46. Ibid., 185–86.

47. Mazarr et al., *Desert Storm*, 34.

48. Munro, *An Arabian Affair*, 14.

49. Luttwak, "The Self-Importance of Saddam," 13–14.

50. Ibid., 15.

51. *Sunday Times*, 26 August 1990.

52. Ibid.

53. Quandt, "The Middle East on the Brink," 13.

54. In Vaux, *Ethics and the Gulf War*, 159.

55. Al-Majid, *Ihtilal al-Kuwait*, 87.

56. Al-Mish'an, *Al-'Udwan al-'Iraqi wal Athar al-Nafsiyya 'ala al-Muwatin al-Kuwaiti*, 26.

57. Ibid.

58. Ibid., 107.

59. Bin Sultan, *Desert Warrior*, 18.

60. Ibid., 155.

61. Ibid., 159.

62. Ibid., 160.

63. The Arab states failed to condemn U.S. and British continuous raids against Iraq. Instead, they repeated the cliché that Iraq must comply with all U.N. resolutions, which induced the United States to applaud the Arab League's call. The communiqué issued at the end of the council of the Arab ministers of foreign affairs held in Cairo on 24 January 1999 expressed regret only about the Anglo-American missile and air strikes against scores of Iraqi targets. In fact, many anti-Iraq air attacks were launched from bases in Saudi Arabia and Kuwait.

7. The Case for Islamic Revival

1. Halpern, *The Politics of Social Change*, 22.

2. Sura *Al-Anfal*, verse 60.

3. This view is ably explained by Hallaq, *Al-Jihad wal Taghyir*.

4. Ibid., 27.

5. Sura *Al-Hajj*, verses 39–40.

6. See, for example, article 10 of the constitution of the Islamic state as proposed by Hizb al-Tahrir al-Islami in *Al-wa'y*, no. 99, July 1995, p. 2.

7. One may argue that radical Muslim groups were not the first to voice resentment of Western values, since traditional Muslims and Arab nationalists had done so earlier. The distinguishing difference between the two types of opposition to the West lies in that radical Muslims see themselves on an unavoidable collision course with the West and genuinely believe in the inherent superiority of Islamic doctrines.

8. *Hukm al-Islam fi al-Qawmiyya wa al-Wataniyya*, 19–21.

9. Sura *Al-'Imran*, verse 103.

10. Al-Faruqi, "Nazariyyat al-Dawla al-Islamiyya wa al-Waqi' al-Mu'asir," 83–86.

11. *Hukm al-Islam fi al-Qawmiyya wal Wataniyya*, 10–11.

12. Sura *Al-Nisa'*, verses 59–61.

13. See, for example, Voll and Esposito, "Islam's Democratic Essence," 3–11.

14. Zallum, *Al-Dimuqratiyya Nizam Kufr*, 5–7. The fragility of this assertion is evident and does not require elaboration as there is a litany of documentation to show the contrary. Although Muslim rulers governed in the name of shari'a, many of them had systematically committed widespread violations of public trust and basic human rights.

15. For a discussion of Muslim grievances against the West, see Khashan, "The New World Order and the Tempo of Militant Islam," 5–24.

16. Sura *Al-'Imran*, verse 118.

17. Jum'ah, *Allah Aw al-Damar*, 5.

18. Ibid., 6.

19. Ibid., 6–7.

20. Ibid., 95.

21. Khashan, "The New World Order and the Tempo of Militant Islam," 12.

22. Dekmejian, *Fundamentalism in the Arab World*, 22.

23. Sayyam, *Al-'Unf wal Khitab al-Dini fi Misr*, 36–38.

24. This does not mean that Islam as a belief system was contested. In fact, religion continued to dominate personal matters and social activities throughout Arab lands. However, the idea of an all-encompassing Islamic state lost its luster and was replaced by pan-Arabism.

25. Khashan, "The New World Order and the Tempo of Militant Islam," 13.

26. See U.S. Department of State, Office of the Coordinator for Counterterrorism, "1995 Patterns of Global Terrorism," April 1996, 1.

27. Esposito, *The Islamic Threat: Myth or Reality?* 19.

28. Pipes, *In the Path of God*, 83.

29. Huntington, "The Clash of Civilizations?" 40.

30. In an effort to consolidate his still-tenuous presidency, Sadat, who needed to contain the Nasserite and leftist challenges, helped revive the long-subdued religious groups in order to countervail the strength of the power elite created by the reign of Nasser.

31. Ansari, "Sectarian Conflict in Egypt and the Political Expediency of Religion," 400-401.

32. Zoubir, "Algerian Islamists' Conception of Democracy," 73–74.

33. Ibid.

34. Abdel Moula, "The 'Fundamentalist' Agenda for Human Rights," 7.

35. Ibid., 8.

36. Ibid., 10–14.

37. Clark, "Islamic Social Welfare Organizations in Cairo," 11.

38. Halpern, *The Politics of Social Change*, 14.

39. Kramer, *Arab Awakening and Islamic Revival*, 142.

40. Ibid., 260.

41. Ibid., 133. In communicating with his wife, Malcolm Kerr expressed worries

about an attempt on his life by Lebanese Phalangists but never made any reference to the Islamists. These thoughts, as well as those of his wife, make Kramer's assertions sound propagandist, despite an otherwise excellently written book. See Kerr, *Come with Me from Lebanon.*

42. Other leading Western scholars such as John Voll, Hrair Dekmajian, and James Piscatori wrote on Islamic fundamentalism and reached conclusions that concur with those of John Esposito.

43. Esposito, *The Islamic Threat,* 4–5.

44. Ibid., 211.

45. Al-Sayyid, "Al-Islam al-Siyasi wal Anzima al-'Arabiyya," 89.

46. Ibid., 90–91.

47. Abu 'Amru, *Al-Haraka al-Islamiyya fi al-Diffa al-Gharbiyya wa Qita' Ghazza,* 11.

48. Salih, *Al-Nahda,* 14.

49. Sura *Al-A'raf,* verse 179.

50. Ibid., 90–93.

51. Rahman, *Islam,* 212.

52. Abu 'Amru, *Al-Haraka al-Islamiyya fi al-Diffa al-Gharbiyya wa Qita' Ghazza,* 30–31.

53. Ibid., 133.

54. Khashan, "The Developmental Programs of Islamic Fundamentalist Groups in Lebanon as a Source of Popular Legitimation," 52.

55. Joffe, "Democracy, Islam and the Culture of Modernism," 134.

56. Khurshid Ahmad, "Islamic Resurgence: Challenges, Directions, and Future Perspectives," in Abu-Rabi, ed., *Islamic Resurgence,* 53.

8. The Arab Impasse

1. Murad, *Al-Waqi' al-'Arabi,* 8.

2. Ibid., 9.

3. Al-Bakkar, *Al-Ma'zaq,* 40.

4. Karanjia, *Arab Dawn,* 64.

5. Ibid., 78.

6. Hafiz, *'Arab bila Ghadab,* 7–8.

7. Ibrahim, *Al-Khuruj min Zuqaq al-Tarikh,* 109.

8. John P. Entelis, "Civil Society and the Authoritarian Temptation in Algerian Politics: Islamic Democracy vs. the Centralized State," in Norton, ed., *Civil Society in the Middle East,* 45–46.

9. 'Id, *Azmat al-Tanwir,* 9.

10. Ibid., 11.

11. Ibid., 12.

12. Al-Bakkar, *Al-Ma'zaq,* 39.

13. In Al-Jabiri, "Al-Haraka al-Salafiyya wal Jama'at al-Diniyya al-Mu'asira fi al-Maghrib," in *Al-Harakat al-Islamiyya al-Mu'asira fi al-Watan,* 212.

14. Al-Hamash, *Al-Nizam al-Iqlimi al-'Arabi*, 88.

15. Jamil, *Huquq al-Insan fi al-Watan al-'Arabi*, 168.

16. *Huquq al-Insan fi al-Khalij al-'Arabi*, 5.

17. Hafiz, *'Arab bila Ghadab*, 7–8.

18. Ibid.

19. Ibid., 9.

20. Al-Hafiz, *Alla 'Aqlaniyya fi al-Siyasa*, 5.

21. Ibid., 6.

22. Kafafi, *Al-Hadara al-'Arabiyya*, 11.

23. Al-Rifa'i, *Hadarat al-Watan al-'Arabi al-Kabir fi al-'Usur al-Qadima*, 62–85.

24. Ibid., 87–103.

25. Sura *Gafir*, verse 60.

26. Al-Sayih, *Adwa' 'ala al-Hadara al-Islamiyya*, 39.

27. Ibid., 195.

28. (Sura *Al-Baqarah*, verse 1).

9. Negotiating the Future

1. For more on Arab and Muslim phobias about the trappings of Western notions such as civil society and human rights, see Fuller and Lesser, *A Sense of Siege*, 38.

2. A keynote speech broadcast by the *CNN World Report* on 19 June 1998.

3. U.N. sanctions against Iraq and Libya reveal the increasing weakness and isolation of Arabs in the new world order. The reemergence of Iran as a powerful regional player (especially in Persian Gulf politics), Arab helplessness in bringing about a dignified solution to the conflict with Israel, Eritrea's belligerency toward Yemen and Sudan, Sudan's embroilment in an unwinnable war in its southern provinces, and Turkish incursions inside Iraqi territory and its provocative water policy in relation to Syria and Iraq confirm the shift in the balance of power to non-Arab regional players.

4. Such as identifying common economic interests, forming inclusive bonds of individual associations, engagement in intellectual pursuits, and development of the idea of anonymous citizenship.

5. Mansfield, *The Arab World*, 504.

6. Ibid., 505.

7. Ibid.

8. Zurayk, "Ghiyab Dawlat al-'Aql," in *al-A'mal al-Fikriyya al-'Amma lil Doktor Costantine Aurayk*, 61.

9. For a good account of fruitless Arab efforts at cooperation, see Maddy-Weitzman, *The Crystallization of the Arab State System 1945–1954*, 179–80.

10. Sayigh, *The Arab Economy*, 141–62.

11. Ibid., 121.

12. *Roz al-Yusuf* (Cairo), no. 3621, 3 November 1997.

13. Bashshur, "Mustaqbal al-Harakat al-Qawmiyya al-'Arabiyya," 8–9.

14. This issue is discussed in detail by al-Jabiri, *Mas'alat al-Hawiyya*, 78.

15. *Nida' al-Watan* (Beirut), 4 November 1997.

16. Ibid.

17. Maynes, "The Middle East in the Twenty-First Century," 11.

18. For further elaboration on the demerits of secularism in the context of Arab politics, see Al-Sulh, "Hisaruna al-Dati Fataka bina wal Hal bi Nizam Thaqafi Awwalan."

Selected Bibliography

Abboushi, W. F. *The Angry Arabs*. Philadelphia: Westminster Press, 1974.

'Abd, Karim. *Al-Dawla Ghayr al-Muthaqqafa* (The uncultured state). Brussels: al-Markaz al-'Arabi lil Funun wa al-Adab, 1995.

Abdel Moula, Adam M. "The Fundamentalist Agenda for Human Rights: The Sudan and Algeria." *Arab Studies Quarterly* 18, no. 1 (1996): 1–28.

Abdelnasser, Walid M. *The Islamic Movement in Egypt: Perceptions of International Relations, 1967–81*. London: Kegan Paul International, 1994.

'Abdul Sayyid, H. *Al-Ruh al-Thawriyya fi al-Mithaq* (The revolutionary spirit of the charter). Cairo: al-Dar al-Qawmiyya lil Tiba'a wal Nashr, n.d.

Abu 'Amru, Ziad. *Al-Haraka al-Islamiyya fi al-Diffa al-Gharbiyya wa Qita' Ghazza* (The Islamic movement in the West Bank and Gaza Strip). Acre, Israel: Dar al-Aswar, 1989.

Abu Izzeddin, Nejla M. *Nasser of the Arabs: An Arab Assessment*. London: Third World Centre for Research and Publishing, 1981.

Ajami, Fouad. *The Arab Predicament: Arab Political Thought and Practice since 1967*. Cambridge: Cambridge University Press, 1981.

———. "The Sorrows of Egypt." *Foreign Affairs* 74, no. 5 (1995): 72–88.

Alani, Mustafa M. *Operation Vantage: British Military Intervention in Kuwait 1961*. Surbiton, England: Laam, 1990.

Allan, J. A. *Libya: The Experience of Oil*. London: Croom Helm, 1981.

Alpher, Joseph, ed. *Nationalism and Modernity: A Mediterranean Perspective*. New York: Praeger, 1986.

Al-A'mal al-Fikriyya al-'Amma lil Doktor Costantine Zurayk (The intellectual works of Costantine Zurayk), vol. 4. Beirut: Markaz Dirasat al-Wihda al-'Arabiyya, 1994.

Al-A'mal al-Qawmiyya li Sati' al-Husry (The nationalistic works of Sati' al-Husry). Beirut: Markaz Dirasat al-Wihda al-'Arabiyya, 1985.

Anderson, Roy R., et al. *Politics and Change in the Middle East: Sources of Conflict and Accommodation*. Englewood Cliffs, N.J.: Prentice-Hall, 1993.

Ansari, Hamied. "Sectarian Conflict in Egypt and the Political Expediency of Religion." *Middle East Journal* 38, no. 3 (1984): 397–418.

Antonius, George. *The Arab Awakening*. Beirut: Khayyat's College Book Cooperative, 1938.

Armstrong, John A. *Nations before Nationalism*. Chapel Hill: University of North Carolina Press, 1982.

'Assasa, Sami. *Watha'iq Harb al-Khalij* (The Gulf War's documents). Beirut: Maktabat Bisan, 1994.

Al-Ayubi, Mahmud N. *Ihdharu al-Sulh Ma' al-Yahud* (Beware of peace with the Jews). Privately printed, 1995.

Badeau, John S. "The Clashing Paths to Modernization." *Journal of International Affairs* 19, no. 1 (1965): 1–7.

Al-Bakkar, 'Abdul Hadi. *Al-Ma'zaq: Misr wa al-'Arab al-Akharun* (The standoff: Egypt and the other Arabs). Damascus: Dar Tlas, 1987.

Al-Bakr, Bashir. *Harb al-Yaman: al-Qabila Tantasir 'la al-Watan* (The tribe wins against the nation). Beirut: al-Mu'assasa al-'Arabiyya lil Dirasat wal Nashr, 1995.

Baram, Amatzia. "Territorial Nationalism in the Arab World." *Middle Eastern Studies* 26, no. 4 (1990): 425–48.

Baram, Amatzia, and Barry Rubin, eds. *Iraq's Road to War.* New York: St. Martin's Press, 1993.

Bashshur, Ma'n. "Mustaqbal al-Harakat al-Qawmiyya al-'Arabiyya" (The future of Arab nationalist movements). *Al-Manabir* 73 (Feb.–Mar. 1994): 4–21.

Bax, Mart, and Adrianus Koster, eds. *Power and Prayer: Religious and Political Processes in Past and Present.* Amsterdam: Vu University Press, 1993.

Beattie, Kirk J. *Egypt during the Nasser Years: Ideology, Politics, and Civil Society.* Boulder, Colo.: Westview Press, 1994.

Ben-Gurion, David. *Israel: Years of Challenge.* New York: Holt, Rinehart and Winston, 1963.

Bill, James A., and Robert Springborg. *Politics in the Middle East.* 3rd ed. London: HarperCollins, 1990.

Bin Sultan, Khaled. *Desert Warrior: A Personal View of the Gulf War by the Joint Forces Commander.* London: HarperCollins, 1995.

Bishai, Wilson B. *Islamic History of the Middle East.* Boston: Allyn and Bacon, 1968.

Al-Bitar, Nadim. *Min al-Tajzi'a ila al-Wihda* (From division to unity). Beirut: Markaz Dirasat al-Wihda al-'Arabiyya, 1986.

Bliqziz, 'Abdul Ilah. *Harb al-Khalij wa al-Nizam al-Dawli al-Jadid: al-Watan al-'Arabi ila 'Ayn?* (The Gulf War and the new world order: Where to the Arab world?). Beirut: Dar al-Tali'a, 1993.

Bloom, William. *Personal Identity and International Relations.* Cambridge: Cambridge University Press, 1990.

Blumberg, Herbert H., and Christopher C. French, eds. *The Persian Gulf War: Views from the Social and Behavioral Science.* Lanham, M.D.: University Press of America, 1994.

Boullata, Issa J. *Trends and Issues in Contemporary Arab Thought.* Albany: State University of New York, 1990.

Brass, Paul R. *Ethnicity and Nationalism: Theory and Comparison.* New Delhi: Sage Publications, 1991.

Burghat, François, and William Dowell. *The Islamic Movement in North Africa.* Austin: Center for Middle Eastern Studies of the University of Texas at Austin, 1993.

Cable, Vincent. "The Diminished Nation-State: A Study in the Loss of Economic Power." *Daedalus* 124, no. 2 (1995): 23–53.

Carmichael, Joel. *The Shaping of the Arabs: A Study in Ethnic Identity.* New York: Macmillan, 1967.

Carter, Stephen L. *The Culture of Disbelief: How American Law and Politics Trivialize Religious Devotion.* New York: Basic Books, 1993.

Castelli, Jim. *A Plea for Common Sense: Resolving the Clash between Religion and Politics.* San Francisco: Harper and Row, 1988.

Cheriat, Boutheina. "The Resilience of Algerian Populism." *Middle East Report* 22, no. 1 (1992): 9–14.

Clark, Janine A. "Islamic Social Welfare Organizations in Cairo: Islamization from Below?" *Arab Studies Quarterly* 17, no. 4 (1995): 11–28.

Cleveland, William L. *A History of the Modern Middle East.* Boulder, Colo.: Westview Press, 1994.

Cohen, Raymond. "Negotiations across the Golan Heights: Culture Gets in the Way." *Middle East Quarterly* 1, no. 3 (1994): 45–53.

Cordesman, Anthony H. *The Iran-Iraq War and Western Security.* London: Royal United Services Institute for Defence Studies, 1987.

Dam, Nikolaos Van. *The Struggle for Power in Syria: Politics and Society under Asad and the Ba"th Party.* London: I. B. Tauris, 1996.

Davenport, John. *An Apology for Mohammad and the Koran.* London: Privately printed, n.d.

Dekmejian, R. Hrair. *Egypt under Nasir: A Study in Political Dynamics.* Albany: State University of New York Press, 1971.

———. *Islam in Revolution: Fundamentalism in the Arab World.* 2nd ed. Syracuse: Syracuse University Press, 1995.

Dessouki, Ali E., ed. *Islamic Resurgence in the Arab World.* New York: Praeger, 1982.

Deutsch, Karl W. *Nationalism and Social Communication: An Inquiry into the Foundations of Nationality.* 2nd ed. Cambridge: MIT Press, 1966.

Deutsch, Karl W., and William J. Foltz, eds. *Nation-Building.* New York: Atherton Press, 1963.

Dirasat fi al-Qawmiyya al-'Arabiyya wa al-Wihda (Studies on Arab nationalism and unity). Beirut: Markaz Dirasat al-Wihda al-'Arabiyya, 1984.

Draft of the Charter. Cairo: Information Department, 21 May 1962.

Eban, Abba. *My Country: The Story of Modern Israel.* New York: Random House, 1972.

Eilts, Hermann F. "The Persian Gulf Crisis: Perspectives and Prospects." *Middle East Journal* 45, no. 1 (1991): 7–22.

Emerson, Rupert. *From Empire to Nation: The Rise to Self-Assertion of Asian and African Peoples.* Cambridge: Harvard University Press, 1960.

Esposito, John, ed. *Voices of Resurgent Islam.* New York: Oxford University Press, 1983.

————. *The Islamic Threat: Myth or Reality?* New York: Oxford University Press, 1992.

Fadil, Salim. *Qadisyyat Saddam: Tabi'at al-Sira' wa Afaq al-Mustaqbal* (Saddam's Qadisiyya and future horizons). Baghdad: Dar al-Hurriyya lil Tiba'a, 1981.

Faraj, Muhammad A. *Al-Farida al-Gha'iba* (The forgotten obligation). N.p., n.d.

Al-Farsy, Fouad. *Modernity and Tradition: The Saudi Equation.* London: Kegan Paul International, 1990.

Al-Faruqi, Suha. "Nazariyyat al-Dawla al-Islamiyya wa al-Waqi' al Mu'asir" (Theories of the Islamic state and the contemporary reality). *Qira'at Siyasiyya* 5, no. 1 (1995): 83–98.

Fawzi, Muhammad. *Asrar Sukut Ta'irat al-Mushir* (The secrets of the crash of the marshal's plane). Cairo: Dar al-Hadaf lil Nashr bi al-Qahira, 1992.

Findlay, Allan M. *The Arab World.* London: Routledge, 1994.

Fuller, Graham E., and Ian O. Lesser. *A Sense of Siege: The Geopolitics of Islam and the West.* Boulder, Colo.: Westview Press, 1995.

Garnham, David, and Mark Tessler, eds. *Democracy, War, and Peace in the Middle East.* Bloomington: Indiana University Press, 1995.

Gellner, Ernest. *Nations and Nationalism.* Ithaca: Cornell University Press, 1983.

Gellner, Ernest, and Charles Micaud, eds. *Arabs and Berbers: From Tribe to Nation in North Africa.* Lexington, Mass.: Lexington Books, 1972.

Gershoni, Israel, and James P. Jankowski. *Egypt, Islam and the Arabs: The Search for Egyptian Nationhood 1900–1930.* Oxford: Oxford University Press, 1986.

Gilmour, David. *Dispossessed: The Ordeal of the Palestinians 1917–1980.* London: Sidgwick and Jackson, 1980.

Glazer, Nathan, and Daniel P. Moynihan, eds. *Ethnicity: Theory and Experience.* Cambridge: Harvard University Press, 1975.

Goldberg, Ellis, et al., eds. *Rules and Rights in the Middle East: Democracy, Law, and Society.* Seattle: University of Washington Press, 1993.

Hafiz, Salahuddin. *'Arab bila Ghadab* (Arabs without anger). Beirut: Dar al-Nafa'is, 1996.

Al-Hafiz, Yasin. *Alla 'Aqlaniyya fi al-Siyasa: Naqd al-Siyasat al-'Arabiyya fi al-Marhala ma ba'd al-Nasiriyya* (Irrationality in politics: A critique of Arab politics in the post-Nasserite period). Beirut: Dar al-Tali'a lil Tiba'a wal Nashr, 1975.

Haj Hamad, Muhammad A. "Al-Mafhum al-Qur'ani lil 'Uruba wa al-Dar fi Muqabil al-Qawmiyya wa al-Watan: Muqaddimat Tahliliyya fi Fawariq al-Nasaq al-Ma'rifi wa Kayfiyyat Tawhid al-Masar al-Mustaqbali lil Shakhsiyya al-'Arabiyya" (Koranic conception of Arabism and the abode against nationalism and the homeland: Analytical introductions to differences in the patterns of knowledge and ways of integrating the future direction of the Arab character). *Qira'at Siyasiyya* 5, no. 1 (1995): 9–25.

Hall, Harvey P., ed. *The Evolution of Public Responsibility in the Middle East.* Washington, D.C.: Middle East Institute, 1955.

Hallaj, Muhammad. "U.S. Gulf Policy: Going the Extra Mile for War." *Arab Studies Quarterly* 13, nos. 1–2 (1991): 1–10.

Hallaq, 'Abdullah. *Al-Jihad wal Taghyir* (Holy war and change). Beirut: al-Dar al-Islamiyya, 1985.

Hallaq, Hassan. *Dawr al-Yahud wa al-Qiwa al-Dawliyya fi Khal' al-Sultan 'Abdul Hamid al-Thani 'An al-'Arsh: 1908–1909* (The role of Jews and international powers in dethroning Sultan 'Abdul Hamid al-Thani: 1908–1909). Beirut: al-Mahrusa lil Tiba'a wal Nashr, 1993.

Halliday, Fred, and Hamza Alavi, eds. *Statehood and Ideology in the Middle East and Pakistan.* New York: Monthly Review Press, 1988.

Halpern, Manfred. *The Politics of Social Change in the Middle East and North Africa.* Princeton: Princeton University Press, 1963.

Hamadi, Sa'dun. *Tajdid al-Hadith 'An al-Qawmiyya al-'Arabiyya wa al-Wihda* (Resuming talk about Arab nationalism and unity). Beirut: Markaz Dirasat al-Wihda al-'Arabiyya, 1986.

Al-Hamash, Munir. *Al-Nizam al-Iqlimi al-'Arabi* (The Arab regional order). Damascus: Dar al-Mustaqbal, 1995.

Hamdan, Hamdan. *Al-Khalij Baynana: Qatrat Naft bi Aatrati Dam* (The Gulf between us: A drop of oil for a drop of blood). Beirut: Bisan lil Nashr, 1993.

Haqqi, S. A. H., ed. *West Asia since Camp David.* Delhi: Mittal Publications, 1988.

Al-Harakat al-Islamiyya al-Mu'asira fi al-Watan al-'Arabi (The contemporary Islamic movements in the Arab homeland). Beirut: Markaz Dirasat al-Wihda al-'Arabiyya, 1987.

Harik, Iliya. "Rethinking Civil Society: Pluralism in the Arab World." *Journal of Democracy* 5, no. 3 (1994): 43–56.

Hasib, Khair al-Din, ed. *Mustaqbal al-Umma al-'Arabiyya: al-Tahaddiyat wa al-Khayarat* (The future of the Arab nation: The challenges and the options). Beirut: Markaz Dirasat al-Wihda al-'Arabiyya, 1988.

Heikal, Mohamed. *Harb al-Khalij: Awham al-Quwwa wa al-Nasr* (The Gulf War: Illusions of might and victory). Cairo: Markaz al-Ahram lil Tarjama wal Nashr, 1992.

———. *Azmat al-'Arab wa Mustaqbaluhum* (The crisis of the Arabs and their future). Cairo: Dar al-Shuruq, 1995.

———. *Bab Misr ila al-Qarn al-Wahid wa al-'ishrin* (Egypt's gate to the twenty-first century). Cairo: Dar al-Shuruq, 1995.

———. *Secret Channels: The Inside Story of Arab-Israeli Peace Negotiations.* London: HarperCollins, 1996.

Heywood, Andrew. *Political Ideologies: An Introduction.* New York: St. Martin's Press, 1992.

Hiro, Dilip. *Holy Wars: The Rise of Islamic Fundamentalism.* New York: Routledge, 1989.

———. *The Longest War: The Iran-Iraq Military Conflict.* London: Grafton Books, 1989.

———. *Desert Shield to Desert Storm: The Second Gulf War.* London: HarperCollins, 1992.

Hitti, Philip K. *History of the Arabs: From the Earliest Times to the Present.* 10th ed. London: Macmillan, 1970.

Hoffe, E. G. H. "Relations between the Middle East and the West." *Middle East Journal* 48, no. 2 (1994): 250–67.

Hopwood, Derek. *Egypt: Politics and Society 1945–1981.* London: George Allen and Unwin, 1982.

Hourani, Albert. *A History of the Arab Peoples.* London: Faber and Faber, 1991.

Hudson, Michael C. "After the Gulf War: Prospects for Democratization in the Arab World." *Middle East Journal* 45, no. 3 (1991): 407–26.

Hukm al-Islam fi al-Qawmiyya wa al-Wataniyya (The ruling of Islam on nationalism and patriotism). Hizb al-Tahrir al-Islami, a series on media awareness, no. 2, 1995.

Huntington, Samuel P. "The Clash of Civilizations?" *Foreign Affairs* 72, no. 3 (1993): 22–49.

Huquq al-Insan fi al-Khalij al-'Arabi (Human rights in the Arabian Gulf). Al-Lajna al-Dawliyya li Huquq al-Insan fi al-Khalij wa al-Jazira al-'Arabiyya, 1994.

Hybel, Alex R. *Power over Rationality: The Bush Administration and the Gulf Crisis.* Albany: State University of New York, 1993.

Ibrahim, Hasanyn Tawfiq. "Azmat al-Khalij al-Thaniya wa al-Amn al-Qawmi al-'Arabi: Qadaya wa Tasa'ulat hawl al-Mustaqbal" (The second Gulf crisis and Arab national security: Issues and concerns about the future). *Shu'un 'Arabiyya* 67 (Sept. 1991): 29–50.

Ibrahim, Sa'd al-Din. *Al-Khuruj min Zuqaq al-Tarikh* (Exiting the narrow lane of history). Safat, Kuwait: Dar Su'ad al-Sabbah, 1992.

'Id 'Abdul Razzaq. *Azmat al-Tanwir: Shar'anat al-Fawat al-Hadari* (The crisis of enlightenment: The legitimization of civilizational backwardness). Damascus: al-Ahali lil Tiba'a wal Nashr wal Tawzi', 1997.

Iskandar, Marwan. *Ghuyum fawq al-Kuwait* (Clouds over Kuwait), translated by Mahmud Zayid. Beirut: Sharikat al-Matbu'at lil Tawzi' wal Nashr, 1991.

Ismael, Tareq Y., and Jacqueline S. Ismael. *Government and Politics in Islam.* New York: St. Martin's Press, 1985.

Issawi, Charles. *The Arab World's Legacy.* Princeton, N.J.: Darwin Press, 1981.

Al-Jabiri, Muhammad 'A. *Takwin al-'Aql al-'Arabi* (The formation of the Arab mind). Beirut: Dar al-Tali'a lil Tiba'a wal Nashr, 1984.

———. *Bunyat al-'Aql al-'Arabi* (The making of the Arab mind). Beirut: Markaz Dirasat al-Wihda al-'Arabiyya, 1986.

———. *Ishkaliat al-Fikr al-'Arabi al-Mu'asir* (The problems of Arab contemporary thought). Beirut: Markaz Dirasat al-Wihda al-'Arabiyya, 1989.

———. *Wujhat Nazar: Nahw I'adat Bina' Qadaya al-Fikr al-'Arabi al-Mu'asir* (Viewpoint: Toward reconstructing the issues of Arab contemporary thought). Beirut: Markaz Dirasat al-Wihda al-'Arabiyya, 1992.

———. *Al-Dimuqratiyya wa Huquq al-Insan* (Democracy and human rights). Beirut: Markaz Dirasat al-Wihda al-'Arabiyya, 1994.

———. *Mas'alat al-Hawiyya: al-'Uruba wa al-Islam wa al-Gharb* (The issue of identity: Arabism, Islam, and the West). Beirut: Markaz Dirasat al-Wihda al-'Arabiyya, series on issues of Arab thought, no. 3, 1995.

Jamil, Husayn. *Huquq al-Insan fi al-Watan al-'Arabi* (Human rights in the Arab homeland). Beirut: Markaz Dirasat al-Wihda al-'Arabiyya, 1986.

Joffe, George. "Democracy, Islam and the Culture of Modernism." *Democratization* 4, no. 3 (1997): 133–51.

Johnston, R. J., et al. *Nationalism, Self-Determination and Political Geography.* London: Croom Helm, 1988.

Al-Juhmani, Khalil. *Al-Masir al-'Arabi min 'Am 1990 ila 'Am 2030: 'Ard Waqi'iwa Nazra Mustaqbaliyya* (The fate of the Arabs from 1990 until 2030: A realistic review and a future outlook). Damascus, Dar al-Mustaqbal, 1993.

Jum'ah, Sa'd. *Allah Aw al-Damar* (God, or destruction). Beirut: Dar al-Katib al-'Arabi, n.d.

Kafafi, Muhammad 'Abdul Salam. *Al-Hadara al-'Arabiyya: Taba'uha wa Muqadimatuha al-'Ama* (Arab civilization: Its character and general constituents). Beirut: Dar al-Nahda al-'Arabiyya, nd.

Kamenka, Eugene, ed. *Nationalism: The Nature and Evolution of an Idea.* New York: St. Martin's Press, 1976.

Kanovsky, Eliyahu. *The Economy of Saudi Arabia: Troubled Present, Grim Future.* Washington, D.C.: Washington Institute for Near East Policy, Policy Paper No. 38, 1994.

Karanjia, R. K. *Arab Dawn.* Bombay: Jaico Publishing House, 1958.

Katibah, H. I. *The New Spirit in Arab Lands.* New York: Privately printed, 1940.

Kedourie, Elie. *Nationalism.* 2nd ed. London: Hutchinson University Library, 1961.

Kelidar, Abbas. "The Wars of Saddam Hussein." *Middle Eastern Studies* 28, no. 4 (1992): 778–98.

Kerr, Ann Zwicker. *Come with me from Lebanon.* Syracuse: Syracuse University Press, 1994.

Khadduri, Majid. *Political Trends in the Arab World: The Role of Ideas and Ideals in Politics.* Baltimore: Johns Hopkins University Press, 1970.

Al-Khafaji 'Isam. "Al-Iqtisad al-'Iraqi ba'da al-Harb ma' Iran" (The Iraqi economy after the war with Iran). *Al-Fikr al-Istratiji al-'Arabi* 32 (Apr. 1990): 177–221.

Khalidi, Rashid, et al., eds. *The Origins of Arab Nationalism.* New York: Columbia University Press, 1991.

Khashan, Hilal. "Are the Arabs Ready for Peace with Israel?" *Middle East Quarterly* 1, no. 1 (1994): 19–28.

———. *Palestinian Resettlement in Lebanon: Behind the Debate.* Montreal: Montreal Studies on the Contemporary Arab World, Occasional Papers Series, no. 1, April 1994.

———. "The Developmental Programs of Islamic Fundamentalist Groups in Lebanon as a Source of Popular Legitimation." *Hamdard Islamicus* 18, no. 1 (1995): 51–71.

———. "The Levant: Yes to Treaties, No to Normalization." *Middle East Quarterly* 2, no. 2 (1995): 3–13

————. *Partner or Pariah? Attitudes toward Israel in Syria, Lebanon, and Jordan.* Washington, D.C.: Washington Institute for Near East Policy, Policy Paper No. 41, 1996.

————. "The New Arab Cold War." *World Affairs* 159, no. 4 (1997): 158–69.

————. "The New World Order and the Tempo of Militant Islam." *British Journal of Middle Eastern Studies* 24, no. 1 (1997): 5–24.

Khashan, Hilal, and Michel Nehme. "The Making of Stalled National Movements: Evidence from Southern Sudan and Northern Iraq." *Nationalism and Ethnic Politics* 2, no. 1 (1996): 111–40.

Al-Khawli, Lutfi. *'Arabs? Na'am wa Sharq Awsatiyyun Aidan* (Arabs? yes and Middle Easterners also). Cairo: Markaz al-Ahram lil Tarjama wal Nashr, 1994.

Khurshid, Ahmad. "Islamic Resurgence: Challenges, Directions, and Future Perspectives." In Ibrahim M. Abu-Rabi, ed., *Islamic Resurgence: Challenges, Directions and Future Perspectives.* Tampa, Fla.: World and Islam Studies Enterprise, 1994, 49–66.

Kimmerling, Baruch, and Joel S. Migdal. *Palestinians: The Making of a People.* New York: Free Press, 1993.

Kohn, Hans. *A History of Nationalism in the East,* translated by Margaret M. Green. London: George Routledge and Sons, 1929.

————. *The Idea of Nationalism: A Study in Its Origins and Background.* New York: Macmillan, 1944.

Kramer, Martin. "Arab Nationalism: Mistaken Identity." *Daedalus* 122, no. 3 (1993): 171–205.

————. *Arab Awakening and Islamic Revival.* New Brunswick, N.J.: Transaction Publishers, 1996.

Kritzeck, James, and Baily R. Winder. *The World of Islam.* London: Macmillan, 1960.

Krooth, Richard, and Minoo Moallem. *The Middle East: A Geopolitical Study of the Region in the New Global Era.* Jefferson, N.C.: McFarland, 1995.

Landau, Jacob M. *The Politics of Pan-Islam: Ideology and Organization.* Oxford: Clarendon Press, 1990.

Lewis, Bernard. *The Arabs in History.* New York: Harper and Brothers, 1958.

————. "The Roots of Muslim Rage." *Atlantic* 266, no. 3 (1990): 47–60.

Lewis, William H. "Algeria at 35: The Politics of Violence." *Washington Quarterly* 19, no. 3 (1996): 3–18.

Long, David E., and Bernard Reich, eds. *The Government and Politics of the Middle East and North Africa.* Boulder, Colo.: Westview Press, 1980.

————. *The Government and Politics of the Middle East and North Africa,* 3rd ed. Boulder, Colo.: Westview Press, 1995.

Longrigg, Stephen H. "The Economics and Politics of Oil in the Middle East." *Journal of International Affairs* 19, no. 1 (1995): 111–22.

Luttwak, Edward N. "The Self-Importance of Saddam." *Times Literary Supplement* (18 Jan. 1991): 8–16.

Maddy-Weitzman, Bruce. *The Crystallization of the Arab State System 1945–1954.* Syracuse: Syracuse University Press, 1993.

Al-Majid, Majid. *Ihtilal al-Kuwait* (The occupation of Kuwait). Damascus: Dar Daniya lil Tiba'a wal Nashr, 1990.

Mansfield, Peter. *The Arab World: A Comprehensive History.* New York: Thomas Y. Crowell, 1976.

———. *A History of the Middle East.* New York: Viking, 1991.

Maqdisi, Antun. *Harb al-Khalij: Ikhtiraq al-Jism al-'Arabi* (The Gulf War: The penetration of the Arab body). London: Riyad al-Rayyis Books, 1992.

Al-Marayati, Abid A. *The Middle East: Its Governments and Politics.* Belmont, Calif.: Duxbury Press, 1972.

Mardin, Serif, ed. *Cultural Transitions in the Middle East.* Leiden: E. G. Brill, 1994.

Marr, Phebe. "The United States, Europe, and the Middle East: An Uneasy Triangle." *Middle East Journal* 48, no. 2 (1994): 211–25.

Marr, Phebe, and William Lewis, eds. *Riding the Tiger: The Middle East Challenge after the Cold War.* Boulder, Colo.: Westview Press, 1993.

Marty, Martin E., and R. Scott Appleby, eds. *Fundamentalisms Observed,* vol. 1. Chicago: University of Chicago Press, 1991.

———. *Fundamentalisms Comprehended,* vol. 5. Chicago: University of Chicago Press, 1995.

Maull, Hanns W., and Otto Pick, eds. *The Gulf War: Regional and International Dimensions.* London: Pinter Publishers, 1989.

Maynes, Charles William. "The Middle East in the Twenty-First Century." *Middle East Journal* 52, no. 1 (1998): 9–16.

Mazarr, Michael J., et al. *Desert Storm: The Gulf War and What We Learned.* Boulder, Colo.: Westview Press, 1993.

The Middle East and North Africa 1997. 43rd ed. Edited by Simon Chapman. London: Europa Publications, 1997.

Migdal, Joel S. *Strong Societies and Weak States.* Princeton: Princeton University Press, 1988.

Al-Mish'an, 'Uwayd Sultan. *Al-'Udwan al-'Iraqi wal Athar al-Nafsiyya 'ala al-Muwatin al-Kuwaiti* (The Iraqi aggression and the psychological effects on Kuwaiti citizens). Kuwait City: Mu'assasat al-'Ilm al-Hadith, 1993.

Moen, Matthew C., and Lowell S. Gustafson, eds. *The Religious Challenge to the State.* Philadelphia: Temple University Press, 1992.

Mohi El Din, Khaled. *Memories of a Revolution: Egypt 1952.* Cairo: American University in Cairo Press, 1992.

Morton, Fried H. *The Evolution of Political Society.* New York: Random House, 1967.

Mufti, Muhammad A., and Sami Salih al-Wakil. *Huquq al-Insan fi al-Fikr al-Siyasi al-Gharbi wal Shar' al-Islami* (Human rights in Western political thought and Islamic shari'a). Beirut: Dar al-Nahda al-Islamiyya, 1992.

Muhammad, ʿAbdul ʿAlim. *Harb al-Khalij: Hasad al-Muwajaha bayn al-Tarikh wa al-Mustaqbal* (The Gulf War: The harvest of confrontation between history and the future). Beirut: Markaz al-Dirasat al-Istratijiyya wa al-Buhuth wal Tawthiq, 1993.

Munassa, Mahmud S. *Harakat al-Yaqaza al-ʿArabiyya fi al-Sharq al-Asiawi* (The movement of Arab awakening in the Asian East). Cairo: Privately printed, 1972.

Munro, Alan. *An Arabian Affair: Politics and Diplomacy behind the Gulf War.* London: Brassey's, 1996.

Murad, Hudaytha. *Al-Waqiʿ al-ʿArabi* (The Arab reality). N.p., n.d.

Al-Nabahani, Taqiy al-Din. *Al-Dawla al-Islamiyya* (The Islamic state). Reprint. Beirut: Dar al-Umma, 1994.

Nairn, Tom. "Internationalism and the Second Coming." *Daedalus* 122, no. 3 (1993): 155–71.

Al-Najjar, Mustafa ʿAbdul Qadir. *Al-Tarikh al-Siyasi li Mushkilat al-Hudud al-Sharqiyya lil Watan al-ʿArabi fi Shat al-ʿArab: Dirasa Watha'iqiyya* (A documentary study on the political history of the problem of the Arab world's eastern boundaries at shatt al-ʿArab). Basra, Iraq: Matbaʿat al-Mawani' al ʿIraqiyya, 1974.

Nasser, Gamal Abdul. *Egypt's Liberation: The Philosophy of the Revolution.* Washington, D.C.: Public Affairs Press, 1955.

Needless Deaths in the Gulf War: Civilian Casualties during the Air Campaign and Violations of the Laws of War. Edited by Virginia N. Sherry. New York: Human Rights Watch, 1991.

Norton, Richard Augustus. "The Future of Civil Society in the Middle East." *Middle East Journal* 47, no. 2 (1993): 205–16.

———, ed. *Civil Society in the Middle East,* vol. 2. Leiden: E. J. Brill, 1996.

Nuseibet, Hazem Z. *The Ideas of Arab Nationalism.* Ithaca: Cornell University Press, 1956.

Nusus al-Harb (Texts of war). Beirut: al-Mu'assasa al-ʿArabiyya lil Dirasat wal Nashr, 1992.

Nutting, Anthony. *Nasser.* New York: E. P. Dutton, 1972.

Owen, Roger. *State, Power and Politics in the Making of the Modern Middle East.* London: Routledge, 1994.

Palmer, Monte. *Dilemmas of Political Development.* Itasca, Ill.: Peacock, 1980.

Pelletiere, Stephen C. *The Iran-Iraq War: Chaos in a Vacuum.* New York: Praeger, 1992.

Perthes, Volker. "Syria's Parliamentary Elections: Remodeling Asad's Political Base." *Middle East Report* 22, no. 1 (1992): 15–18.

Pipes, Daniel. *In the Path of God: Islam and Political Power.* New York: Basic Books, 1983.

———. *The Hidden Hand: Middle East Fears of Conspiracy.* New York: St. Martin's Press, 1996.

———. *Syria beyond the Peace Process.* Washington, D.C.: Washington Institute for Near East Policy, Policy Paper No. 40, 1996.

Piscatori, James P. *Islam in a World of Nation-States.* London: Cambridge University Press, 1986.

Presthus, Robert. *The Organizational Society.* New York: Alfred A. Knopf, 1962.

Primakov, Y. M. *Anatomy of the Middle East Conflict,* translated from the Russian by H. Vladimirsky. Moscow: Nauka Publishing House, 1979.

——. *Muhimmat fi Baghdad* (Assignments in Baghdad), translated from the French. Limassol, Cyprus: Sharikat al-Ard lil Nashr al-Mahduda, 1991.

Al-Qabbani, 'Abdul 'Alim. *Mawqif Shawqi wal Shu'ara' al-Misriyyin min al-Khilafa al-'Uthmaniyya* (The position of Shawqi and Egyptian poets from the Ottoman caliphate). Alexandria: al-Hai'a al-Misriyya al-'Ama lil Kitab, 1988.

Al-Qadhafi, M. *The Green Book, Part One, The Solution of the Problem of Democracy.* Arabic and English ed. London: Martin Brian and O'Keeffe, 1976.

Quandt, Bill. "The Middle East on the Brink: Prospects for Change in the 21st Century." *Middle East Journal* 50, no. 1 (1996): 9–17.

Qutub, Muhammad. *Madhahib Fikriyya Mu'asira* (Contemporary intellectual schools). Cairo: Dar al-Shuruq, 1991.

Raffer, Kunibert, and M. A. Mohamed Salih, eds. *The Least Developed and the Oil-Rich Arab Countries: Dependence, Interdependence or Patronage?* London: St. Martin's Press, 1992.

Rahman, Fazlur. *Islam.* 2nd ed. Chicago: University of Chicago Press, 1979.

Al-Rasheed, Madawi. "God, the King and the Nation: Political Rhetoric in Saudi Arabia in the 1990s." *Middle East Journal* 50, no. 3 (1996): 359–71.

Al-Rayyis, Riyad Najib, ed. *'Awdat al-Isti'mar: Min al-Ghazw al-Thaqafi ila Harb al-Khalij* (From cultural conquest to the Gulf War). London: Riyad al-Rayyis lil Kutub wal Nashr, 1991.

Record, Jeffrey. *Hollow Victory: A Contrary View of the Gulf War.* Washington, D.C.: Brassey's, 1993.

Reich, Bernard, ed. *Arab-Israeli Conflict and Conciliation: A Documentary History.* Westport, Conn.: Praeger, 1995.

Renfrew, Nita M. "Who Started the War." *Foreign Policy* 66 (Spring 1987): 98–108.

Riad, Mahmoud. *The Struggle for Peace in the Middle East.* London: Quartet Books, 1981.

Richards, Alan. "Economic Imperatives and Political Systems." *Middle East Journal* 47, no. 2 (1993): 217–27.

Al-Rifa'i Anwar. *Hadarat al-Watan al-'Arabi al-Kabir fi al-'Usur al-Qadima* (The civilization of the great Arab world in ancient times). Beirut: Dar al-Fikr, 1972.

Rishani, Nazi. "Al-Siyasa al-Kharijiyya al-Amirikiyya ma bayn al-Matraqa al-'uruppiyya wa Azmat al-Khalij" (American foreign policy between the European hammer and the Gulf crisis). *Al-Fikr al-Istratiji* 35 (Jan. 1991): 91–101.

Rivlin, Benjamin, and Joseph S. Szyliowics, eds. *The Contemporary Middle East: Tradition and Innovation.* New York: Random House, 1964.

Roy, Olivier. *The Failure of Political Islam,* translated by Carol Volk. Cambridge: Harvard University Press, 1994.

Al-Sabbah, Salem Abdullah al-Jaber. "The Gulf Cooperation Council and the Security of the Gulf 1981–1989." Master's thesis, American University of Beirut, 1991.

Safadi, Muta'. "Muhawala fi al-Bahth 'an Mu'adil Siyasi li Harakat al-Qawmiyya al-'Arabiyya" (An attempt to search for a political equivalent to the Arab nationalist movement). *Al-Fikr al-'Arabi* 11–12 (1979): 122–32.

Safwat, Khadija. *Al-Islam al-Siyasi wa Ra's al-Mal al-Harib: al-Sudan Namudhajan* (Political Islam and the flight of capital: The Sudanese example). Cairo: Sina lil Nashr, 1994.

Said, Edward W. *Peace and Its Discontents: Essays on Palestine in the Middle East Peace Process.* New York: Vintage Books, 1996.

Salame, Ghassan. "The Middle East: Elusive Security, Indefinable Region." *Security Dialogue* 25, no. 1 (1994): 17–35.

Salih, Hafiz. *Al-Nahda* (The renaissance). Beirut: Dar al-Nahda al-Islamiyya, 1988.

———. *Al-Dimuqratiyya wa Hukm al-Islam Fiha* (Democracy and the ruling of Islam on it). Beirut: Dar al-Nahda al-Islamiyya, 1992.

Sayigh, Yusif A. *The Arab Economy: Past Performance and Future Prospects.* London: Oxford University Press, 1982.

Al-Sayih, Ahmad 'Abdul Rahim. *Adwa' 'ala al-Hadara al-Islamiyya* (The Islamic civilization in the spotlight). Riyadh: Dar al-Liwa', 1981.

Sayyam, Shihata. *Al-'Unf wal Khitab al-Dini fi Misr* (Violence and religious discourse in Egypt). Cairo: Sina lil Nashr, 1994.

Al-Sayyid, Radwan. "Al-Islam al-Siyasi wal Anzima al-'Arabiyya: al-Istiqtab Yuhaddid al-Halaqat a-Da'ifa" (Political Islam and the Arab regimes: Polarization determines the weak links). *Shu'un al-Awsat* 41 (May–June 1995): 85–96.

Sciolino, Elaine. *The Outlaw State: Saddam Hussein's Quest for Power and the Gulf Crisis.* New York: John Wiley and Sons, 1991.

Al-Shahir, 'Abdullah. *Al-Ittijahat al-Fikriyya wal Siyasiyya fil Watan al-'Arabi* (Intellectual and political trends in the Arab homeland). Damascus: Manshurat Dar Mu'ad lil Tiba'a wal Nashr wal Tawzi', 1995.

Sharabi, Hisham B. *Nationalism and Revolution in the Arab World.* New York: Van Nostrand Reinhold, 1966.

———, ed. *The Next Arab Decade: Alternative Futures.* Boulder, Colo.: Westview Press, 1988.

Shibutani, Tamotsu, and Kian M. Kwan. *Ethnic Stratification: A Comparative Approach.* New York: Macmillan, 1965.

Shuqayr, Rashid. "Azmat al-Khalij: Judhur wa Afaq" (The Gulf crisis: Origins and horizons). *Al-Fikr al-Istratiji* 35 (Jan. 1991): 11–43.

Sidahmed, Abdel Salam, and Anoushiravan Ehteshami, eds. *Islamic Fundamentalism.* Boulder, Colo.: Westview Press, 1996.

Sinai, Anne, and I. Robert Sinai, eds. *Israel and the Arabs: Prelude to the Jewish State.* New York: Facts on File, 1972.

Sivan, Emmanuel. *Radical Islam: Medieval Theology and Modern Politics.* New Haven: Yale University Press, 1985.

Smith, Anthony D. S. *Nationalism in the Twentieth Century.* Oxford, England: Martin Robertson, 1979.

Smith, Charles D. *Palestine and the Arab-Israeli Conflict.* 2nd ed. New York: St. Martin's Press, 1992.

Statistical Yearbook. 41st issue. New York: United Nations Department for Economic and Social Information and Policy Analysis, 1996.

Al-Suwaidi, Jamal S., ed. *The Yemeni War of 1994: Causes and Consequences.* London: Saqi Books, 1995.

Tatawur al-Fikr al-Qawmi al-'Arabi (The evolution of Arab nationalist thought). Beirut: Markaz Dirasat al-Wihda al-'Arabiyya, 1986.

Thawrat al-'Arab Did al-Atrak: Muqaddimatuha, Asbabuha wa Nata'ijuha (The Arab rebellion against the Turks: Its beginnings, causes and results). Revised ed., anonymous author. Beirut: Dar al Tadamun lil Tiba'a wal Nashr wal Tawzi', 1993.

Torrey Gordon H., and John F. Devlin. "Arab Socialism." *Journal of International Affairs* 19, no. 1 (1965): 47–62.

Vaux, Kenneth L. *Ethics and the Gulf War: Religion, Rhetoric, and Righteousness.* Boulder, Colo.: Westview Press, 1992.

Veer, Peter Van Der. *Religious Nationalism: Hindus and Muslims in India.* Berkeley: University of California Press, 1994.

Voll, John O. *Islam: Continuity and Change in a Modern World.* Boulder, Colo.: Westview Press, 1982.

———. "Sudan: A State and Society in Crisis." *Middle East Journal* 44, no. 4 (1990): 575–8.

———. *Islam: Continuity and Change in the Modern World.* 2nd ed. Syracuse: Syracuse University Press, 1994.

Voll, John O., and John L. Esposito. "Islam's Democratic Essence." *Middle East Quarterly* 1, no. 3 (1994): 3–11.

Von Der Mehden, Fred R. *Politics of the Developing Nations.* Englewood Cliffs, N.J.: Prentice-Hall, 1964.

Vryonis, Speros, Jr., ed. *Islam and Cultural Change in the Middle Ages.* Wiesbaden, Germany: Otto Harrassowitz, 1975.

Ward, Barbara. *Five Ideas That Change the World.* New York: W. W. Norton, 1959.

Yapp, M. E. *The Near East since the First World War.* London: Longman, 1991.

Yetiv, Steve A. *The Persian Gulf Crisis.* Westport, Conn.: Greenwood Press, 1997.

Zallum, 'Abdul Qadim. *Al-Dimuqratiyya Nizam Kufr Yuharram Akhdhuha aw Tatbiquha aw al-Da'wa Ilayha* (Democracy is a system of incredulity that must not be adopted, implemented or advocated). Hizb al-Tahrir, 1990.

———. *Kaifa Hudimat al-Khilafa* (How the caliphate was destroyed). Beirut: Dar al-Umma lil Tiba'a wal Nashr wal Tawzi', 1990.

Zanoyan, Vahan. "After the Oil Boom: The Holiday Ends in the Gulf." *Foreign Affairs* 74, no. 6 (1995): 2–7.

Zartman, William, and William M. Habeeb, eds. *Polity and Society in Contemporary North Africa.* Boulder, Colo.: Westview Press, 1993.

Zdzislaw, Mach. *Symbols, Conflict, and Ideology.* Albany: State University of New York Press, 1993.

Zisser, Eyal. "Negotiations across the Golan Heights: Asad Inches toward Peace." *Middle East Quarterly* 1, no. 3 (1994): 37–44.

Zoubir, Yahia, H. "Algerian Islamists' Conception of Democracy." *Arab Studies Quarterly* 18, no. 3 (1996): 65–85.

Index

Hilal Khashan is professor of political science at the American University of Beirut. He is the author of *Inside the Lebanese Confessional Mind* (1992) and *Partner or Pariah?* (1996).